LANGUAGE IN TIME OF REVOLUTION

Nostalgia Jewishness is a lullaby for old men
gumming soaked white bread.

J. GLADSTEIN, *modernist Yiddish poet*

CONTRAVERSIONS

JEWS AND OTHER DIFFERENCES

DANIEL BOYARIN,

CHANA KRONFELD, AND

NAOMI SEIDMAN, EDITORS

The task of "The Science of Judaism"
is to give Judaism a decent burial.

MORITZ STEINSCHNEIDER,

founder of nineteenth-century

philological Jewish Studies

LANGUAGE IN TIME OF REVOLUTION

BENJAMIN HARSHAV

Stanford University Press · *Stanford, California*

Stanford University Press

Stanford, California

© 1993 by the Regents of the University of
California

First published in 1993 by the University of
California Press

Reprinted in 1999 by Stanford University Press

Printed in the United States of America

ISBN 0-8047-3540-9

LC 99-71317

This book is printed on acid-free paper.

Original printing of this edition 1999

Last figure below indicates year of this printing:

08 07 06 05 04 03 02 01 00 99

CONTENTS

PART II: THE REVIVAL OF THE HEBREW LANGUAGE
Anatomy of a Social Revolution

PART III: SOURCES ON THE HEBREW LANGUAGE REVIVAL
Translated from Hebrew by Barbara Harshav

PREFACE

This book deals with two remarkable events—the worldwide transformations of the Jews in the modern age and the revival of the ancient Hebrew language. It is a book about social and cultural history addressed not only to the professional historian, and a book about Jews addressed not only to Jewish readers. It tries to rethink a wide field of cultural phenomena and present the main ideas to the intelligent reader, or, better, present a "family picture" of related and contiguous ideas. Many names and details are mentioned, which may not all be familiar to the uninitiated; their function is to provide some concrete texture for this dramatic story, but the focus is on the story itself.

The last hundred, or hundred and twenty, years have witnessed a radical transformation of Western civilization, and of humanity as a whole. The transformations of the Jews were, essentially, part of that process. They manifested the transitions from a "medieval" to a modern, Western-type civilization; the tensions between cultural tradition and modern sensibility and between ethnicity and cosmopolitanism; the rise of a lower-class population to the centers of sophisticated culture; the crucial role of language in group identity; processes of urbanization, immigration, secularization, democratization, mass education; the new centrality of science and communications; and so on. But among the Jews, the same processes came later than among the established nations of Europe, were more rapid and drastic, and enveloped wider circles. The transformations of the Jews often clashed with other trends—notably, the totalitarian regimes—that emerged in the same radical age; and they were heavily "overdetermined" (to use Freud's term) by the peculiar characteristics of Jewish tradition, mentality, and destiny.

The very fact that it was a nation without its own territory, with a slanted selection of professions, a people on the move with no certainty about its moorings, with a penchant for constantly asking (or actively refraining from asking) about its own identity—all this shifted the problem from the political to the ideological and cultural domain. A culture of an extraterritorial caste had to survive in a world of politically monolingual, centralized nations, and change or melt into them. It was a small but sufficiently significant group, tainted by history, carrying several private languages around the globe, and producing in a short time a centrifugal explosion of contradictory tendencies, which appeared like a whirling, restless kaleidoscope, enclosed in its own orbit. All that made the transformations of the Jews not just a more intense example of general tendencies but a very peculiar case indeed. And, from the internal point of view, it totally changed the nature of Jewish history.

The book consists of two concentric essays. The first examines the nature of what we may call the *Modern Jewish Revolution*. This revolution, emerging from the internal responses of Jews to the challenges of history, brought about the total transformation of the Jewish people in the century of 1882–1982. The period is overshadowed by dramatic events—the migrations of the Jews, the Holocaust in Europe, and the creation of the State of Israel are the most obvious examples—yet I analyze here not the well-known external history but the internal responses in culture and consciousness. Such responses, implemented by many individuals and in many directions, resulted, on the one hand, in the creation of a modern, secular Jewish literature and society and a Jewish State and, on the other hand, in assimilation to other languages and important contributions made by "Jews" and their descendants to general culture and science. In this essay, I draw the map as a whole, including both its wings, but focus primarily on the internal culture, leaving the external ("assimilated") direction for another study. Special attention is given here to the creation of a new Hebrew society in Palestine/Eretz-Israel, in the context of this revolution.

Part II is a close investigation of one aspect of that revolution: the almost "miraculous" revival of the Hebrew language and its emergence as the base language of a new, Hebrew society. Indeed, of all the cultural creations of this age, what remains is a rich secular Yiddish and Hebrew literature, as well as a partly "Jewish" literature in other languages (Bruno Schulz, Joseph Roth, Philip Roth, Saul Bellow, and many others); but what *continues* is the living Hebrew literature and culture of Israel, based on the Hebrew revival. Language was at the center of interest in modern philosophy, literary criticism, human sciences, and politics; Modernism in all the arts was focused on a revolution in the "languages" of art; in the Hebrew case too there was a sense that an entirely new language will create a "New Man" and a new society. But here the upheaval was radical, changing not just the secondary language of ideology but the natural language of society itself. A recent sociological book describes Israel as the result of "an ideological trend that created a society that became a State" (Horowitz and Lissak 1990: 9). It would be even more correct to say: "*an ideology that created a language that forged a society that became a State.*" And each of these four stages was not automatically entailed in its predecessor but required an immense effort at transcending its boundaries.

While Part I draws a rather general and comprehensive map, Part II

provides a detailed analytical study of one historical phenomenon in all its ramifi-
cations. It shows the language revival to be not a magic trick of one stubborn
idealist (the mythologized Eliezer Ben-Yehuda) but a highly complex interaction
of historical, social, ideological, psychological, and linguistic clusters of facts.

The subject of this book is immense; many scholars have investigated various
aspects of the history of this period, filled with events, trends, and documents. I
shall rely on the relevant scholarship (without burdening the reader with endless
details and footnotes), but my purpose is different: I intend to present an overall
conception of the problem as I see it. This is basically a phenomenological essay:
I am concerned here not with the multitudes of numbers, witness accounts, and
individual biographies, but with the understanding of the interwoven, complex
phenomena, the general tendencies that cut across the many individual ideologies,
facts, and persons. The book deals with the relations between ideological trends
(explicit and implicit), semiotics of culture, individual psychology, and changes
in history. The boundaries between literary scholarship, history of ideas, sociolin-
guistics, and analysis of a society cannot be preserved in such a framework. In
other words, this is an essay that tries to rethink aloud many facts known in
isolation; the gloves of disciplinary methodologies are dropped.

In recent years, there has been a strong positivist trend in Jewish historiography, encouraged by the multitude of facts and stories waiting to be uncovered
and the conventions of academic discourse. No doubt, valuable studies have been
published and our knowledge has increased immensely. But no matter how many
facts we uncover, we still have to erect a *construct* to justify our selection and
explain the historical trends. This book tries to erect the construct itself: it provides a network of generalizations, which may be seen as hypotheses, to be
falsified or further refined by others.

The essay on the revival of the Hebrew language (Part II) deals primarily with
its sociocultural and ideological aspects. For the most part, I have not pursued
any narrow linguistic analysis—and in those passages where I have, the reader
can understand the point without knowing the language. This part is accompanied
by a selection of telling documents, *Sources on the Hebrew Language Revival*, written
by salient figures of the period and translated from Hebrew by Barbara Harshav.

Another, formerly central and now almost extinct, creation of the revolutionary
period was the worldwide literature and culture of Yiddish, which I treated in my
book *The Meaning of Yiddish* (Harshav 1990a). In that study, I first outlined some
of the conceptions developed in the present book.

The other side of the coin is the massive influx of Jews into the national cultures
of various countries and the question of a possible "Jewish" contribution to general
culture and science in the modern age. I discussed this question in lectures titled
"The Jewishness of the 'Non-Jewish Jew'" (referring to Isaac Deutscher's term)
and "The 'Jewish Discourse' Hypothesis." Though raised in general terms in Part
I, this topic is much too complex to be dealt with properly here; it deserves a
separate study.

Strange as it may sound, though this book deals with quite recent trends and events, the revolutionary spirit and the period of transformations of the Jews are over. The urbanization and assimilation of European Jewry, and the role they played in German, Russian, Polish, and other cultures in the twentieth century, are gone with the Jews themselves. Only in America did a major center of assimilated Jewry survive. Likewise, the exuberant flourishing of Jewish secular ideologies and social and cultural institutions, including a rich literature in Hebrew and Yiddish written around the world, is gone too. A secular Jewish culture and society survived only in the Hebrew State of Israel.

All that remains is an interesting chapter of history and a library of fascinating texts.

And a point of caution: some of the issues discussed here in historical perspective are still alive in the present. In this book, however, I intend to describe and not to prescribe. In the beginnings of Jewish emancipation, equality was granted to the individual and not to Jews as a group or cultural entity. Now that both possibilities are open in democratic societies, it is up to the individual to decide whether he wants to shed his Jewish identity altogether, embrace ultra-Orthodox religion, or act on anything in between. I come not to judge but to show what transpired in this turbulent, perhaps transitional, but creative century. I believe it is one of the interesting periods in the history of cultural change.

This is especially true for the second part of the book. The current political situation, including various actions of Israeli governments, often obstructs the historical perspective. Nevertheless, we must recognize that the creation of Israel was the greatest internal response that changed the nature of Jewish history as it subsisted in the last two thousand years, and it may yet provide the only base for the continuation of a viable, secular Jewish culture in the future. The revival of the Hebrew language enabled it all—and it is a fascinating story in its own right.

A NOTE ON TERMINOLOGY AND SPELLING

The book describes a movement in Jewish history from the past into the future, hence the use of such terms as *intrinsic* versus *extrinsic* trends, as seen from the internal perspective; they are meant not in a judgmental but in a purely descriptive sense. Similarly, the term *Diaspora* (dispersion)—as opposed to *Eretz-Israel* (Palestine)—is not meant to impose on the description a Zionist ideology but simply to refer to the existential situation of the Jewish minority throughout the world (actually, the traditional and Zionist term for "Diaspora" is *Galut*, "Exile"). The term *Eretz-Israel* ("The Land of Israel") is the traditional Jewish name for Palestine; since the label "Palestine" (which used to be a Zionist name for that country) became Arabized, I often resort to the Hebrew term when referring to the land before the creation of the State of Israel in 1948. However, the new Jewish society that emerged in Eretz-Israel before 1948 is called *Yishuv* (a loaded word, meaning "a stable settlement," as opposed to the "Exile" of the "Wandering Jew") or the "new *Yishuv*," as opposed to the "old *Yishuv*," the Orthodox community that lived or settled in the cities of Palestine throughout the ages and hardly participated in the Zionist revival.

A frequently used term in this book is *Aliya* (pl. *Aliyot*). *Aliya* means immigration to the Holy Land, or to Israel (literally, "climbing up a mountain," from the image of ascending Mount Zion; the opposite, leaving Israel, is called *yerida*, "descent"). When qualified by a number, it refers to the waves of modern, Zionist immigration to Eretz-Israel/Palestine, each delimited in a specific period and characterized by a dominant group of people and source of origin. In the period of each *Aliya*, people of various types and origin arrived, but the *Aliya* is known for the group that gave its special tone.

The *First Aliya* (1881–1903) came after the pogroms in Russia in 1881–82; it consisted mainly of Russian and Romanian Jews, who built new, Jewish agricultural settlements, with private farmers.

The *Second Aliya* (1904–1914) began in the wake of the Kishinev and Homel pogroms in 1903 and the failed Russian Revolution of 1905, and brought intellectual youth from the Russian Empire (especially from Poland and Byelorussia) who created the labor movement and the first collectives in Eretz-Israel.

The *Third Aliya* (1919–1923) came after the Balfour declaration of 1917, the two Russian Revolutions, the Russian Civil War of 1918–1922, and the exterminating pogroms in Ukraine in 1919. They brought a more massive influx of Socialist-oriented youth from Russia (especially Ukraine) and the former Austro-Hungary (Galicia), who built roads and established the kibbutz movement.

The *Fourth Aliya* (1924–1928) brought middle-class families, especially from Poland, who built the cities, primarily Tel Aviv.

The *Fifth Aliya* (1929–1939) brought German Jews in the time of Hitler.

All passages quoted in this book have been translated by its author, unless excerpted from sources in English (as indicated in the list of References).

The transcription of Hebrew words and names is straightforward, assigning a fixed letter to each sound, and not attempting any adaptation to English spelling. For some sounds, two or three letters were used: **sh** (as in English), **ts** (like zz in *Pizza*), **tsh** (like *ch* in *chair*), **kh** (like *ch* in *chutzpah*). But whenever a Hebrew *ḥet* is distinguished from a *khaf*, the first is represented by **ḥ** and the second by **kh**. Vowels are used as in Italian, German, and other European languages. The same vowels appear in diphthongs: **oy** (like *oy* in *boy*), **ay** (like *uy* in *guy*), **ey** (like *ay* in *day*).

For the sake of uniformity, I have transcribed names directly from the Hebrew or Yiddish, irrespective of the various spellings they have been represented by in the past. Hence: *Berditshevski* rather than the German *Berditschewski*, the Polish *Berdyczewski*, or the Anglicized *Berdichevsky*; *Dubnov* rather than *Dubnow*; *Tsemakh* and not the German *Zemach* (which would sound in English like *zebra*); *Tsvi* and not *Zvi* or *Zwi*.

But in several cases exceptions have been made: we use the accepted (German) spelling of *Eretz-Israel* (for what should be *Erets*); and *Yitzhak* rather than the normative *Yitshak* (because the combination **sh** would make it read *Yit-shak*). We also preserved the author's own spelling of *Jabotinsky* instead of the proper transcription *Zhabotinski*, for readers who know this name might otherwise not be able to identify it.

In representations of sounds the stressed syllable of a word is in capital letters wherever relevant. For example, the Israeli pronunciation **daVID** is officially stressed on the last syllable, but affectionately on the first: **DAvid**.

ACKNOWLEDGMENTS

Parts I and II of this book are based on two earlier essays published in Hebrew. The first began as a lecture at Harvard University in December 1980, titled "1881—A Watershed in the History of Jewish Culture and Consciousness," and continued as a lecture at a conference on "Culture and Society in Eretz-Israel" at the Open University at Tel Aviv. It was published in a book edited by Nurith Gertz (Harshav 1988). The second essay was commissioned by the most stimulating of editors, Nitza Drory-Peremen, for a new Israeli intellectual periodical, *Alpayim* (Harshav 1990b). I would like to thank Robert B. Alter, Nitza Drory, Itamar Even-Zohar, Nurith Gertz, Irving Howe, Chana Kronfeld, Yakov Shavit, and many others with whom I exchanged ideas on these issues. I am grateful to Hagi and Vered Kenaan for compiling the index. Barbara Harshav, as before, was my first and indispensable reader and editor.

PART I: THE MODERN JEWISH REVOLUTION

An Essay on the History of Culture and Consciousness

ONE

Transformations: Extrinsic and Intrinsic

As we look around us in contemporary America, we see large numbers of "Jews" or persons of Jewish origin (many of whom shed their recognizably Jewish names) in such areas as law, medicine, psychoanalysis, mathematics, theoretical physics, economics, linguistics, the academy in general, as well as in the communications and entertainment industries, in trade and political thought, and very few among farmers, industrial workers, or soldiers. A similar picture is revealed if we observe the small Jewish populations of England and France today, even the Soviet Union (despite long-standing attempts to bar Jews from higher education and positions of power); and certainly if we look at the cultures of Germany and Soviet Russia in the 1920s. With some exaggeration, we may say that, if observed as one social group, such "Jews" derive from a religion but strive to the condition of a "class," occupying large parts of certain social domains and professions with no proportionality to their percentage in the population as a whole. As is well known, this situation resulted in important contributions made by individuals of Jewish origin to modern culture and science. After Hitler's racism, especially vis-à-vis the Jews, this is a sensitive issue, though it serves as a favorite topic in Jewish insider whispering. But the striking statistical imbalance, often accumulating in a very short period, and despite most individuals' fully assimilated behavior and sincere professionalism, make those "Non-Jewish Jews" (as Isaac Deutscher dubbed them)—justly or unjustly—"Jewish" again in the eyes of the beholder. Though antecedents of this phenomenon can be found in earlier centuries, the massive influx of Jews into general culture is a product of a very short period, at the end of the nineteenth and the beginning of the twentieth century.

Simultaneously, especially after 1882, a new secular culture emerged in the internal Jewish domain, giving rise to a rich and variegated literature written in Yiddish and Hebrew (which, for many reasons, is open in its full flavor only to those who master the intricate layering and universe of allusions of those languages). Hand in hand with this new literature, a rainbow of ideological and

3

social movements showed a vigorous life among the Jews and gave ideological and cultural momentum to a whole generation and their children, until it disappeared; one branch of this trend survived and culminated in the stunning creation of a new, Hebrew society, the *Yishuv*—the organized Jewish community in pre-independent Palestine (1882–1948)—which eventually led to the establishment and flourishing of the State of Israel.

Both those directions—which we may call the extrinsic and intrinsic respectively—exhibit a total transformation of the modes of existence of Jews and their descendants in the post-Christian modern world. It was a period of the rejuvenation of the Jews, which took many forms and directions and endowed people weary of suffering with a nervous creative energy. Whatever the results, the process itself is as rich in meanings as a work of fiction. Indeed, it was thematized in the multilingual Jewish fiction that was, at the same time, part of the process itself.

Today, it is hard to believe that just recently, about a century ago, Jewish literature had captured the essence of Jewish existence in the fictional image of the primitive *shtetl,* the East European Jewish small town. Sholem Aleichem (Rabinovitsh, 1859–1916) had immortalized it in the image of Kasrilevke:

> The town of the little people into which I shall now take you, dear reader, is exactly in the middle of the blessed Pale[1] into which Jews have been packed as closely as herring in a barrel and told to increase and multiply. [. . .] Stuck away in a corner of the world, isolated from the surrounding country, the town stands, orphaned, dreaming, bewitched, immersed in itself and remote from the noise and the bustle, the confusion and tumult and greed, which men have created about them and have dignified with high-sounding names like Culture, Progress, Civilization. ("The Town of the Little People," Sholom Aleichem 1956:28)

The irony, of course, is double-directed, but the *shtetl* is unmistakably reconstructed from a distance, much as James Joyce reconstructed Dublin. Both the writer and his readers are already modern city-dwellers who believe in "Culture, Progress, Civilization" and look back at the small town as at a museum exhibit. When we read the memoirs of Solomon Maimon (1753–1800) or the writings of Mendele Moykher Sforim (Abramovitsh, 1835–1917), we are amazed at how wretched, dirty, degenerate, illiterate, or ugly our ancestors appeared—only three or four generations ago. Here, for example, is a typical description by the master of Yiddish and Hebrew literature, Mendele Moykher Sforim, following *The Travels and Adventures of Benjamin the Third* from his small *shtetl* of Teterevke to the regional "metropolis" of *Glupsk* (i.e., "Fooltown"):

---

1. "Pale of Settlement"—former Polish territories, comprising central Poland, Ukraine, Byelorussia, Lithuania, occupied by Russia at the end of the eighteenth century and turned into a large geographical ghetto beyond which only a few Jews were permitted to live. The Pale included thousands of small towns, many of them predominantly Jewish.

First of all, when you arrive in Glupsk, by the road from Teterevka, you must leap over—I apologize for mentioning it—a mud hole; a little farther on you must leap over another, and still farther on a third, the largest of the lot, into which all the sewage of the town flows. If the gutters are filled with yellow sand used for scrubbing floors, with chicken and fish guts, with fish scales and chicken heads, you know it is Friday and time to go to the steam bath; if, on the other hand, they show egg shells, onion skins, radish parings, herring skeletons and sucked-out marrow bones—why, good Sabbath to you, you Jewish children! (Mendele 1968:89)

This metonymic description of the mire of Jewish uncivilized existence was supposed to be symbolic for the whole Jewish Pale of Settlement in Russia. And Mendele's readers in the early twentieth century, themselves born in Jewish small towns, thought that was an appropriate portrait. Without foreseeing the Holocaust, the Hebrew literary critic David Frishman (1859–1922) wrote that, if the Jewish world were destroyed, it would remain alive in the writings of Mendele Moykher Sforim. Similar images, influenced by Mendele's perception of the *shtetl*, were repeatedly used by those who revolted against traditional Jewish existence, such as the British chemist, Zionist leader, and later President of Israel, Chaim Weizmann (1874–1952), who described his hometown Pinsk (capital of Polesye, Byelorussia) as a sleepy swamp. The transformation since then has been enormous.

What was clear to the children of the *shtetl* was that, to regain the dignity of human existence, they would have to embrace the culture and ideas of the "civilized"—that is, Western European—world. And this could be done in one of two ways: either join it or imitate it. In other words: either go to the center of culture (in both the physical and spiritual sense), master its language, literature, ideologies, behavior, and science, and become a member of that language community (German, Russian, English); or create a parallel culture in Jewish languages, that would have similar genres, norms, ideas, institutions, and achievements. Through either of those, you join cosmopolitan European culture as a whole. (We may note that the ideological background of this striving can be found in the fermentation that had engulfed Russian literature and the intelligentsia in the nineteenth century, confronted by the challenges of Western European culture, and divided between "Westernizers" and Slavophiles.)

The extraordinary leap of a whole nation from that mire existence to both the creation of a new Jewish civilization and participation in the general culture of modernity can be understood only as a radical revolution, driven by a complex of extraordinary historical circumstances. Revolutions are usually sudden political and military acts of overthrowing an old regime that governs a society (and often end up with a new regime, worse than the old one). Here, the revolution was first of all internal, it passed through the minds and hearts of each individual, it had to be reworked and regained time and again, and hence, after many sacrifices and failures, the final result was so successful. This *Modern Jewish Revolution* was not directed against a political power structure but rather against a governing semiotics, a set of beliefs, values, and behavior, and toward internalized ideals of a new world culture. In this respect, it is similar in time and nature to the revolution that occurred in Modernist art and literature in the same period.

David Ben-Gurion (1886–1973) formulated it thus: "All other revolts, both past and future, were uprisings against a system, against a political, social, or economic structure. Our revolution is directed not only against a system but against *destiny,* against the unique destiny of a unique people" ("The Imperatives of the Jewish Revolution," 1944, in Hertzberg 1973:607). Ben-Gurion was talking about the realization of Zionism, but the same could be said about all other transformations of the Jews in the modern age.

TWO

The Internal Response to History

In his famous story "The Sermon," the Hebrew writer Hayim Hazaz (1898–1973) describes a usually silent kibbutz member, Yudke, who suddenly makes an impassioned speech declaring to the Committee that he is opposed to Jewish history: "Because we didn't make our own history, the *goyim* [i.e, Gentiles] made it for us" (Alter 1975:274; see the analytical discussion in Yerushalmi 1989:97–101). Indeed, it is hard to deny that "they did" a lot to the Jews. In the period that concerns us here, in the nineteenth and twentieth centuries, there were waves of pogroms and persecution; world wars and expulsions; the British White Paper of 1939 that barred further Jewish immigration and settlement in Palestine; the gates of Western countries closed to refugees from Nazi persecution. And there was the total destruction of the nation in Europe, the center of its life for a millennium.

But people often overlook the fact that there were also crucial positive conditions: Jews achieved civil rights in Western Europe in the nineteenth century and in Russia in 1917; the big cities were opened to Jews; the Russian Pale of Settlement was abolished by the February Revolution of 1917; the universities in the West and in Soviet Russia were opened to various extents; and millions of Jews emigrated overseas—the emigration that, in fact, guaranteed the survival of the Jewish nation in the period of the Holocaust. There were conditions that enabled masses of Jews in various countries—not without a struggle—to rise to the middle and upper classes, to practice trade and open chains of department stores, and to reach the centers of culture and science. And there were conditions that enabled the establishment of the State of Israel, the rapid development of its economy, culture, and military force. In sum, there were sweeping and comprehensive historical circumstances—some of them intended directly for the Jews, most not related to them at all—that enabled the Jews, in the final analysis, to change the very nature of their hovering, transnational existence.

Nevertheless, Yudke was wrong. General history, indeed, did determine the conditions of Jewish survival; but everything we see today in the existence of Jews

7

or descendants of Jews in the world resulted, to a considerable extent, from the *internal responses* to these historical conditions, persecutions and opportunities. The responses—both individual and collective—grew out of Jewish society itself, and in this sense it is the Jews who made their own history. The changes went through the consciousness of each individual, who realized them by responding to situations and options encountered in his own life and in light of various ideological attitudes, explicit or implicit, hovering in the air. To be sure, it was a consciousness filled with contradictions and prejudices but also with recurrent self-criticism and the mobilization of every individual's resources. History was made by girls and boys who left their home, abandoned their parents' house, their language and religion, and came to the difficult land of Eretz-Israel or the no less difficult New York or Moscow, in order to "build and rebuild themselves" (*anu banu artsa livnot u-le-hibanot ba*, "we came to our Land to build and be rebuilt by it," as the Hebrew song says): to build a new life, a new solution for themselves and, at the same time, often inadvertently, also for Jewish history. It was made by individuals like Rachel (1890–1931), a fragile poetess in Russian, living on the banks of Lake Kineret, suffering from tuberculosis and unfulfilled love, reading the Bible and inventing a language for a new poetry in Hebrew; or by Mani Leyb (1883–1953), a shoemaker in New York, with no formal education, writing sonnets and translating from world poetry into Yiddish. Every trend, every solution had its own hundreds and thousands of Yudke's.

We can date the beginning of this revolution in the year of the pogroms, 1881–82 in Russia. What happened from then on completely changed the nature of the lives of Jews and their descendants in the world. It was the most radical change in the historical situation of the Jews in the last two thousand years, entirely transforming their geography, modes of living, languages, professions, consciousness, culture, politics, and place in general history.[2] It was borne by a multifaceted, centrifugal movement with many directions and varying outcomes. Prominent failures, brutal disappointments, and dreadful sacrifices were part and parcel of these transformations. Individuals who experienced the change in their own bodies and souls paid an extraordinary emotional price for leaving their hometown, their parents' home, their childhood language, their beliefs, their ways of talking, and for the conquest of new modes of behavior, a new language, new traits, conventions, and beliefs. A salient example is *Portnoy's Complaint* by Philip Roth. But, from a historical perspective, the results are amazing: thanks to those

---

2. In December 1980, at a conference at Harvard on the centennial of the pogroms, I delivered a lecture titled "1881—A Watershed in the History of Jewish Culture and Consciousness." When Jonathan Frankel's masterpiece (1981) appeared, I saw that he used the same word, "watershed," though he too examined some roots of the change in earlier generations. The same extraordinary importance of this critical date in Jewish history was seen from the point of view of American Jewry by Irving Howe, in his monumental *World of Our Fathers* (1976). It is also a cornerstone of Zionist historiography which counts the waves of Zionist immigration to Eretz-Israel (*Aliyot*) from the First *Aliya* beginning in 1881 (some earlier antecedents notwithstanding).

transformations, Jews exist now, and exist in the center of consciousness of general society.

The renaissance of Hebrew culture and literature in the Diaspora and its immigration to Eretz-Israel, the rise of a full-fledged society in the Hebrew language, the establishment of the State of Israel on that basis, and its economic and cultural growth were part of that historical momentum.

Time and again throughout history, individual Jews have returned to Eretz-Israel; but the revival of the homeland in the modern age, based on secular ideology and politics, can be understood only within the framework of the Modern Jewish Revolution: the world of concepts, ideologies, debates, literature, consciousness, the whole imaginary space of society, and all the transformations that have taken place among the Jews during the last hundred years, especially in Eastern Europe and wherever immigrants from Eastern Europe landed: in London, New York, or Palestine. The "return" to Jewish history and to the Hebrew language are part of this complex. Most of the founders of the *Yishuv*, the immigrants of the Second and Third Aliyot, came from what was then the Russian Empire (and a minority from Austrian Galicia and elsewhere). They brought with them a world of literary and popular concepts and values evolved in that great fermentation. Even if they came to the land of Israel out of protest and negation of the Diaspora, they shaped themselves in continuation of and in opposition to notions that were crystallized there.

Their option was not the only remedy—either personal or collective—for the Jewish situation, and they were aware of it. A handful of young people in strange landscapes, in a desolate and hostile world, the first generation of a budding society, a society without parents and grandparents, they surrounded their precarious existence with a brand-new fence—a fence of an emotionally perceived ideology and a new Hebrew language. Behind the fence, every person was expected to bury his first language and early emotions, ingrained modes of behavior, conventions and beliefs, subtle gestures and pithy sayings, family warmth and instinctive fears, which had all been accumulated in the Diaspora for hundreds of years. The ideology that served as a foundation for the new edifice was a substitute for the land of a tribe that stays in its own place for centuries until the place becomes part of the language of its existence. The ideology, which justified the radical break cutting through the life of every individual, was formulated as the only correct position in a multifaceted debate.

THREE

A New Period in History

There are no neat boundaries in history. If we look at broad movements like "Zionism," "Romanticism," "Futurism," or "Hasidism," we see that they are characterized by a heterogeneous but intertwined cluster of institutions, ideas, and features, expressed in specific persons, actions, and texts, and located in a given time and place. If we analyze such a complex, we see that for almost every individual phenomenon, motif, or idea, we can find both roots and antecedents in preceding periods. A new trend in history is marked not by the novelty of each detail; instead, we have a new *framework* that reorganizes various elements in a new way, selects and highlights previously neglected features, adds conspicuous new ones, changes their hierarchies, and thus makes the complex a totally new global entity. When such a framework is perceived as a new trend, it can win a broad following and become a dominant force in society. Such a framework may be established by means of a label or crucial dates. It may be the name of an intellectual movement or a social cluster or a new political institution, either given at the time or assigned later; it may be a date indicating an event that inaugurated the change or is thought to determine it; or all of those combined. Such labels are, for example, "Modernism" in poetry and art, "Zionism," "The Period of Revival" in Hebrew literature, or events like World Wars I and II, the Russian Revolutions of 1905 and 1917, and the pogroms of 1881–82.

Specific ideas and phenomena that characterize this period after 1882 also appeared earlier. Indeed, it is convenient to project back from the watershed date of 1882 and adopt Professor Yosef Klauzner's (1874–1958) periodization of the Hebrew enlightenment, beginning with the edict of Austrian Emperor Joseph II in 1782 and extending a full century. In that edict, Joseph II imposed elementary education in German on Jewish children, thus opening their way to general culture and scandalizing the traditionalists at the same time. The Enlightenment, the assimilation of Jews in Western Europe, several harbingers of Zionism and

Socialism, Hebrew and Yiddish writers in the nineteenth century and, even earlier, the Golden Age of Hebrew literature in medieval Spain, Jewish intellectuals and Hebrew poets in Italy after the Renaissance—all of them planted ideas and set precedents of secular culture and changes in the life of the individual. Ideologically, we can demonstrate how some writings of the Enlightenment period prepared or predated the ideas of the new period; and Heine or Marx preceded Trotsky, Freud, and Einstein in their place in general culture. Closer to our date, the "unexpected" pogrom in Odessa in 1871, like an early tremor before an eruption, sent ripples of nationalism and unease among Jewish writers and assimilated students. But those were isolated phenomena affecting individuals, even many individuals, or groups of Jews in some places. It was not until after 1881–82—the wave of pogroms in Russia and Ukraine that Mendele dubbed "Storms in the Negev [South]"—that the winds of change encompassed the entire Jewish people, particularly the considerable masses in Eastern Europe and their branches in other countries. Only after 1882 did the great Jewish immigration from Russia to America and the Zionist immigration to Eretz-Israel begin. And no less important: a new literary, cultural, educational, ideological, and political Jewish establishment arose which could justly claim to be the heir to the old religious establishment.

No event in Jewish history since the destruction of the Second Temple has changed the nature of Jewish existence as much as this revolution. The physical and symbolic expression of this change—and even its basic condition—lies in the decisive shift in the geographical centers of Jewish life: from the *shtetl* heartland in Eastern Europe to the West and overseas, on the one hand, and to Central Russia and the Soviet East, on the other; and from the Arab countries and North Africa to Israel or the West. Indeed, the remnants of previous forms of life, symbolized by the small Eastern European town, were finally destroyed by the Nazis. But the alternatives that replaced them were all crystallized before the Holocaust. They include alternatives that ultimately failed or declined—such as Yiddish literature and its cultural and educational institutions, or the rise of Jews in the Communist establishment—and those that eventually prevailed and met with success: the State of Israel and the prominent position of Jews in the United States today.

The pogroms of 1881–82 did not do it all. There were additional waves—waves of pogroms and waves of revolutions and upheavals (with critical dates being 1891–92, 1903–1905, 1917, 1919, 1933, 1945, 1948)—which renewed or accelerated that process and carried new waves of Jews through similar transformations. The cultural and ideological alternatives were developed in their own, autonomous evolution; but external events triggered their wider implementation. Furthermore, the multi-wave character of these transformations was essential to their success, contrary to what is normally perceived as a one-shot, revolutionary change of history.[3] Indeed, any phenomenon in time must be a multi-wave process to be perceived, digested, and established by a living society. Thus the settlements of the First Aliya (Zionist immigration to Eretz-Israel, 1881–1903) would not have left a *Yishuv* in Palestine any more stable than that of their cousins, the Jewish agricultural settlements in Argentina, if more waves of immigration had not arrived time and again, none of them as an organic continuation but as a new impulse from the Diaspora. For such waves to be repeated, they must of course be carried by one ideology (which is also transformed in time).

But 1881–82 does seem to be the decisive historical watershed. At the end of the nineteenth century, most Jews lived in Eastern Europe and in the centers of immigration recently spawned by it (Vienna, Berlin, London, New York, Boston, Philadelphia, Rishon Le-Tsiyon). The largest community was still under the rule of the Russian Empire. According to the census of 1897, there were about 5.2 million Jews in Russia, that is, over half of world Jewry. Almost 98% of them declared Yiddish as their native tongue, which means that most of them grew up in the traditional world of an extraterritorial culture whose spoken language was Yiddish. That too was overthrown within two or three generations.

We must emphasize that each individual phenomenon characterizing the modern Jewish revolution was not unique to the Jews. Jews moved to the big cities, migrated overseas, joined revolutionary movements, moved up the educational ladder, or entered modern science—and so did millions of non-Jews. In fact, Jewish immigration and entrance into new professions was made possible by the opening of opportunities in the world as a whole. It was especially the accelerated expansion of new professions, fields, and disciplines, inviting new and imaginative originators and carriers, that encouraged alert Jews to apply their energies and find a place in the general world. The special case consists of the fact that the Jewish transformations were more rapid, higher in proportions, enveloped most of the nation, and were connected not only with the consciousness of upward mobility of a class but with a new self-understanding of the Jews as a nation.

If observed from the outside, it may seem to be just a more intensive expression of general trends; if, however, observed from an internal, Jewish perspective, this was a total transformation of the nature of the entity "Jews" as a social group. Millions of Germans or Italians had immigrated to the United States and assimilated to the English language, but the German and Italian nations and cultures remained in their places, and assimilation of their immigrants to English-American culture makes no difference in that fact. But this is not the case with the Jews: if their assimilation is complete, they won't exist any longer. In this sense, their assimilation to a new *Hebrew* culture in Israel was "deluding" the spirit of history: the same move of immigration and assimilation indeed canceled the old nation

---

3. This *dynamic* view of history is neglected by those who describe it as a one-time upturn: the October Revolution of 1917 or the declaration of independence of the State of Israel. Such a view invites stagnation and causes melancholy nostalgia and eventual collapse.

but created a new Jewish secular nation instead. The concept "Jew" itself shifted: from a religious category to the designation of a culture and a nation, on the one hand, or a racial-ethnic origin, on the other. Nevertheless, even though the very concept of "Jews" has changed, this was a crucial chapter in Jewish history (which continues in spite of its shifting subject).

This chapter is, furthermore, different from similar cataclysms in Jewish history itself. There was a sense of shock among Jews also after the Spanish expulsion of 1492; it relocated the surviving refugees, produced an important religious literature, yet did not change the essential nature of the Jewish Diaspora. And there were similar shocks in the slaughters of Jews by the Crusaders in Germany in the eleventh and twelfth centuries and after the pogroms of 1648–49 in Ukraine; but, eventually, Jews went back and settled in the same places. Now, however, a general upheaval really did take place, exploiting the dynamic opportunities of the modern world in Europe and the United States and producing in this period what looks like a new Jewish nation built on a bipolar axis of two quite different entities: Israel and a new Diaspora.

FOUR

The Centrifugal Movement

What occurred in this period was a multidirectional, centrifugal movement away from the old existence, symbolized by the religious culture of the Eastern European small town, the *shtetl*, as mythologized in Jewish fiction. As mentioned above, the movement went in two basic directions: intrinsic and extrinsic. Extrinsically, Jews entered en masse into the education and culture of other nations and, in some fields, made outstanding contributions, in terms of both quality and quantity; they were also prominent in the international leftist movement. Intrinsically, they founded three interconnected establishments: 1) a rich literature and culture in Hebrew, Yiddish, and a third language (varying with the country); 2) a gamut of ideologies and political movements; 3) a network of cultural and social institutions based on models of European, post-Christian society. All those cultural expressions—both intrinsic and extrinsic—were intertwined with the existential level, the migrations and transformations of every person's life, which encompassed most of the nation and included shifts in geographic settlement (mainly from the small town to the city and from East to West) and linguistic, educational, and professional changes.

I am concentrating on the Ashkenazi Jews of Eastern European origin a) because they constituted the overwhelming majority of world Jewry at the beginning of this period[4] and b) because it was primarily in this group that the organized

4. Present-day proportions, including the large numbers of Oriental Jews living in Israel, must not mislead us about the picture of the past. In the 1880s, only 10% of world Jewry were Sephardic and Oriental Jews (Ben-Sasson 1976:791). At the outbreak of World War I, about 11 million Jews lived in Eastern Europe and the United States (most of whom were of East European origin), compared to 1 million in Western Europe (including a large part who were also of East European origin) and only 800,000 in the Near East and North Africa (see Ben-Sasson 1976:860). It was only after the Holocaust, which destroyed the original European Ashkenazi communities, and the almost total evacuation of Jews from Oriental countries to Israel that Oriental and Sephardic Jews constituted 50% of Israeli society. Coupled with the cultural centrality of Israel itself in the Jewish world, their political place became prominent. But this was not the case at the beginning of the modern movements, which Oriental Jews joined gradually.

intrinsic responses to the historical situation—literature, ideologies, and the social network—took shape. However, the phenomena on the individual level, particularly modernization, moving from small towns and villages to the cities, changing professions, dropping Yiddish (or its equivalent) and embracing the dominant language, and entry into the world of general culture, took place in all Jewish communities, either before this revolution or after it. In this respect, Western Europe preceded Eastern Europe, and the rise of North African Jews in France came later. The structure of the phenomenon was basically similar in different times and places (with obvious differences of context), and there is no space here to describe the specific case of each country and community.

Among the Jews of Eastern Europe, too, events did not take place all at once but in waves, enveloping ever new groups. It is important to note that, in terms of the institutions themselves, we can talk about one history continuing for several generations (e.g., the history of Zionism or of Hebrew literature); but every individual participating in it entered that stream at a different time and place—usually from the outside, separating from his old life on the one hand and coping, on the other, with phenomena very new to him. In terms of the individual, this was a one- or two-generation revolution, with the second generation digesting and consolidating the irrevocable change made by its fathers.

In this sense, Jewish history is a staggered history: what happened to one Jewish group earlier happened to another group later. And, since various groups at different stages of transformation immigrated and often met in one place or on one level of debate, tensions arose which assumed the form of simultaneous, often irreconcilable attitudes and modes of behavior. This pattern is evident in the attitudes of the westernized Jews of Vienna or Berlin (who had perhaps assimilated one or two generations earlier) toward their brothers who had just come from small towns and from the East ("Ostjuden"); or in the attitudes of old-time immigrants to the United States toward the "Greenhorns"; or in the attitude of the established *Yishuv* in Eretz-Israel toward each new wave of *Aliya*—and vice versa. Much of what was created in this period came from both the tensions and the collaboration of such groups on different levels.

From this perspective, the collaboration of the "Westernized" Jews with their Eastern European cousins produced important intrinsic results as well. Thus, a Zionist movement emerged in Eastern Europe and in Palestine in the 1880s, but it was the formal and organizational tradition of the West that gave rise to a political Zionist organization in 1897—to be resuscitated by a movement in the East that gave Zionism mass support and saved it from Herzl's idea of building a Jewish state in Uganda. The prestige of "Dr. Theodor" Herzl in the general world and his Western manners made him "King of Israel" in the eyes of the Vilna masses. But Herzl himself was an immigrant from the relative East (Hungary), with a religious family background; and the Zionist movement became what it was because of the collaboration between Western Zionists (often of East European background, e.g., Martin Buber or Nakhum Goldman) and the mass movement in Eastern Europe. Another example: the *Educational Alliance* was formed in New York by rich and assimilated uptown Jews of German origin with the aim of educating and assimilating some of their Eastern brethren flooding the city, and it became an important school, at first teaching in Yiddish, and raising American graphic artists born in Eastern Europe, such as Rafael Soyer, Chaim Gross, Jacob Epstein, Ben Shahn, Leonard Baskin, Louise Nevelson, Barnett Newman, and Mark Rothko.

Within the period itself, the alternative solutions often seemed unbridgeable. An abyss gaped between different options for the new form of life to be embraced by the individual and the community. The hostilities between all the intrinsic trends and the assimilationists, between the Socialists and the Zionists, between the labor Zionists and the bourgeois Zionists, between Yiddish and Hebrew, between Western Jews and Eastern Jews, were in the center of social consciousness and public debate. No Jew in this secularized period seemed able to live without active consciousness, and in Jewish behavior there was no consciousness without a position in a debate. The semiotics of the Talmudic world, which was essentially a debating discourse and debating learning, has been internalized in Jewish folklore; no ideological position could be expressed without arguing against a real or hypothetical counterposition. The "other" was not just an enemy, he was an opposite alternative included in your self-definition and riding the same wave of change. In retrospect, however, we can see common patterns of thinking and behavior among all those feuding alternatives.

FIVE

The Force of Negation

Every movement of change in this period, either institutionalized or personal and existential, was borne by two powerful impulses: negative and positive. The negative impulse was shared by all the trends, although it assumed different forms. It can be described in semiotic concepts as the negation of the three deictic axes of the old Jewish existence. Deictics are linguistic tools that have no lexical meaning of their own but relate the meanings of words and sentences to the coordinates of a specific act of communication. The three basic deictics are: *I, here,* and *now,* relating the discourse to the speaker, and the place and time of speech. All other deictics are derived from those (*you, he, there, two years ago,* etc.). For example, "here" and "now" attach the content of the words to the place and time in which they are uttered; but also "then," "yesterday," "next year," or "in the past" relate the content not to a given chronological time but to a point relative to the time of the specific speech act.

In these terms, we can say that all the trends declared in one form or another: *Not here, Not like now, Not as we are* (though the interpretation of those negations varied widely). "*Not here*" was the response of the Zionists and the Territorialists as well as the instinctive response of millions who left the *shtetl* or turned to immigration. Even the Bundists, who ostensibly stood for "hereness" ("*doikeyt*") in the Diaspora, meant a decidedly different "here" from the old "here" of *shtetl* culture: an urban setting, an organized working class, an educational movement steeped in secular Yiddish culture. "*Not like now*" was expressed in the struggle for political change—either in Socialism (turning to the future) or in Zionism (turning to the future as a revived past) and, on the personal level, in the future-oriented aspiration for learning and personal education and professional change of every individual for himself and his children. Hence the endless ideological debates in Jewish society, especially at the beginning of the century—ideology is future-oriented—and the many factionalizations over the formulations of "*programs maximum*" and "*programs minimum*" which emerged from the orientation

17

toward a utopian or wishful future rather than from a need for current political blocs of power.

Of the three deictic axes, the hardest one for a person to negate is the personal: "*Not me.*" Some did say it and were devoured by self-hatred, like the Viennese genius Otto Weininger (1880–1903), who drew the logical conclusion and committed suicide. The prototypical image of Jewish life located in the topography and iconography of the *shtetl* and in the past, as vividly evoked in Jewish literature, enabled the critical and nostalgic distancing from such a collective "we." Hence, the negation of the personal deixis was usually translated into: "*not as we were*" or "*not like the public image of 'us.'* " Practically, this meant a sharp dissociation from all that was "wrong" with the Jews themselves—from the negative "other" both outside and inside a person's self. First, every trend cast the negation onto other manifestations of Jewish life or onto alternative trends that, in its view, embodied all that was negative in Jewish stereotypes. Second, the individual tried to repress in his own emotions and behavior every manifestation of the negative "*we*" ("don't yell like a Jew," "don't be pushy," "don't talk with your hands," etc.). The infamous "*Jewish Self-Hatred*"—a concept introduced in a book of that title by Theodor Lessing (1930) (1872–1933)—is not really hatred of the self but hatred of manifestations of "Jewish" behavior in one's personality which are negative in your own eyes.

The expressions of this attitude in the various trends coincide amazingly with one another. Hatred of the "wheeling-dealing" Jew and rejection of the "Diaspora mentality" in Eretz-Israel were not essentially different from hatred of the "Ost-jude" by German Jews, contempt for the provincial "yokel" among modern city Jews, or for the "petit bourgeois" among the Socialists. For both assimilationists and Zionists, Yiddish language and "behavior" symbolized the contemptible world of the *shtetl*. The aspiration of the Realizing Zionists[5] to create a "New Jew," healthy in mind and body, came from the same perception (one might ask: What's wrong with the "old Jew?"). Indeed, the negative traits were often seen not as changeable behavior but as symptoms of a negative essence, and subsumed under the label "Jew" or "Judaism," hence the appearance of a "Jewish self-hatred."

Examples are many, often showing up in biographies of individuals as a "strange" deviation (and accompanied by uneasiness on the part of the biographer). No doubt, a person's specific behavior, beliefs, and expressions are grounded in his own biography and in the development of his own consciousness; but it is hard not to see here a more general trend, inherent in the semiotic breakdown of a whole social group. Thus, Stefan Grossman (1875–1935), a Viennese Jew who became one of the leading journalists of the German Weimar Republic and editor of the German weekly *Das Tagebuch*, tells in his memoirs how his own parents "spoke a different language" than his, and saw the highest

---

5. I use "realization" for the key term of *hagshama*, referring to those who did not just preach but came to Palestine to implement personally the ideals of Zionism.

value in "money, money, money." His own poor and worried mother appeared to him "as the incarnation of capitalist thinking," and though he admits she had no money, "money was the most important word in her vocabulary." Even in retrospect, from 1930, he was grateful to his own "instinctive antisemitism" which helped him in his youth to liberate himself from his family (Grossman 1930: 24–25). Grossman also published Karl Marx's wildly antisemitic papers, written from a similar position. But the derogatory slogan "money, money, money" is used already by Sholem Aleichem's Tevye the Milkman. Furthermore, such a hatred for the capitalist mentality of one's parents does not have to identify it as "Jewish," but so it was. And the Russian Social-Democrat Lev Deytsh (1855–1941) tells in his memoirs (published in Berlin in 1923) about the reaction of his intellectual circle and family to the pogrom in Odessa in 1871: "our own fellow Jews give enough reasons for the hostile relation toward them, the major reason being their preference for unproductive, easy, and more financially reward-ing jobs"; the Jewish intelligentsia "must encourage the people to undertake hard, physical work [not intended for themselves!—B.H.] and help them get rid of superstitions, prejudices, bad habits; in short, one must pull the Jews out of darkness and poverty in which their majority lives" (Deytsh 1923:34–35).

Like many others, Walter Lippmann (1889–1974) echoed these words in America in 1922: "The rich and vulgar and pretentious Jews of our big American cities [. . .] are the real fountain of antisemitism. [. . .] You cannot build up a decent civilization among people who, when they are at last, after centuries of denial, free to go to the land and cleanse their bodies [sic!], now huddle together in a steam-heated slum." Though a Jew himself and the son of a real-estate developer (whom he did not like to remember), he opposed "too great a concen-tration" of Jews at Harvard, because of their inferior "manners and habits." (How far is this from the views of T. S. Eliot, perceived as antisemitic?) Lippmann was the most influential American journalist during World War II, but he never mentioned the Nazi extermination of the Jews. (See Ronald Steel's [1980] biog-raphy of Lippmann and the review in *New York Review of Books*, Oct. 9, 1980.)

Yet, if it is "self-hatred," it is matched in many texts of Hebrew literature itself. The fictional and journalistic writings of the great Hebrew writer Y. H. Brener (1881–1921) are filled with expressions even sharper than these. In his famous essay of 1914, "Our Self-Evaluation in Three Volumes," celebrating Mendele's *Collected Works*, he extrapolates a view of the Jews from Mendele's writings taken almost as gospel. To begin with: "A 'living' people whose members have no power but for moaning and hiding a while until the storm blows over, turning away from their poorer brethren to pile up their pennies in secret, to scratch around among the *goyim*, make a living from them, and complain all day long about their ill will—no, let us not pass judgment upon such a people, for indeed it is not worth it." He talks of "our sick character" and the "universal and understandable hatred of such a strange being, the Jew," and praises the function of Hebrew literature: "The literature of self-criticism since Mendele says: *Our function now is*

to recognize and admit our meanness since the beginning of history to the present day,
all the faults in our character, and then to rise and start all over again" (my
emphasis—B.H.). This caustic negation, however, is a purifying move that lays
the groundwork for a positive purpose: "we need our own environment" and "our
character must be radically changed," and he sees that solution in the small groups
of pioneers in Eretz-Israel: "Workers' Settlements—this is our revolution. The
only one." (See Hertzberg 1973:307–312.) Indeed, pioneers of the Labor Zionist
movement adored their prophet Brener precisely for the sharpness and "honesty"
of that negation, as we can see from Rachel Katznelson's (1888–1975) essay
"Language Insomnia" (in this volume). Shlomo Tsemakh (1886–1974), one of
the first workers of the Second Aliya, wrote in his memoirs: "The generation was
educated by the naked truth of Mendele and the atrocious truth of Elyakum and
his wife in Brener's 'In Winter' and the emotional truth of Bialik's poems, every
word of which carried a meaning several times greater than what was written"
(Tsemakh 1965:148).

Needless to say, the features criticized in such negations—by Jews and anti-
semites alike—are not "Jewish" in themselves and are not all negative: for example, trade facilitates the economy; intellectual work cannot be so bad in itself;
striving toward "financially more rewarding jobs" is hardly a Jewish monopoly or
an evil justifying pogroms; and the symptoms of upward mobility of people with
lower-class behavioral patterns are not exclusive to Jews. But when such features
were condensed in a cluster, matching widespread stereotypes, and were coupled
with a massive "push" of Jews into a very different culture, the clash of semiotic
systems was laid bare and foregrounded the criticism from the outside and from
the inside. Furthermore, it is precisely the belief of Jews in lofty Western culture
(without many contacts with the concrete life of the carriers of that culture) that
prevented them from assuming that antisemitism was altogether groundless—and
sent them off to find internal therapies.

The hatreds, tensions, and contempt that characterized relations between various Jewish groups who had different existential and cultural solutions (even
between members of different waves of *Aliya* to Eretz-Israel) thrived on that split
of the "we" that passed through the heart of every individual. The other person
or trend appeared so negative because they demonstrated one side of the "we" of
ourselves or our parents which was not completely repressed in us, or because
they represented an alternative road not taken by us. And that split was com-
pounded by the debate on the specific positive solution to the slogans "not here"
and "not now," a debate that was sometimes fatally bitter since it seemed as if the
very existence of the Jews or their descendants as well as your own personal
existence depended on it.

The problem of the three deictics, representing three axes of orientation in the
world, was especially acute within Jewish society for two reasons: a) the lack of
an identifiably Jewish existential base in a specific territory, and b) the foundation

of Jewishness itself in a world of discourse. In other words, this society was not rooted in existential axes in a geographic area of its own—a physical *here* and *now* and a stable *we* of a normal nation.[6] On the contrary, in their everyday awareness—as Jews—they were connected to a *universe of discourse*, a "fictional world" outside of history and geography, based on a library of texts and their interpretations (or, at least, instinctive beliefs and responses derived from that). Hence the centrality of discourse (rather than love of the land) for their self-understanding. When this universe of discourse lost its moorings (the two thousand years of "dead books" which M. Z. Fayerberg [1874–1899] denounced in *Whither*), the anchoring of a universe of discourse vis-à-vis the "real," historical world became the most important existential question for any alternative, any mode of Jewish culture, and for every individual. Hence the fervor of the rejection, the sharpness of the criticism, and the eagerness to grasp every specific new solution as if it were of paramount concern: whether it was the tiny kibbutz Eyn Harod in the Jezreel Valley, or Yiddish literature, a pure German accent, or the Sephardi pronunciation of Hebrew.

Instead of a religious world that was rejected or became meaningless, every new solution strove eagerly to grasp a new "*here*," "*now*," and "*I*," to adopt an acquired set of values as new axes of life, demanding ideological justification and fanatic loyalty. The break with the past was compensated by a person's being anchored in a new island, even if it eventually turned out to be a temporary island at the crossroads. The importance of Yiddish or Hebrew literature, in the eyes of their adherents, as a new territory for Jewish existence was part of that phenomenon (in retrospect we can see that those were islands on the way to another continent). And those who found their new "here" and "now" and "we" in the culture of another language, intensely embraced both the high culture and the daily semiotics of that language. Saul Bellow (b. 1915), in a tribute to Bernard Malamud (1914–1986), after his death in 1986, wrote: "Well, we were here, first-generation Americans, our language was English and *a language is a spiritual mansion from which no one can evict us*" (quoted by Robert Giroux, "Introduction," in Malamud 1989:15; my emphasis—B.H.).

The revival of the *Yishuv*, the new Jewish community in Eretz-Israel, was also formulated to a large extent in contrasting oppositions: Zionism as opposed to a Socialist solution in the Diaspora; Jewish secular culture as opposed to assimilation; Hebrew as opposed to Diaspora Yiddish; the "Sephardi accent" as a "pioneer" and "masculine" language as opposed to the "moaning" and religious Ashkenazi Hebrew; a "Hebrew" people and "Hebrew" work as opposed to the distorted

---

6. Of course, in their non-Jewish aspect—as "Germans," "Russians," and so on—the same people were part of a State and a language-based nation anchored in a specific territory and concrete political situation. And within this framework, Jewish politics throughout history tried to find accommodations with the specific political powers. But in no case was it felt to be a Jewish "ancestral land," even when Jews lived there for many centuries.

"Jewish" character; return to nature as opposed to the (imaginary) "ghetto" walls of the *shtetl*; return to the land as opposed to life up in the air (people who lived in the air and on the air were called *luftmentshn*, which Kafka described as *Lufthunde*, "soaring dogs," in his "Investigations of a Dog"); bearing arms as opposed to the impotence of the Diaspora Jew;[7] admiration of youth as opposed to the culture of the fathers; and idolization of the *sabra* (Israeli-born youth) as a new man or woman and a new Jew, healthy in body and mind, a young wholesome person who does not brood or hesitate. Berl Katznelson (1887–1944) thus finished "From Inside," his first published, programmatic article, written in Hebrew in Palestine, 1912:

> Only with the actual exit from the ghetto will Zionism find a way for its fullfilment. *The change of the geographical center* in itself, by an internal imperative, [. . .] gradually turns into *a change of a moral and vital center*. The forefathers' heritage, the suffering of generations and the distortions of history, little by little, give way—though with considerable resistance—to the new forces that revolted against them. The expected change of all values in the inspiration of Hebrew poetry, the change of all values of matter and spirit, are imminent. Instead of the murky matter of ghetto life—life on soil and labor; instead of the spiritual life of the old and renewed ghetto—man born straight. (1912:19; my emphases—B.H.)

That is why Brener, the prophet of the pioneers, wrote, in a review published in the journal of the Eretz-Israel labor movement, words that caused quite a stir: "*We, free Jews, have nothing to do with Judaism* [anakhnu [. . .] ha-yehudim ha-khofshim, eyn lanu ve-la-yahadut klum]" (Brener 1910:8; my emphasis—B.H.). Though they would hardly suspect it, Berl's and Brener's words could be expressed by Jewish Communists, assimilationists, and Yiddishists as well. If Jews succeeded in a short time in breaking out of their material and spiritual "ghetto"—in Berlin or Warsaw, New York or Boston, Moscow or Tel Aviv—it is because of such a strongly felt negative impulse. However, those who joined a foreign culture rarely explained their position in the open, for dealing with their Jewishness would not be part of the expected behavior in their new culture.[8] Those who tried to create an intrinsic cultural alternative certainly had to erect an ideology for that purpose.

The question is only what positive impulse was chosen instead. Brener's—in the same article—was the intrinsic, secular choice. The radical statement quoted above actually continues thus: "and nevertheless, we are part of the collective [=

---

7. In fact, what was internalized here as an ideal was the two defining features of the feared Cossack: settling in a borderland village and bearing arms. The change was so successful that agricultural products and arms became the main exports of the State of Israel (along with the "Jewish" diamonds, promulgated by an international Jewish network rather than an authentic Israeli culture).

8. Hence, people like Kafka and Freud, who were preoccupied with their problematic Jewish identity, discussed it primarily in private communications.

nation]—by no means less than those who lay tefilin and grow sidelocks," and he concludes:

> We, the living Jews, [. . .] do not stop identifying ourselves as Jews, living our Jewish lives, working and creating Jewish modes of work, talking our Jewish language, accepting our spiritual nourishment from our literature, toiling for our free national culture, defending our national honor, and fighting the war of our existence in every form this war assumes. (Brener 1910:8)

Of course, the ideals of "not here" and "not now" can be described as basic tenets of Romanticism. Indeed, both the new Hebrew poetry and the political ideologies can be said to derive (by different routes) from Romanticism, in a broad sense of that term. The difference is that, in this revolutionary period, such Romantic ideals are no longer yearnings and evocations of poetic or fictional worlds but attempts at their realization in the actual life of the "I" and the collective "we," in actual history.

SIX

The New Cultural Trends

In terms of political awareness, the break with the old universe of discourse entailed a departure from both the ahistorical perception permeating the ideology of religious Jewry and the collective nature of that ideology (with the slogan of "all Jews are responsible for each other")—and acceptance of two alternative principles essential to modern European culture: historicism and individual consciousness.

Mendele's Benjamin the Third or Sholem Aleichem's Tevye the Milkman still view specific historical events in ahistorical (or pan-historical), folklorized yet text-related terms. The belief in an abstract "destiny" as governing the lot of the nation and the individual, to the minutest detail, is reflected in that repeatedly used Yiddish word *bashert* ("it was so designed," "it was destined").[9] The new trends are manifested in a return to history. Solomon Maimon admires the beauty of history as opposed to the dreariness of the Talmud (see Mendes-Flohr and Reinharz 1980:215). A return to history means actively interfering in its events and in the human and Jewish fate in a given context—for example, voting in elections, participating in demonstrations and strikes, or immigrating illegally to Eretz-Israel. Hence the importance of political organization, political awareness, and a personal decision on one's own destiny in light of one's understanding of a given political situation. Indeed, the two major movements influential among Jews—Zionism and Socialism—both set out to interfere in the process of history. Yet, paradoxically, both intended to interfere in history in order to stop history altogether: to end the two-thousand-year history of the Diaspora or the five-

---

9. Of course, Jews acted on specific issues in specific historical circumstances, but their consciousness of themselves *as Jews* was attached to an ideology outside of the given historical situation. Hence the role of the *shtadlan*, the influential Jew in the present who can intercede with the authorities for the people as a whole.

thousand-year history of class struggle. If, with time, they encountered trouble, it is because history cannot really be stopped.

The second new principle was the value of the individual's personal consciousness, his analytic understanding of his own life and consciousness, of human life in general, and the life of the group. "The most awful disease [. . .] is the war man fights in his own soul and heart," writes M. Z. Fayerberg in *Whither* (1899), and it is hard not to recognize in that the torments of the Russian soul and, specifically, the influence of Dostoevsky's "Notes from the Underground," popular in Russia at the time. Hence, the utmost importance of literature, a kind of discourse in which the individual's consciousness of the dimensions of his social and metaphysical being, entangled in the most concrete situations, is central to its nature as discourse.

As indicated above, the intrinsic trends of the modern Jewish revolution created a *three-pronged cluster* of new cultural modes modeled on European secular culture. Let us examine these three major areas in some detail.

1. A new Jewish literature and textual culture emerged in Hebrew, Yiddish, and a third language (Russian, German, Polish, and now English, French). This culture was expressed in the genres, themes, modes of discourse, trends, publishing institutions, and so on, as developed in European languages. Typically, in Russia at the end of the nineteenth century, a powerful fiction emerged in Yiddish, poetry and essays in Hebrew, and essays and historiography in Russian (with the other languages trailing behind in each of those genres). At the beginning of this revolution, the idea of a trilingual Jewish culture (Hebrew, Yiddish, and the language of the State) was raised by a literary critic, "Criticus," in an article in Russian published in 1888 (see Slutski 1961:57).[10] "Criticus" was the pen name of Simon Dubnov (1860–1941), who later became one of the great historians of the Jewish people and who formulated the theory of wandering centers as characteristic of that history. (This is a typical phenomenon of the period: awareness of the vitality and the problematics of Jewish literature in the present leads to the question of the nature of Jewish history; a literary critic becomes a historian. This, too, is part of a broadly conceived Romanticism that permeated both literature and ideology and eventually had to emphasize their relative, historical nature.)

The conception of Jewish literature as trilingual was blurred for a long time, during the infamous "war of languages," supported by ideologies for which language (one language!) was the foundation of national identity. It was overtly an often vicious war between Hebrew and Yiddish, and, subterraneanly, between each of those and the languages of assimilation, and vice versa. The ideological dimension of language was indicated by the concept of "Yiddishland" (the sense

---

10. This notion of a trilingual Jewish culture was later resumed in an important paper by Chone Shmeruk.

of a surrogate homeland their language provided Yiddish writers and readers), on the one hand, and concepts like "Hebrew Work," "Federation of Hebrew Workers," and "Hebrew Youth," on the other, indicating a new conception of social being, marked by language. The trilingual theory, however, was not a whim but reflected the actual trilingualism of Jewish society at the beginning of the centrifugal movement; it was logical and maximalist at the same time: the new Hebrew literature established a beachhead to the secular world in the European mode while maintaining its linguistic attachment to the traditional library of texts; Yiddish literature raised the spoken language of the masses to a respectable level and embodied the new populism, the positive relation to folk vitality and the potential strength latent in the masses; while Jewish writings in Russian and German built a bridge to the culture and science of the dominant society and to the Jewish youth who were rapidly assimilating and coming back from assimilation.

A typical example of the trilingual culture can be seen in the "Sages of Odessa," a group of cultural figures who gave the tone and determined standards of Jewish culture at the turn of the nineteenth and in the beginning of the twentieth century (though only some of them actually lived in Odessa for a longer period of time): Aḥad Ha-Am (1856–1927) was a Hebrew essayist and philosopher; H. N. Bialik (1873–1934), a Hebrew poet (who sometimes wrote Yiddish); Mendele, a Yiddish novelist, who recast his own works into Hebrew; Sholem Aleichem, a Yiddish fiction writer (who also wrote Hebrew); Simon Dubnov, a historian who wrote primarily in Russian (but also in Yiddish and Hebrew).

The new Jewish literature may seem to be almost a direct continuation of Jewish Enlightenment literature of the nineteenth century, the *Haskala*. The three classical masters, Mendele Moykher Sforim, Sholem Aleichem, and Y. L. Peretz (1852–1915), began as Enlightenment writers. Indeed, if mature writers had not existed at the time of the shock (of 1881–82), there would not have been an immediate literary response. But only the changes that took place in their writing after the shock made them what they are and guaranteed the high level of their writing perceived as such to this day. During the Enlightenment, Jewish writers were active and books were published, but there was hardly a full-fledged literary-cultural establishment including journals, continuity, and a network of publishers. Moreover, European literary standards—involving a) tension between the internal world of the individual endowed with a complex consciousness, on the one hand, and the reflection of significant social and philosophical trends on the other, and b) a writer's confronting the challenges of the "language of literature" and its specific nature—such standards were fully achieved in Jewish literature only in the modern period.

At the turn of the century, both in Hebrew and in Yiddish, there was a new sense of literary and cultural creativity emerging from nowhere, almost *ex nihilo*, since the concepts of literature and poetry were derived not from the internal tradition but directly from the dominant culture (Russian and German) that became classic and canonized before their treasures were opened to Jewish youth.

This sense of beginning is indicated, for example, in Bialik's essay, "Our Young Poetry" (1907), or in the nickname, "Grandfather of Yiddish Literature," given to Mendele Moykher Sforim by younger members of his own generation, like Sholem Aleichem, who himself was pronounced a "Classic" of Yiddish literature even during his own lifetime. In the 1920s, such a sense of innovation recurred, this time under the impact of Modernism after World War I.

It was indeed a real beginning, for Hebrew or Yiddish writers in that period did not learn the history of their own literature in school, as writers do in other nations, nor was literature part of the canonical Jewish tradition, but, rather, each of them "leaped" out of the religious library straight into the European conceptual world—and from there, returned to secular writing in their own language (perhaps relating to a few models from the internal literature of the generation preceding them). Only later, from the position of a self-conscious, mature literature, did Hebrew and Yiddish construct an honorific past for themselves and foster the study of literary history. Many writers and most of their readers participated at least in the two internal literatures, Hebrew and Yiddish, and often in three or four; but the institutions—journals, newspapers, poetry books, publishers, and so on—were separate for each language and built autonomous linguistic cultures which, in time, separated entirely from each other.

For the sake of creating in a rich literary language, as required by European norms—by Romanticism and Realism as well as by Modernism—a tremendous ongoing effort was made to develop and enrich the language itself. This occurred in Yiddish—ostensibly a living language but, at the end of the nineteenth century, still primitive and dubbed the "*tsholent* language" by its poet Shimon Frug and "*jargon*" (i.e., "slang," "medley") by its leading writers Sholem Aleichem and Y. L. Peretz. And it occurred in the "dead" Hebrew, which was revived to express, in principle, all modes of international secular culture. This effort was invigorated by the extensive enterprise of translations into the two languages and the expansion of Jewish writing to the areas of politics, science, nature, poetics, education, psychoanalysis, and so on. A Hebrew or Yiddish writer had to develop the instruments of his art during the very act of creating: he had to work out the genres suitable to his specific fictional world, the modes of expression, the language of literature, and the terminology of politics, nature, and science. Within a short time, Jewish literature attempted to catch up with the developments of the European literary tradition since the Renaissance (including its flashbacks toward classical literature) and to spread out over the whole range of genres, both in original works and in translation. And, at the same time, it endeavored to break through to the contemporary trends of Modernism which were turning that very tradition upside down.

Shaul Tshernikhovski (1875–1943) and Uri-Tsvi Grinberg (1894–1981), both living in Germany in the 1920s, represent this range between paradox and eclecticism. Tshernikhovski had extended the scope of Hebrew lyric poetry, as launched by Bialik in the 1890s, to the political poem, the ballad, the narrative and descriptive long poems; he revived in Hebrew the German eighteenth-century idyll and grafted onto it the principles of Romantic figurative language; he developed the sonnet and the sonnet ring in a conscious double reference: to his contemporaries, the Russian Symbolist poets and to the fourteenth-century Hebrew poet Imanuel of Rome; he translated Homer's epic and the Finnish and Babylonian epics, an ancient Russian (*Igor's Tale*) and an American narrative poem (Longfellow's *Hiawatha*), German lyrics, and a whole book by the Greek poet Anacreon. Uri-Tsvi Grinberg responded by placing *Anacreon on the Pole of Melancholy* (the name of one of his volumes of poetry published in 1928); wrote anticlassical Expressionist manifestos, attacking the sonnet and the idyll in the name of the fate of the Jewish people; and, as he said, "brought the American Walt Whitman to the workers' Eretz-Israel." Thus, the history of European literature was discovered by Jewish writers at the end of its development, when it was challenged from within. For the exultant discoverers, that history appeared not as a history but as a synchronic "imaginary museum" where all displays were placed in adjacent rooms, from which they could pick models and influences with no historical order. Else Lasker-Schüler and Nietzsche were translated concurrently with Homer, Shelley, and Rabindranat Tagore.

The aspiration was to create Hebrew or Yiddish literature that could measure up to world literature and be included in it. As the Introspectivist Manifesto of Yiddish poetry in New York in 1919 put it:

> Poetry is, to a very high degree, the art of language. [. . .] And Yiddish poetry is the art of the Yiddish language, which is merely a part of the general European-American culture. [. . .] Yiddish poetry is merely a branch, a particular stream in the whole contemporary poetry of the world. (Harshav 1986:780)

And vice versa: an immense effort was made to include world literature within the domain of Jewish literature. The place of translated literature in the collected writings of the Hebrew poets Shaul Tshernikhovski, David Frishman, Abraham Shlonski (1900–1973), or Natan Alterman (1910–1970) far exceeds what is typical for a poet in the major languages and often surpasses the extent of their own poetry. The Yiddish poet, short-story writer, and editor Avrom Reyzen (1876–1953) wrote in 1905, in the prospectus to his semi-Modernist periodical *Dos yudishe vort* ("The Yiddish [meaning also: Jewish] Word"):

> Yiddish is not just a means to educate the masses but a goal in its own right. It will serve the Jewish intelligentsia and will thus reflect all the trends and tendencies of the great world, so that the Jewish intellectual interested in higher questions will not have to resort to other literatures in other languages, a move that alienates him from the Jewish people. (Lexicon 8:462)

Reyzen published a Yiddish weekly, *European Literature*, including Yiddish translations from Byron, Thomas Mann, Baudelaire, Charles Dickens, Knut Hamsun, Leonid Andreev, and many others. The prestigious Hebrew periodical *Ha-Tekufa*, founded in 1918 in Moscow and published intermittently until 1950 in Warsaw, Berlin, Tel Aviv, and New York, was filled with translations from the best of world literature, especially epic and lyric poetry. Its first editor himself, David Frishman, translated hundreds of works by Pushkin, Nietzsche, Rabindranat Tagore, Byron, Goethe, Heinrich Heine, Oscar Wilde, Anatole France, and others. The translations included works from their countries of origin or acculturation and the cultures they aspired to, as well as other cultures and periods mediated by those. If Goethe's concept of *Weltliteratur* ("World Literature") was ever implemented, it was done in Yiddish and Hebrew in the Modern period. To this day, literary journals, publishers' lists, and library bookshelves in Israel reflect this tendency—to combine original and translated, classical and contemporary literature, in more or less equal proportions.[11]

All this has occurred within a hundred years or less. In this period, Yiddish and Hebrew literatures created the most powerful contribution to Jewish culture since the Bible. There is no greater sense of the culture of a nation and national identity than this achievement.

In terms of Jewish culture as a whole, we must also not underestimate the importance of the "third" language. Modern histories of the Jews were written in German by Heinrich Graetz (1817–1891) and in Russian by Simon Dubnov (for many years, German was a required language for students in Judaic disciplines at the first ever "Hebrew University" in Jerusalem). The "Science of Judaism" that began in nineteenth-century Germany also gave rise to the magnificent *Evreyskaya Entsiklopediya* ("Jewish Encyclopaedia") in Russian, published just before and after the 1917 Revolution, and the *Encyclopaedia Judaica* in English in the last generation. Today, in English and French, there is a widespread revival of literature on Jewish topics: research, journalism, translations of secular and religious texts from Hebrew and Yiddish, and original fictional works. With the linguistic assimilation of most Jews and the demise of Yiddish literature—which had served as an autonomous junction between the Hebrew tradition and the general European cultures—the "third" literature also fills this function. At one and the same time, it can be seen as part of the literature in the language it is written in (American, Russian, French, etc.) and also as an expression of a partial Jewish identity, either in its themes or in its mode of discourse.[12] The Tel Aviv–New York axis (and the less-known Tel Aviv–Paris axis) in fact is manifested in the renewal of a Jewish bilingual culture, at times with an additional nostalgic attachment to the third, Yiddish, limb peeping out from the cellar. This bilingual nature is manifested both in the dependence of Jewish Diaspora culture on the Israeli center of literature

---

11. See, for example, the "thick journal" *Siman Kriya* and its influential book series, *The Library (Ha-Sifriya)* or the *Popular Library (Sifriya La-am)*, published by "Am Oved."

12. Thus, Saul Bellow can be seen as an American writer focusing on Jewish characters, as well as a "Jewish" writer in a non-Jewish language. Similarly, studies in Jewish history in the English language are both part of American historiography and part of Jewish historical research.

and scholarship, and in the orientation toward reception in English and other languages, characterizing much of Israeli creativity.

We discussed literature in detail because this is the most language-dependent art or kind of discourse, and it also was in the center of the revival in this verbally oriented society. But all other arts and modes of discourse emerged in this society as well. Mark Chagall (1887–1985), Chaim Soutin (1893–1943), El Lissitzky (1890–1941), Max Weber (1881–1961), and many other Jewish artists of the period were Yiddish speakers, most from small towns, and many of them began with connections to Yiddish literature and drew illustrations to Yiddish books. They were all ideologically aware of the fact that there was no Jewish art before them, and Chagall saw the creation of a "Jewish art" as a historical challenge. But since art needs no language, and the new Jewish art and literature strove toward international standards anyway, the best of that generation were absorbed by the general art scene, thus bridging between the intrinsic and the extrinsic worlds.[13] The same Russified Yiddish city of Odessa that harbored the center of Hebrew literature in the beginning of the twentieth century, also produced the Jewish Russian writers Isaac Babel (1894–1941) and Edvard Bagritski (1895–1934) and the tradition of raising virtuoso violinists such as the Moscovite David Oistrakh (1908–1974) and the American Jascha Heifetz (1901–1987).

2. Within this period, a gamut of competing political ideologies and parties arose among the Jews (crystallizing especially in 1897, 1905–1907, 1917–1922), formulating all the possibilities and combinations of possibilities for a solution to the Jewish and/or human problem. These included varieties of Anarchism and Socialism (notably, the "Bund"); *Sejmism* (i.e., "Parliamentarism," calling for separate Jewish parliaments); *Revivalism* and *Folkism*, which variously promoted Jewish political and cultural autonomy in the Diaspora; Territorialism, seeking a Jewish State outside of Eretz-Israel (some thirty-six different territories, including Uganda, Surinam, Western Australia, and Birobidzhan, were considered for such a purpose); many shades of Zionism; several ideologically competing varieties of Socialist Zionism (pro-Soviet left Marxist, anti-Soviet left Marxist, Freudian left Marxist, Social-Democratic anti-Marxist, Tolstoyan Agrarian Socialist, Yiddishist); a Zionist religious movement (*Mizrakhi*) and an anti-Zionist religious movement (*Agudas Isroel*); and labor varieties of those (*Ha-Poel Ha-Mizrakhi* and *Poaley Agudat Israel*); as well as extensive Jewish activism in general political trends, especially in the Socialist and Communist movements. All such parties had their

---

13. Just one example: Chagall's use of the Crucifix and the image of Christ in the 1920s, and later in paintings responding to the Holocaust, was severely attacked by Jewish critics. But this iconography came directly from Yiddish literature in the twenties, where Christ as our suffering brother was a major symbolic figure, notably in the nationalist poetry of Uri-Tsvi Grinberg, published in the same journals in which Chagall participated. See his cross-shaped poem "Uri-Tsvi before the Cross," beginning with the line: I N R I.

affiliated youth movements, which often were ideologically independent and deviated from their adult party line.[14] All these were formulated and hotly debated within the narrow confines of the Jewish communities. The *General Jewish Workers' Union in Lithuania, Poland, and Russia (Bund)* was founded in Vilna in 1897, before its Russian counterpart, and members of the Bund assisted in launching in 1898 the Russian Social-Democratic Party, which led to the Revolutions of 1917. The competition between the Bund and the labor Zionists for the support of the Jewish laborers and intellectuals produced not only hatred but also mutual influence. Uri-Tsvi Grinberg's move from Yiddish poetry and Left labor Zionism to Hebrew poetry and rightist Zionist "Revisionism" (or: from a "Hebrew *Revolution*" to a "*Hebrew* Revolution") is just one example indicating that the two poles were in the same field of debate.

3. No less important was the rise of a network of cultural, educational, social, and political organizations attached to competing ideological and linguistic trends, some of them starting in the *Haskala* period: the society of "Disseminators of Education" (*mefitsey haskole*); the organization devoted to promoting health among Jews (*OZE, or TOZ*); the "Society for Dissemination of Labor among Jews" (*ORT*), which maintains a network of technical schools in Israel and around the world even now; the network of secular *Tarbut* schools in Hebrew; schools of CYSHO (mostly Bundist-inspired) and *Shulkult* (Labor Zionist) in Yiddish, especially strong in Poland between the two world wars; the modern religious schools (*Ezra* or *Beys Yakov* for girls); public libraries in every town and kibbutz; theaters, sports associations, newspapers, publishing houses, Jewish professional unions, and so on. The fountainhead of all this activity was in Eastern Europe, but it spread throughout the world, changing shape and reorganizing every so often. Moreover, the ideas and the participants came from Russia and Poland, but only in the West did they have the full freedom to organize and flourish: Yiddish newspapers and strong, international labor unions, as well as poetry in the Russian-inspired accentual-syllabic meters, emerged on a large scale for the first time in America, initiated by the same circles—to be rejoined by Eastern Europe only after 1917. Yiddish (and, to a lesser degree, Hebrew) newspapers, publishers, and schools literally covered the globe: they could be found not only in Poland, Lithuania, Latvia, the USSR, and Romania, but also in America, Canada, Argentina, England, France, South Africa, China, or Australia, wherever first- (and sometimes second-) generation immigrants found themselves.

---

14. For a long time, *Ha-Shomer Ha-Tsa'ir* ("The Young Guard") had no adult party at all and remained "Young" until its leaders reached the age of 90. Itzhak Zuckerman (Antek), leader of the Warsaw Ghetto Uprising, describes dramatically how the Zionist-Socialist youth movements organized the revolt, disregarding the adult Party, even though they were beyond the age of a youth movement, and took destiny in their own hands. (See Zuckerman 1993.)

Such a three-pronged network—literature, ideologies, and Jewish social and cultural organizations—was in part brought from the Diaspora and in part reestablished in Eretz-Israel from the start of the new Jewish settlement. There it flourished easily and by dint of the reality of a place that seemed to the newcomers to be a social desert: the new immigrants perceived the country as theirs and paid little attention to any social life and language of another nation that might have existed there, as Jews did in all other countries of immigration. This trend reached its apogee in the consolidation of the Hebrew *Yishuv*—which really was a Jewish nation-State without territorial power—as a separate ("consociational") entity in Mandatory Palestine, and its eventual transformation into an independent State.

SEVEN

The Secular Polysystem

The expression "secularism" does not exactly account for this three-pronged cultural cluster. To explain this idea, we may introduce the concept of "polysystem," as suggested by Itamar Even-Zohar.[15] We may define a polysystem as a network of interrelated textual genres and social and cultural institutions in a society, each one of which is a flexible system in its own right; that is, a polysystem is a dynamic *system of systems*, as the Russian Formalist Yury Tynyanov described literature, but covering the whole cultural network.

We may say that traditional Jewish life in the past was not reduced to religious life only, but rather was grounded in a social and cultural polysystem exclusive to the Jews—under the aegis of their religion—and encompassing all areas of life. The Jews of the Middle Ages were not a "minority" in the conventional sense (or as they are now in the United States), even though they did not cover a continuous territory, as other subordinate nations did, but were scattered among majority populations. Thus, in the greater Poland, especially between the sixteenth and eighteenth centuries where two-thirds of world Jewry was concentrated, the Jews in fact had administrative autonomy (symbolized by a kind of Jewish parliament, the "Council of Four Lands"). They had their own religious, legal, and administrative system, tax collection (for the King or noble landowners and for themselves), professional organizations, societies for mutual help, medicine, burial societies; moreover, they had a separate, trilingual culture (in Hebrew, Aramaic, and Yiddish) with a separate library of texts, a separate educational network, an ethical movement, and a separate conceptual world. Within this polysystem, they were not a "minority" (like other national minorities) but rather an exclusive *totality*. What was lacking for the existence of a complete national society was the aspect of territorial power: a State, a government, an army, foreign

15. See his collected and revised papers in Even-Zohar 1990.

policy, and so on—and, in that respect, they were not a minority but a *nullity*. A similar structure, perhaps in a less comprehensive form, embraced Jewish life in other places and at other times (for example, in Babylon in the Talmudic period). All this was possible in the pluralistic framework of feudal societies, based on the coexistence of several social classes and professional guilds, in which the Jews constituted a kind of social "class" of their own—that is, before the modern, centralized nation-State took over.

What held this social and cultural polysystem together was a religious framework. Religion was a legal and defining property of persons and communities; it marked the boundary between the internal social-cultural network and the outside world. Hence this network can be described as a *Jewish Religious Polysystem* that established an extraterritorial existence spread over many territories dominated by other nations. But, within the framework of this Religious Polysystem, all aspects of life were accounted for, including aspects that are essentially secular such as medicine, criminal law, speech in a separate language, studying writing and arithmetic, a tailors' organization (or synagogue), or writing poetry in Hebrew. Religion was only the all-encompassing—legal and identifying—ideological framework for the whole polysystem. Its force as a framework is even more impressive when we realize the lack of any unified and hierarchical organized religious authority ruling over all the Jews (like the Roman Catholic Church). Even in small and detached communities it worked, by dint of the dense and intensive *Jewish universe of discourse*: it was a separate semiotic system, that is, a "private" language of culture that absorbed many elements from the outside, and combined them in its particular core.

On this background, the modern Jewish revolution was expressed not only in the formulation of new ideologies but also in the establishment of a multitude of new, mutually reinforcing social, political, and cultural institutions—a whole new *Jewish Secular Polysystem*. It was a classical example of the idea of an ethnic or national cultural autonomy, based on language rather than on territorial power, especially as formulated by the Austro-Marxists in the beginning of the twentieth century (with the purpose of providing equality to the many language groups in the Austro-Hungarian Empire without dissolving the Empire itself). It was, indeed, an absolute example, because it was the only such group that had no territory in which it was a majority at all and to which it could claim power. This autonomy was legally reinforced between the two world wars by the rights of the minorities protected by the Treaty of Versailles and the League of Nations. Poland, Lithuania, and the Soviet Union, where these principles were implemented, became the centers of worldwide Jewish culture.

At the beginning of the period, Simon Dubnov, the theoretician of autonomy, understood the necessity of building on such a wide front: "The internal autonomy of the Jewish nationality rests on a threefold basis: *the community, the language, and the school*" (the first term referring to an elected autonomous municipal body, the *Kehila*) (Dubnov 1958:143). The actual implementation was even more diversified. In a very short time, networks of new Jewish schools emerged: secular and religious, in Yiddish, Ashkenazi Hebrew, and Sephardi Hebrew, as well as in the languages of the respective states; scientific institutions, publishers, libraries, newspapers, political parties, youth movements, labor federations, welfare and medical societies, schools for professional education, cooperatives of craftsmen and so on—a veritable "Jewish State," separate and voluntary, though without ownership of land or a government. (In this respect, today's Jewish minorities are radically different: they participate in the elected bodies, parties, schools, trade unions, and other institutions of the general polysystem.)

Most of these institutions arose voluntarily, without any tradition at all, according to the models and under the influence of trends in the general society. For example, youth movements, which played a central role in reeducating the young generation and in the ferment and change in the Diaspora, and which fed the pioneer *Yishuv* in Eretz-Israel, were formed under the influence of general youth movements, particularly German ones, with their ideals of going out to nature, making bonfires in the field,[16] group singing, ideological and literary debating, and scouting. The same is true of the cooperatives, journalism, publishing, the educational structure (primary, secondary, university), and so on. This dense network, in which every individual participated in several systems at one and the same time, was what enabled the existence of a minority nation on a voluntary basis and, *ipso facto*, took the place of the Religious Polysystem. Religious institutions and cultural expressions continued to exist, but they were absorbed in the all-encompassing new, secular framework, as they would be in any modern secular State.

In sum, the definition of Jewishness in the Religious Polysystem was *legal* and *essentialist*: a Jew was defined by *being* a Jew and was included in the whole network; whereas in the new, Secular Jewish Polysystem it is *voluntary* and *aspectual*. The system itself may contain all aspects and institutions of modern life, but the individual may join voluntarily only some of those and join the polysystem of another nation for other aspects. It is not his total being but some aspects of his conscious world and social affiliation that are Jewish. Thus, he or she may attend a Jewish elementary school and a French university, read Jewish literature as well as literature in other languages, be a member of a non-Jewish health organization or political party, and so on. This openness of coterritorial systems was convenient for the trend of assimilation to other societies, which increasingly enveloped more descendants of the Jews. In other words, the existence of a Jewish Secular Polysystem, even in its heyday in Poland and the Soviet Union between the two world wars, was not coextensive with the Jewish population. Yet it also enabled assimilated Jews to turn (or return) to some aspects of Jewish culture and knowledge whenever they chose.

16. That was not an invention of the Israeli *Palmakh* and youth movements, as it seemed to them.

This was a central problem of the Jewish Secular Polysystem from its beginnings: will it provide all facets of human culture in the intrinsic language, or only the "Jewish aspects" of a person's conscious world? In the latter case, the individual will have to bifurcate his field of consciousness and resort to both the internal and external cultures—very different from each other in their intellectual tenor—as most "Jewish" Jews do in America today. In the first case, however, all human experience is organically encompassed in his natural language and at his level of culture, as in prewar Poland and in contemporary Israel; unconcerned with this problem, Hebrew literature may thematically not appear as Jewish at all, and its readers may be as cosmopolitan as they like. This choice was the key issue in the argument between M. Y. Berditshevski (1865–1921) and Aḥad-Ha-Am in the first days of *Ha-Shiloaḥ*. And the arguments were repeated time and again. The "maximalist" or "cosmopolitan" position was also promoted by A. Leyeles (1889–1966) and the Introspectivist Yiddish poets in New York (see Harshav 1986:780, 789–790): Leyeles argued, against the Yiddish critic Sh. Nigger (1883–1955), that there is no Russian, French, or German "essence" in the respective literatures but that they are the sum total of everything written in those languages, hence one must not demand of Jewish poetry any exclusively "Jewish" content but include in it all of human experience, or, in his words: "Everything a Jewish poet writes [in a Jewish language] is Jewish poetry."

Even the ultranationalist V. Jabotinsky (1880–1940) fought for the same principle in Hebrew education:

> The center of gravity of the concept of "education" today lies in general studies. A small child, especially a *healthy* child, is not interested in national questions. Very different issues stir his curiosity: Why aren't horses harnessed to a train? What is the bright electrical light in the lanterns on the marketplace? Where do heat in the summer and cold in the winter come from? Where is America, from which his older brother's letters arrive? [. . .] Write down for a few months all the questions your little son asks, and you will see that only a small part of them concerns Jewish topics, whereas the majority belongs to "general" disciplines. Hence, the *basic* language of school is the language in which *general* studies are conducted. [. . .] The language of school—only it—will always remain his language of culture and education. (Jabotinsky 1914:408)

Hence, while promoting a full-fledged Hebrew education in Diaspora, Jabotinsky observes that children's literature must also not be "national" in its content and spirit: "an *interesting* book in the *Hebrew* language—this is the desirable type for our children's library" (Jabotinsky 1914:411). For, as Jabotinsky explains, in other nations too, often the father is a nationalist and the son a cosmopolitan who does not believe in nationalism; "but in those nations there is a stronger link than emotion which links the individual to the nation, namely the link of *language.* [. . .] *In national education, language is the essence and content is the chaff*" (Jabotinksy 1914:406; my emphasis—B.H.).

This was the position that characterized the Jewish Secular Polysystem when it flourished—its literature, ideologies, and institutions—and this position won out in Israeli culture; whereas in the present-day Diaspora, Jewish education confined itself to "Jewish" topics only, hence to an apologetic, quasi-religious identity teaching, allowing its participants to enjoy secular culture and critical thinking only in the non-Jewish framework.

It was the combination of these three—ideology, literature, and the social network—that created the Jewish "State in the making" or "State on the Road" (*medina she-ba-derekh*). Without it, neither a rootless literature nor abstract ideologies would have survived. Their existence was characterized by a dialectical tension and a constant flow of people and ideas between the different alternatives. Thus, the revival of Hebrew drew a great deal on the renaissance of Yiddish. Mendele Moykher Sforim, the father of the new, synthetic Hebrew, combining various historical layers of the language in one text, developed the synthetic Hebrew "style" as a response to the synthetic Yiddish, a strong blend of its linguistic components, of which he himself was the great master. Also, many elements of Yiddish penetrated the spoken language in Israel, the journalistic style, and so on, as a subtext. In addition, various phenomena in the revival of Israel may be explained by the models of Russian culture: the poetics of Shlonski's and Alterman's poetry, even of the poetry of the Canaanite ideologue Yonatan Ratosh (1908–1981): the revolutionary ethos of the Third Aliya coming after the October Revolution; or the period of "Progressive Culture" flourishing in Israel in the 1950s.

Modern Jewish literature lived only because of the support of this network: newspapers, libraries, schools, and political movements grew and developed a community of readers and writers. Nevertheless, there were latent tensions between literature and the ideological and political establishment close to it: between Hebrew literature and political Zionism (without Zionism, Hebrew literature would not have had a base, but literature was not inclined to be its direct mouthpiece) and between Yiddish literature and the political establishment that supported it (especially the Bundists and the Communists). The tensions came from the conflict between contradictory concepts of cultural discourse proper to these genres and adopted from the outside, especially from Russian culture: on the one hand, the schematic, consistently "logical," indeed totalitarian, concept of discourse of the political movements—as opposed, on the other hand, to the subtle and ambivalent individualism that determined the fictional worlds of high literature. True, Russian literature fulfilled a critical social function in tsarist Russia, as it does today. In Russian society, however, literature could be independent of the political establishment, both in government and in the opposition, since it relied on its own audience which lived within a language and State framework anyway. But in Jewish society, complete independence of literature would have sawed off the branch the writer sat on (since he didn't have a "State" other than the ideological framework). This was even further complicated by the fact that some Hebrew writers (notably David Frishman) were not Zionists and some

Yiddish writers (notably Sholem Aleichem) were Zionists. In Yiddish—in Warsaw or New York—moreover, there was the pretentious superficiality of mass journalism (for a people whose young intellectuals went off to other languages), which threatened the writer's language with banality, sentimentality, and rhetoric—and it was precisely this journalism which gave the writers a livelihood.

This clash between two major modes of discourse intersected with the high-tension network of competing political trends and social and language institutions, while the entire complex was in constant motion: losing to assimilation, drawing new audiences from the crumbling small town or from waves of immigration, struggling with the heavy pressures of a foreign authority, and moving in migrations from country to country.

This dynamic Jewish Secular Polysystem flourished in Eastern Europe and saw a partial life in the West and in the United States. Under its umbrella, there were also religious forms—for example, religious poetry, a language of religious images (used by secular people and writers as well), religious schools, or religious political parties. Thus, the change did not lie necessarily in abandoning religion or rebelling against it (although that too was a powerful motivation in this period—for Freud as for Ben-Gurion, for Perets Markish as for Tshernikhovsky) but rather in the nature of the new framework, as a polysystem whose general form and particular genres are now secular: European in conception and voluntary in organization.

This Secular Polysystem was tri- or multilingual at first (Jewish intellectuals, typically, read Yiddish, Hebrew, Russian, German, and Polish). In Poland between the wars, the language polysystems were separate but still lived side by side; in the Soviet Union and the Americas, Yiddish became dominant; and in Eretz-Israel, Hebrew became the officially exclusive language. Thus, several autonomous Secular Polysystems evolved, each to each language; and today there is a Jewish network in English as well, though it is only a partial network on the margins of the general American Secular Polysystem.

The founders of the Hebrew *Yishuv* in Eretz-Israel, perhaps instinctively, understood the necessity of creating such a three-pronged base for their existence. They all came from the Diaspora, where they shed religious garb and eagerly joined the revolutionary Jewish Secular Polysystem emerging there: they participated in its institutions in Europe and America and read its texts. It was not ideology alone that built the Jewish State. The combination of existential pressures in the "social desert" of Palestine/Eretz-Israel and the internal need for such institutions—a need imported from the regenerated Diaspora (not from the religious world of the *shtetl*!)—engendered construction along a broad front.[17]

This entire three-pronged network erected in Palestine was modeled in the words of the revived Hebrew language, which developed ways of expression and concepts to contain all the areas of life and culture and served as mortar to unify

17. See the more detailed discussion in Part Two, especially in chapter 26.

it all in one society. Without the revival of the Hebrew language and its domination of the whole social network, it is doubtful that the State of Israel would have come into being. The German speakers of Herzl's utopian "Old-New Land" would have lived on Mount Carmel as isolated and overnight guests, as did the German writer Arnold Zweig (1887–1968) in the 1940s (who returned in 1948 from the Carmel to Communist East Berlin). The new society that took shape in Eretz-Israel, particularly from the Second Aliya on, was a Hebrew-speaking society whose intellectual sustenance came from the new Hebrew literature and ideology—young and abstract bodies of expression that filled the world of consciousness, supplanting the universe of discourse, the notions of *realia*, beliefs, and folklore accumulated over generations and now cast overboard. It was, as Berl Katznelson stressed (in the quotation above), the radical geographic move that enabled the rise of a new culture and morality.

EIGHT

Assimilation

The intrinsic institutions established throughout the Jewish world in this revolutionary period attempted to include all areas of human existence, experience, and creativity under the slogan "like all other nations" (*ke-khol ha-goyim*) or, in Brener's version, "like the perfect among them" (*ka-metukanim she-ba-hem*); and some went beyond that, ambitious to emanate a Biblical "light to the nations" (*or la-goyim*, a goal Ben-Gurion projected for the society and science of Israel). Their framework was Jewish: an exclusively Jewish language, literature in Hebrew or Yiddish, schools for the technological education of Jews, Jewish hospitals, and even a Jewish State. But much of the contents that filled such a Jewish framework were not inherently Jewish at all. Take the State of Israel: the bureaucracy and the universities, the slums and the hospitals, the highways and the cinemas, the tanks and the airplanes, and so on, are not essentially Jewish. It is the framework, the Jewish polysystem itself, the State, and the language, that enables its participants to identify as Jews. But within this framework they live a full life that includes a personal selection from everything offered a person (and forced on him) in this age—and, if you like, forms of life can be cosmopolitan in every respect.

The same is true of Hebrew and Yiddish literature: the ambition was to express all human desires, to develop a modern, innovative, or scientific language, to write iambs, sonnets, and novels in Hebrew or Yiddish; to write about love and death and cypress trees, and to include the best of world literature in that language. Hence, most Israeli literature today is not essentially "Jewish" except for its language and readership—as the literature of any other nation is not necessarily "national" in its essence.[18] The framework is "Jewish," but the content is "human" or, better, "literary." And to the extent that literature can be said to be expressive,

---

18. Would a literary critic ask an American writer to express his "Americanness"?

in the broad sense, of the mental "worlds" of its writers and readers, this cosmopolitan aspect represents them too; this is true for Israeli society today as it was
for Yiddish culture in Warsaw, Moscow, and New York in the 1920s. Even most
of the scholarship of Jewish texts or history is not "Jewish" but cosmopolitan in
its nature; Gershom Scholem's studies of the Kabbalah used the methodologies
of the German Humanities (*Geisteswissenschaften*), including that of Carl Jung.
Naturally, thematic and linguistic "Jewish" elements are an integral part of the
consciousness and world of the writer and his characters and may become central
to their concerns in specific texts and periods.

For Jewish writers in other languages, the opposite is true. In the Diaspora
today, when Jews are integrated into the polysystem of the general society, Jewish
institutions are mostly reduced to purely "Jewish" issues (although here, too,
there are a few neutral activities like "singles groups" within the Jewish community). The individual divides his life between such Jewish institutions (if at all)
and participation in the institutions of the general society. Moreover, writers in
the "third" language (e.g., Kafka, Philip Roth, or Saul Bellow) are identified as
Jewish writers only if some "Jewish" ingredients can be found in the style and
thematics of their writings—something that does not oblige the Israeli writer.

Hence the word "assimilation"—like its counterpart, "secularism" (discussed
above)—also cannot be accepted literally. For, in important respects, all Jews are
assimilated into general modern culture. The intrinsic directions of the revolution
aimed at creating a Jewish equivalent to that culture—an equivalent *freed of the
"obligation of Jewishness."* Rachel Katznelson expressed it when she wrote: "By
coming to Eretz-Israel, we wanted to liberate ourselves from nationalism as an
idée fixe. In Diaspora, nationalism hindered us in living." And even the Lubavitsher
Hasidim who would focus exclusively on the "obligation of Jewishness" have
embraced modern electronics and modern advertising in the *New York Times.*

NINE

A Jewish Century

What stands out on the extrinsic plane is the massive entrance of Jews or their descendants into the general economy and into the world of culture and science. In certain times and places, within an amazingly short period, unusual concentrations of descendants of Jews emerged in specific professions, concentrations that included a third or half or sometimes even a majority of a given field. About 50%–60% of the participants in the Expressionistic journals in the German language were of Jewish origin. So were many of the new German publishers and all prominent theater critics in Berlin in the 1920s. A large part of the audience in the Viennese theaters and many of its writers and directors were Jews. Most of the writers of the "Young Vienna" literary movement at the beginning of the twentieth century were born Jews or half Jews, and their identity crisis was part of a whole cluster of identity crises they embodied (see Pollak 1984). Psychoanalysis was at first a predominantly "Jewish" movement as was most of the Frankfurt School of Sociology, though in their language and goals they were as "general" as can be. A book by a German writer, Bernt Engelmann, *Germany without Jews* (1984), surveys the massive penetration of Jews and "Nuremberg Law Jews" (i.e., half and quarter Jews) into German culture and society. Among the builders of the Hollywood film industry, they formed a decisive majority. They were prominent in the ranks of modern linguistics, mathematics, and physics, among Soviet chess champions, among Russian and American violinists, among American winners of the Nobel Prize in Economics in the last generation, and in American culture and academic life in general, starting especially in the late 1960s.[19]

This statistical density in specific areas produced the reverse of the situation most of its participants aspired to. For every individual, whether he was aware

---

19. The reasons for the rise of Jews in these fields and the problem of possible "Jewish" factors in their behavior and contributions are too complicated to be analyzed carefully here and will be the subject of a separate study. Here I shall merely indicate the phenomenon itself.

and proud of his Jewish origin (an accepted attitude today) or whether he tried to deny it or ignore it (as often happened in previous generations), set out to be a secular, ethnically neutral, physicist in the general physical sciences, linguist, filmmaker, revolutionary, German or American writer, and so on, as an individual. Such Jews made an effort to adapt to the rules of the general cultural domain they embraced, whether it was science, modern fiction, or painting. If there is something to the notion of "Jewish" talent, it was revealed only when descendants of the Jews entered the rigorous frameworks of Western ("Christian") logic, science, and organized, institutionalized culture. It was only after the fact, that such a "Jew" discovered that many of his neighbors and friends were also individuals who had abandoned similar Jewish origins and that, in some sense, their "Jewishness" was not blurred but again became conspicuous. Often, the statistical concentration of such former Jews, or several conspicuous representatives, led others, as well as the Jewish descendants themselves, to discover their "Jewishness" in a different perspective.

One area we tend to talk less about (especially since the McCarthy era in the United States) is the role of Jews in implementing the Communist Revolution in Russia and in the Communist and leftist movement in the world. Indeed, in the Russian Social-Democratic Workers' Party before the Revolution, Jews were prominent in the leadership of the Social-Democratic wing (Bund and Mensheviks) and less represented in the Bolshevik wing (of Lenin); reporting on the party Conference in London in 1907, Stalin even suggested, "jokingly," that a pogrom in the party might tip the scale toward the Bolsheviks. But, right after the Revolution, the situation changed and many Jews entered the new Bolshevik power structure. After Lenin's death, Stalin took power, enlisting Zinovyev (1883–1936; Secretary of the Third International) and Kamenev (1886–1936; one of the leaders of the Soviet government) against Trotsky (1879–1940; founder of the Red Army). But if we peel off the Russian underground aliases, we find that it was Djugashvili (a Georgian) who enlisted Apfelbaum and Rosenfeld against Rosenfeld's brother-in-law Bronshteyn, all three of them Jews. This topic became conspicuous in the political arguments in Russia today, and it is high time we examine it again in a non-apologetic manner.

Jews were prominent in the ranks of the early Soviet governments, and the antisemitic expression "Judeo-Bolshevism" is not without foundation. When the Pale of Settlement was suddenly opened, masses of Jews left the obsolete and class-negative *shtetl* (only the classes of proletarians and peasants had voting rights) and went inside Central Russia, studied in the universities, and filled the new governmental network, which needed a loyal intelligentsia. Many of them changed their names, intermarried with Russians, or behaved like Russians in every respect. Solzhenitsyn blamed the Jews for organizing Soviet concentration camps (the "Gulag") and identified several Jews among the leaders of the Soviet secret police in the early years. But Jews were equally prominent in the top echelons of many other areas of the young Soviet regime: the administration, the

party, education, medicine, Russian literature, physics, the sciences, the collectiv-
ization of the villages and the industrialization of Russia, and also—with particular vengeance—among those purged and liquidated by the regime. Even in World
War II, their prominent position as industrial engineers and factory managers was
visible (as witnessed by the Jewish names in Stalin's "Decrees" commending
heroes of the rear in the war effort). The same is true of the leftist movement in
the world, including the leadership of the Soviet revolutions in Bavaria and Hungary in 1919; such figures as Joffe (1883–1927; conducted the peace talks at
Brest) and Borodin (Gruzenberg, 1884–1951; advisor to Sun Yat-Sen); or Karl
Radek (Sobelson, 1885–1939), who carried out Stalin's policies in Germany,
helping Hitler's rise to power. All were liquidated by Stalin.

Both in Weimar Germany and in Soviet Russia, the massive influx and rise of
the descendants of Jews was the product of a very short period (with important
but individual precedents in the nineteenth century), and in both these cases they
rose not as Jews but as Germans or as Russians, essentially nonreligious. But in
both countries, they were perceived socially as Jews, a perception that now could
only be racial.

In Germany the Jewish issue was truly central to the ideology of Hitler, Rosenberg, and Goebbels: it was the negative pole of a bipolar social mythology (or
phantasmagoria). In Communist ideology, which emphasized the multinational
Soviet state and the international workers' solidarity, it was impossible to include
open negation of a nation or a race as an organic part of the system of Marxist
argumentation. But here too, the role of assimilated Jews as aliens was central in
consciousness. The major example Stalin analyzed in his programmatic pamphlet
on "Marxism and the National Question" (1913) was the Jewish example, and
the enemy was the Jewish Socialist "Bund."

The purges in the Soviet Union in the late 1930s did in fact destroy the power
of most Jews in the party and the government under the guise of a war on
"leftist deviationism" (a typical Jewish ailment) and on "Trotskyism." In the official
textbook, *History of the All-Soviet Communist Party (of Bolsheviks)*, written in Stalin's
name, Trotsky was called "Yudushka-Trotsky," that is, Judas-Trotsky, ostensibly
adapting the name of the hero of a nineteenth-century Russian social satire by
Saltykov-Shtshedrin, but really alluding to Judas Iscariot and the demonic "Judaism." And in the late 1940s, they were suppressed in all areas of culture under
the guise of a war against "Cosmopolitanism" (whose protagonists were dubbed
"passportless nomads"). For many years, not Marxism but rather anti-Trotskyism
and anti-Cosmopolitanism were the truly central issues in actual Soviet ideology,
propaganda, censorship, and State terrorism; they were the negative banner of
Stalin's regime, concrete and targeted *ad hominem*. Those campaigns were not
openly or exclusively anti-Jewish, but the anti-Jewish thrust was enveloped in
them. Then, in the 1950s and later, Jews were oppressed with the excuse of
fighting the most satanic religion of "Judaism" and the racist and Nazi "Zionism."
After the fall of Nazi Germany, Communist Russia was the only country in the

enlightened world which maintained de facto discrimination against Russians of Jewish origin (even half Jews) both in the government and in higher education. Today, the opposite myth—of the Jews as the perpetrators of Communism in Russia—plays a similar role in the ideology of large parts of the Russian right, the cultural establishment, and the old party apparatus.

In sum, in the two major ideological-totalitarian regimes, the figure of the Jew has loomed large in the self-consciousness of the authorities and their mass-supported propaganda, as if Jewish assimilation had never existed.[20] Similar attitudes prevailed in smaller totalitarian states, like Poland and Romania in the late thirties.

This negative mega-experience, and the numerical imbalance of individuals of Jewish origin in various professions in the modern world, requires an explanation of why the descendants of Jews may be felt to be different even when they assimilate, in fact or in popular perception. The study of modern Jewish history should not be reduced to Jews who participate in Jewish institutions (the Jewish State, religion, literature, organizations) while the rest are included only when they are exterminated. The prominent Polish poet, Julian Tuwim (1894–1953), wrote during the Holocaust (while in Exile in London): I am a Pole when the blood flows in my veins and a Jew when it flows out of my veins (Tuwim 1981). Albert Einstein said similar things. But modern mythologies did not exempt them from Jewry as a whole. Jewish historiography must not exclude them from its scope either.

The prestigious "Jerusalem school" of Jewish history tended to be teleological: every minor expression in the past that could be read as leading to Zion became significant. The historian Bentsiyon Dinur (Dinaburg, 1884–1973), who promulgated such an approach in Jerusalem, might have been influenced by post-Revolutionary Russia (he was a student in Petrograd): instead of history, they taught the "history of revolutions," and any local peasant uprising was glorified as a step toward the Communist Revolution, that is, openly applying an ideological, hence teleological (fed by hindsight) filter to history. But we can look at history differently: from the past toward the present. When we ask not "How did we get here?" but "What happened to the Jews in the nineteenth century? Where did they go?"—we discover an enormous outburst expressed in a centrifugal movement which, in wave after wave, produced the gamut of manifestation of Jewish existence today. (Indeed, even in Jerusalem, historiography has opened up to those areas.)

From a Jewish perspective, the century of 1882–1982 in general history can be called a "Jewish Century": in no period in the past did Jews assume such a

20. On the contrary, assimilation was suspected as a sly strategem of the Jewish conspiracy to rule the world, as we can see in the Jews who shave their beards and externally appear as Germans, but are the same rats as before, in the Nazi film *The Eternal Jew*; or in the second-class treatment accorded half-Jewish students in the Soviet Union during the Brezhnev years of discrimination.

prominent role in general culture, not in just one country but in Western civilization as a whole. It is hard to describe the modern world without Marx, Husserl,
Einstein, Freud, Kafka, Jakobson, Lévi-Strauss, Chomsky, Derrida, and a long list
of other figures in science and culture, though their own Jewish identity was
vague, problematic, or indifferent to many of them. Moreover, Jews and the image
of the Jew played a role in the imagination and consciousness of the period
beyond any proportion to their numbers in the population. The Holocaust and
the State of Israel too were present in general consciousness. And it was not only
in the negative mythology of Hitler and Alfred Rosenberg that Jews played a
central role (Rosenberg stole Jewish libraries in countries occupied by the Nazis
intending to set up an "Institute for the Study of Jewry without Jews" after the
war). The Jewish question attracted the interest of Veblen, T. S. Eliot, Ezra Pound,
Lenin, Stalin, Toynbee, C. P. Snow, J.-P. Sartre, and others. One might say that
the Jews in the twentieth century, to paraphrase the Israeli literary critic Dov
Sadan (1902–1989), "were sitting in a corner in the middle of the room."

TEN

The Continuous Rainbow

These changes in intrinsic and extrinsic culture took place along with changes in the physical, geographic, linguistic, professional, and educational makeup and the very modes of existence of the Jews in the world. The shock of the pogroms of 1881–82, in combination with other circumstances and other shocks, uprooted the masses of the people from their places. In the generation before World War I, over a third of the Jewish people in Eastern Europe migrated overseas (it is estimated that between 1882 and 1914 two million out of over five million Jews left Russia for the West). At least another third moved to the cities. There was a massive internal migration: from the village and the *shtetl* to the district town (Bobruisk, Zhitomir, Pinsk, Minsk, Bialystok) and further, to the big city (Vilna, Lodz, Lemberg, Warsaw, Odessa), and to cities outside the Pale of Settlement (Kiev, Moscow) and to Western Europe (Vienna, Budapest, Berlin, London) and many countries overseas; and, after the Russian Revolution, from the *shtetl* in the Pale of Settlement which was opened—to Moscow, Leningrad, and smaller cities of Russia proper, as well as to Central Asia and other Soviet territories.

A new Jewish proletariat was formed in Warsaw, Kharkov, New York, Tel Aviv, and other cities, encouraged by ideology and social pressures, but it dissolved everywhere within one generation. The Jewish proletarians worked mostly in small, Jewish-owned artisan shops and "sweatshops," and hardly in heavy industry. Rather than being individual tailors, they may have joined a women's garment factory. Indeed, it was hard for Jewish workers to penetrate industry proper: even in the 1920s in the Soviet Union, antisemitism among non-Jewish factory workers limited their absorption on the lower levels of industry. The children of the new "proletarians" moved everywhere into new areas of trade and industry, medicine and science, communications and art. That means that, within the sight of one generation, masses of Jews traveled from a feudal to a capitalist economy, and from there again to the new, scientific and electronic age. They obviously expressed the general shifts, but in a more rapid and massive way, and their consciousness and behavior were influenced by it; and so was the perception from the outside, which needed to feel the empty Jewish stereotypes.

Within one generation, Jews learned Polish, Russian, German, Hungarian, Romanian, French, English, or Hebrew. It was often a crude language, but the next generation mastered a literary language in contrast with their immigrant-sounding parents (since even the most careful student has a hard time getting rid of the intonation of the language he was born into). Indeed, Yiddish literature was written everywhere by first-generation immigrants: all Yiddish writers came as young men and women from a *shtetl* to Warsaw, Vilna, Kiev, or Moscow, or from Eastern Europe to New York, Chicago, or Los Angeles. Jewish painters made a similar road to Petersburg, Moscow, Paris, and America. But great literature in another language was written, with a few exceptions, by the second generation (Pasternak, Mandelshtam, Kafka, Buber, Feuchtwanger, Bellow, Malamud, Philip Roth).

In a CBC film, made shortly before his death, the Israeli-born General Moshe Dayan (1915–1981) talked about his parents, who came to Eretz-Israel with the Second Aliya and wanted to do three things: speak Hebrew, work in agriculture, and defend themselves. But, in the eyes of their children, they stammered in all three; it was the second generation that completed the personal triple revolution. The torments of that adaptation can be seen in the Jewish literature of immigration throughout the world.[21] The Hebrew poet Yehuda Amichai captured it in his poem, "My Parents' Migration":

> And the migration of my parents has not subsided in me.
> My blood goes on sloshing between my ribs
> Long after the vessel has come to rest.
> And the migration of my parents has not subsided in me.
>   (Amichai 1987)

An entire people moved away from its place and its language; the movement to Eretz-Israel and to Hebrew was only a small part of this larger trend. For example, agriculture was the pride and the territorial foundation of the *Yishuv* in Eretz-Israel. The move to the village was one of the manifestations embodying a whole cluster of new tendencies: the desire to create a new Jew, including a Jewish "peasant," innocent, honest, healthy, and productive—the opposite of the *luft-mentsh* who "lived in the air" and "on the air" and gambled on the stock market; the desire to go out to nature, the antithesis of the imaginary "walls" of the metaphorical "ghetto" of the Jewish *shtetl*; the dream of returning to the soil, where the nation can strike roots, in the image of the nation as a tree; and the utopian dream of rehabilitating the desert and through that purgatory work rehabilitating the desolate settlers themselves. That was a trend opposed to the worldwide movement from village to city. It drew on pre-capitalist notions of

---

21. A good example is *Portnoy's Complaint* by Philip Roth.

"health," "productivity," and morality, as embodied by the farmer who produces tangible products *ex nihilo*; on ideals of an aristocratic society of landowners, internalized in the consciousness of a bourgeois intelligentsia (an obvious example is Lev Tolstoy, who influenced the Hebrew revival); and on the utopia of a return to the "soil" and to a primeval condition of wholeness and health of the race (the German alliterative *Blut und Boden* was replicated by Uri-Tsvi Grinberg in the paranomastic *dam ve-adama*, "blood and soil"). Indeed, the metaphor of the *shtetl* as a ghetto with walls (whereas actually most small towns never had a ghetto and were wide open to nature) was underscored by Sholem Aleichem, when he wrote that the only "field" the people of *Kasrilevke* could enjoy was their old cemetery ("field" in Yiddish is a euphemism for a graveyard); hence Bialik's poem, "In the Field," describing only nature, was perceived as a Zionist manifesto. And A. D. Gordon's (1856–1922) "*Religion of Work*" (i.e., physical work) was combined with a Tolstoy-inspired "*Religion of the Soil*," by which the worker's movement was influenced.

But the move of Jews to agriculture was propagated in the *Haskala* as early as Isaac Baer Levinson's (Rival, 1789–1850) book *Teuda Be-Israel* (1828), and its implementation was not exclusive to Eretz-Israel. In Russia, after the Revolution, according to various accounts, some three hundred thousand Jews settled in villages in the 1920s, at a time when, in Eretz-Israel, there were only a few thousand or tens of thousands of farmers; the settlement organization "*ICA*" (*Jewish Colonization Association*) supported agricultural settlements in Palestine, Argentina, and Brazil; and there was a movement to settle Jewish farmers in New Jersey, Nebraska, and other American states, with a journal in Yiddish, *The Jewish Farmer* (1908–1959). For various reasons—like the industrialization of the Soviet Union, which was rapid and more enticing than the early industrialization of Israel; enforced "internationalization" of the Jewish *Kolkhozes* in Russia (by inserting pigs in their pens); assimilation and urbanization in the West; higher education which the second generation everywhere was devoted to; and, finally, the Holocaust—most of the other agricultural attempts eventually disappeared, while Israeli agriculture survived and is one of the finest achievements of the Jewish State. Yet, if we look not from the end of a historical trend but from its beginning, it was one centrifugal movement with similar ideals realized in different directions and countries.

This centrifugal movement, in which New York and Eretz-Israel may be seen as extensions—and, I would add, implementations—of the Jewish fermentation in Russia, has been described in detail by Jonathan Frankel in his classic study *Prophecy and Politics* (1981). The book focuses on ideological debates and political organizations and does not discuss the full consciousness of these debaters, including the fictional worlds of literature and ideology which molded their perception of the world and themselves. Sholem Aleichem, Mendele, Dostoevsky, Tolstoy, Nietzsche, and others were basic assets in their awareness, almost taken for granted, no less than the writings of Aḥad Ha-Am, Syrkin (1868–1924), or Borokhov (1881–1917). All political movements, as well as popular consciousness, shared an opposition to the world of the *shtetl*, to the "Diaspora," "provincial," "primitive" Jew. But this notion of the *shtetl* itself was crystallized in Jewish literature, symbolized by Sholem Aleichem's *Kasrilevke*. This new literature was written by intellectuals living outside the *shtetl*, from a modern, rational position, and with a satirical and "forgiving" glance backward. The ideologues, the politicians, and their audiences were steeped in the world of Jewish and non-Jewish literature and molded their identity under its influence. Berl Katznelson said it was Jewish literature that brought him and his generation to Eretz-Israel. Yitzhak Tabenkin (1887–1971), the leader of the largest kibbutz movement, described the impact of Jewish and general literature in a strong, personal memoir, "The Roots" (1947, see translation in this book). Borokhov, the theoretician of Marxist Zionism, was also a Yiddish linguist and one of the founders of modern Yiddish standard spelling. And there was a brilliant group of young intellectuals who formed a short-lived party in 1905–6 with the Russian name *Vozrozhdenie* ("Revival") based on the spectacular revival of Hebrew and Yiddish literature and culture. Even during the Holocaust, literature had a formative influence on the youth who shouldered the resistance movement—witness the literary activities of the "Youth Club" in Vilna Ghetto and the *Dror* underground gymnasium in Warsaw Ghetto.[22]

Even in an issue where the sharpness of the debate was extreme, we can find images common to the opposing trends. For example, the Bundists sneered at the Zionists: You're going to Palestine, a "carcass of a kingdom" (*di gepeygerte melukhe*), while Uri-Tsvi Grinberg, the Yiddish poet who suddenly went from Berlin to Eretz-Israel in 1924 and switched from writing Yiddish poetry to Hebrew, wrote a hymn of revival that begins:

> This land the Hebrew God chose for atrocious torture as a sadist tormenting a
> woman's body, covering her with leprosy from Egypt to the Syrian border—
> ("Tur Malka")

The connections also existed on a personal level. Jonathan Frankel (1981:93) describes an excited encounter between two young Russian Jews in the spring of 1882: Yisrael Belkind (1861–1929), a member of Bilu (an idealist immigrant group that launched the First Aliya), and Abraham Cahan (1860–1951), a Russian Socialist Revolutionary on his flight from the Russian police, intending to go to Switzerland; as Cahan put it in his memoirs: "Belkind, the *Palestinyets*, made me into an *Amerikanyets*." Belkind convinces the Russian revolutionary Cahan—not to go to Eretz-Israel, no chance of that—but rather to become an "Amerikanyets" and devote himself to serving his people in free America (the terminology is Russian, like the language of culture and ideology, although both their roots were

---

22. See the memoirs of Yitzhak Zuckerman (Antek) 1993, and Abba Kovner's interviews (in my possession).

in the discourse of Yiddish and both are about to abandon Russia). In fact, the young Russian revolutionary Cahan is influenced by the Zionism of the Bilu Belkind, goes to America, participates in the struggles of the Jewish and general American Socialist movement in New York, edits the influential Yiddish newspaper *Forverts* for half a century, and writes novels about the lives of the immigrants in English and a huge history of the United States in Yiddish.

Those very circles of *Poaley Tsiyon* (Labor Zionists) in Poland and Russia, which split in 1905–1907 into three trends, produced such leaders of the *Yishuv* in Eretz-Israel as Ben-Gurion, Yitzhak Tabenkin, and Zrubavel (1886–1967), and such party leaders and cultural figures in the Diaspora as the Jewish demographer Jacob Leshtshinski (1876–1966), the Yiddishist theoretician Dr. Zhitlovski (1865–1943), and the linguist Nokhum Shtif (1879–1933), one of the founders of the Jewish section of the Academy of Sciences in Soviet Kiev. Berl Katznelson admired Avrom Lyesin (1872–1938), the American Yiddish poet and editor of *Tsukunft* (a central Yiddish literary and cultural journal in New York), whom he knew from the movement in Byelorussia. The radical ultrarightist Uri-Tsvi Grinberg, in the 1970s in Israel, spoke fondly of Perets Markish (1895–1952), his fellow Expressionist in Yiddish poetry in Warsaw and Berlin in the early 1920s, although the latter went to the Soviet Union and became a distinguished Communist writer (until he perished in Stalin's purges).

Another example: one of the participants in the self-defense movement in Homel (Gomel) in Byelorussia during the pogroms of 1903 was a youth who assumed the underground name of Virgilius (what an idyllic ideal of a socialist Jew loyal to the concepts of the Enlightenment!). Virgilius Kahan became one of the leaders of the Bund in Vilna. Naturally, Virgilius named his son Arcadius. But the self-defense groups in Homel included both Bundists and Zionists. Virgilius's sister, Rosa Kahan, fled to Palestine and took part in organizing the defense of Jewish Jerusalem during the Arab riots of 1920. Her son is the Israeli general and prime minister Yitzhak Rabin, while his cousin, the late Arcadius Kahan, was a Professor of Economics at the University of Chicago. Also, Virgilius's uncle was Mordekhai Ben Hillel Ha-Cohen, a Hebrew writer and early Zionist, who came to Eretz-Israel with the Second Aliya, in 1907, and was among the founders of Tel Aviv; and his son, David Ha-Cohen, was a leader of the labor union construction company, *Solel U-Bone*, a liaison officer between the Jewish underground, *Hagana*, and the British Army, and from his home in Haifa, in World War II, the Free France transmitter broadcasted to the Vichy forces in Syria. All in one family.

Indeed, the whole concept of "*Self-Defense*" emerged in Russia during the pogroms of 1881–82. After the Kishinev pogrom of April 1903, it was taken up again. The Odessa writers, including Aḥad Ha-Am, Bialik, and Dubnov, issued a statement calling for the organization of Jewish self-defense, for "it is degrading for five million people [. . .] to stretch out their necks to be slaughtered [. . .] without attempting to protect their property, dignity, and lives with their own hands." This was a direct challenge to the religious precept of passive heroism, *kidush ha-shem*, dying for God's name, accepted in the Ashkenazi religious tradition, as well as a challenge to the Russian authorities. And in the same vein, Bialik wrote his influential poem "In the City of Slaughter," chastising the Jewish males who were hiding from their persecutors while their wives and daughters were raped. An illegal self-defense movement emerged all over Russia, in spite of the odds and the hostility of the authorities. The self-defense of the Jewish settlements in Israel took over that tradition; the name of the Jewish underground, *Hagana*, is a direct translation of the Yiddish term for "self-defense" and is preserved to this day in the name of the army, *Israel Defense Forces*. The *Ha-shomer* group, which organized in the Galilee at the time of the Second Aliya, came from that conceptual background. One of its founders, Manya Shokhat, in her youth a labor leader in Russia, had been arrested and had become friendly with Zubatov, the Russian union organizer and police chief, before she fled to build Zionism in Palestine. She tried to settle land on the east side of the Jordan River, went to Paris to enlist Rothschild's financial aid, but learned of revolutionary ferment in Russia and smuggled arms there before returning to Eretz-Israel.

And a very different example: Isaac Nakhman Shteynberg (Steinberg, 1888–1957) was People's Commissar for Law (= Minister of Justice) in Lenin's first Soviet government; he was a member of the Left S.R. (Socialist-Revolutionary Party), who took part in Lenin's first coalition, and at the same time a believing and practicing Orthodox Jew. When he fled Russia in 1923, he lived in Berlin, London, and New York, was leader of the Jewish Territorialist movement and editor of its journal *Frayland* ("Free Land"), and tried to get land for a Jewish State in Australia, Surinam, and elsewhere. All three trends that he believed in—the paradoxical opposites of the Russian Left S.R., Jewish religious Orthodoxy, and Yiddish Territorialism—were consistently anti-Bund and anti-Zionist! Before he became Lenin's minister, he was thrown out of Moscow University for revolutionary activity, then went to Heidelberg and wrote a dissertation in German on criminal law in the Talmud; he published books and articles in Russian, German, and Yiddish (his son is the American art historian Leo Steinberg). Isaac's brother Aaron Shteynberg (1891–1975), combining a profound interest in Russian religious-philosophical trends with Jewish religious moralism, taught philosophy at St. Petersburg, went to Berlin in 1922, then to London. He translated Dubnov's *World History of the Jewish People* from Russian into German, wrote a brilliant book in Russian on *Dostoevsky's System of Freedom*, and dozens of essays in Yiddish, and eventually became the head of the Cultural Department of the World Jewish Congress.

The debates between the trends were often extremely bitter, the alternatives seemed unbridgeable, but they were hewn out of the same quarry.

ELEVEN

The Individual

The intelligentsia is a class of people who constantly try to question and formulate ideas and beliefs, or express them in works of fiction. Social ideologies are crystallizations of such attitudes, systematic and logical constructs. What we did in the previous chapters was not to describe individuals but the trends of the time that influenced many individuals and were manifested or voiced by them at one time or another.

Both attributes of the change in Jewish involvement—action in history and personal consciousness—require awareness and decision by each individual. No doubt, individuals act under various influences and are swept up by social trends and political organizations. Nevertheless, in many situations, there was a voluntary element to a person's choice among available alternatives, in which convictions and personal action played an important role. That was especially true for a society at a time of upheaval, with many options of physical and geographic change and cultural and ideological orientation. Paradoxically, Jews in this period had a great deal of freedom of choice, because they could move across boundaries of countries, languages, and cultural trends.

The individual cannot be seen simply as an embodiment of an ideology. The still persistent essentialist fallacy often derives a person's whole being from his political or professional affiliation: X is a Socialist, a Zionist, an assimilationist, a liberal, an antisemite, a Jew, a poet, and so on, and such a label is supposed to account for all his actions, positions, or statements. A statement—or even a casual expression—by Sigmund Freud or T. S. Eliot, or any other figure, is elevated from its specific context and taken as a generalization about his whole life or attitudes, identifying ideology and personality, with no regard for the specific setting, frame of mind, and kind of discourse, and for the factor of a person's changing in time. In this respect, many critics still pay dues to the age of ideology.

To be sure, individuals often embrace ideologies or various beliefs, and some hold to them for a long time. Yet, in principle, it would be more appropriate to see the individual as an open semantic field through which various tendencies crisscross: some of them are involuntary and some he himself embraced and helped formulate, some become dominant and others merely hover in the field of consciousness. Moreover, we are dealing here with sensibilities and attitudes, which are often fuzzy and ambivalent and not as systematic and consistent as ideologies would like to be. Individuals, even highly articulate ones, are often undecided on various matters, inconsistent, compromising between opposite ideas, changing their position with time, explicit and committed on some issues and silent on others (perhaps no less important to them). And even well-defined, logically grounded ideologies keep changing in time (as we can see, for example, in the evolution of Freud's theory or in the abstract and logical arguments of the Marxist Zionist Ber Borokhov [1881–1917], which kept shifting throughout his short life [see Frankel 1981]). Saul Bellow understood it when he pitched the creative individual's "distraction" against the organized "destruction" (*Herzog*, p. 50).

Thus, in general terms, we may describe a cultural situation as a result of the interaction of two kinds of entities: social, cultural, and ideological *trends* and individual *junctions*. A junction is a cluster of and a selection from intersecting tendencies that constitute an autonomous existential unit, such as a *text* or a *person*. A text, however, is not simply a given intersection of relations, ideas, or poetic principles, but an individualized body of language, marked by partial coherence, and reader-dependent. In this sense, a person may be seen as a text, but unlike a text, he is open-ended in time, has the ability of shifting and changing, actively reshuffling his own hierarchies, reaching out for material from the outside, explicitly formulating experiences, and reunderstanding himself. In a person, furthermore, biological, physical, economic, and social aspects of existence are intermingled with ideational, linguistic, and semiotic elements.

Both a text and an individual human being, indeed, exhibit various manifestations of the social, ideological, or semiotic trends of the time and may give them voice. But those manifestations are subordinated to the partial cohesion of the individual being, be it the fictional world and the structure of a literary text or the quasi-"organic" internal relationships and continuities of a living person. Hence the importance of individual biographies and interpretations of individual texts for the history of ideas: precisely because the ideas and conceptions are contextualized in an individual junction and "impure" as ideological constructs. The biography of an individual exhibits a unique, unpredictable combination and evolution of heterogeneous elements, embedded in the circumstances of his life, and combining receptivity and activity in interaction with other individuals and trends.

Having taken this stand, I think we can make a generalization that the Jews in this period of transition—and I stress both "Jews" and "period"—were especially prone to vacillating between different options. An extreme statement often just means exaggerating a meaningful point, or *foregrounding* a position, while leaving in the background other options, which may reappear in time. With all the radical statements, for example, negating the Jewish past and religion, many individuals came in time to a compromise, became nostalgic and penitent, or embraced some of the notions suppressed in their unarticulated consciousness. Our analysis of historical trends must not imply that any of the negations or innovations were implemented in a pure and full form—either in a person's life or in a given cultural situation—but simply that those were moving forces in the field of social reality and cultural argument, as well as in the field of each individual's personality.

The same Hebrew writer Hazaz who made Yudke deny Jewish history and hate the past, and who wrote a play with the slogan "*Burn the Diaspora!*" opened a revised version of one of his books with the words: "Oh, Jewish *shtetls*, who slandered you!" (Well, of course, Hazaz himself did.) And many of the ideologues and writers of the period went through quite a few political trends in their youth, as we can see from the autobiographical narratives of Tabenkin or Berl Katznelson. The Yiddish poet Mani Leyb, for example, was an apprentice to a shoe-stitcher in a small town in northern Ukraine; one after another, he joined the Ukrainian Socialists, the Russian Socialist-Revolutionaries, the Anarchists, the Social-Democrats; then was arrested, fled to England and America, became a Yiddishist and a major Yiddish poet, and grew nostalgic about the East European religious Jewish world after it disappeared.

Interestingly enough, many young intellectuals first embraced Russian culture and then went back to Yiddish and Hebrew, especially after the pogroms and revolution of 1903–1905. Ber Borokhov, whose mother tongue was Russian, became a Yiddish writer and linguist and a Marxist-Zionist theoretician and leader; the Christian-born (though of Jewish origin) and Russian-speaking Vladimir Medem (1879–1923) became a brilliant Yiddish public speaker and leader of the Bund; the Russian journalist and poet Vladimir Jabotinsky became a Hebrew ideologue, poet, military leader, and founder of the radical rightist Zionist movement. In an earlier generation, the Russian poet Dovid Edelshtat (1866–1892), born into a Russian-speaking family outside of the Pale of Settlement, emigrated in 1882 with *Am Olam* to the United States and became a popular Yiddish poet, political journalist, and anarchist; the ideologue of the Hebrew language revival, Eliezer Ben-Yehuda, under the influence of the Russian-Turkish war in the Balkans in 1877–78, first became a Russian nationalist and Slavophile, and only when he read *Daniel Deronda* did he aim his nationalist spirit at Zionism and Hebrew; Dr. Ḥayim Zhitlovski was a Russian S.R. before becoming the theoretician of Yiddishism in the United States; Pinhas Rutenberg was a Russian S.R., assassinated the Russian Minister of Interior, then helped organize the Jewish Legion in London in World War I, then fought on the "White" side in the Russian Civil War, and eventually built the Palestine Electric Company and was elected President of the Jewish parliament in Mandatory Palestine, the *Va'ad le'umi*. It is from the Russian or European culture that such intellectuals brought back the ideals of secular culture to the Jewish milieu, and, in spite of all their fanatic ideologism, they vacillated between opposite orientations. Jabotinsky expressed it in his sharp manner: "They are chained with iron chains, the people of my generation who grew up on the Russian language and turned into national Hebrews, with iron chains are they enslaved to the foreign culture. [. . .] The [Russian] language with which my teacher poisoned me—there is no balm for it in all of Gilead!" (Jabotinsky 1914:406).

Most achievements of this period were actually made by small groups of youth: typically, they would leave home in their teens, study in a yeshiva and abandon it, or study a trade, try out various ideological trends, then move to a different place and launch a new trend in their early twenties. Eliezer Ben-Yehuda (1858–1922), the standard-bearer of the revival of Hebrew, left his home at the age of 13 for a yeshiva, then went to another city for a Russian *Gimnasya*; at the age of 20 he moved to Paris, and immigrated to Palestine at the age of 23. Theodor Herzl (1860–1904) came to Vienna from Budapest at the age of 18. The *Biluyim*, the ideological group that launched the Zionist migration to Israel in 1881–82, were youths. The "workers" of the Second Aliya and their leaders came at a similar age: Ben-Gurion at 20, Aleksander Zayd (Seid) at 18, Yitzhak Tabenkin at 23 (after several years as activist in Warsaw and Vienna), Berl Katznelson at 22. Most Yiddish poets in America came to the United States at the ages of 18–22: Jacob Glatshteyn was 18, A. Leyeles was 20 (but left his home in Lodz for London at 16), Moyshe-Leyb Halpern was 22 (but left his home for Vienna at the age of 12), H. Leyvik was 25 (at 18 he was arrested as a revolutionary and exiled to Siberia). They were often children when they left their home in a small town and were all young when they came to a new place and began a new cultural movement. The same is true for most other creative and political trends of the period.

Of course, there are decisions in a person's life, like going overseas or being educated in a new language, which create new physical facts, change the whole existential context, and are not easily reversible. But, given such an existential framework, on the level of consciousness the matter is more flexible. Jews who assimilated to this or that new culture may have abandoned or suppressed the old modes of behavior and discourse and embraced new ones, but often some of the old reappear with the new. And the same is true for beliefs and persuasions. Furthermore, the tendencies articulated by writers and intellectuals are implemented by masses of people who do not fully articulate them, in various combinations of the new and the old, the pro and the con, the committed and the fuzzy.

That said, we may return to the history of ideas and trends, as abstracted from—and exemplified by—many individuals and texts, and crystallized in comprehensive constructs.

TWELVE

Flashback: Collapse and Victory of the Enlightenment

Let us now return to the background of this great fermentation. In the sixteenth century, about two-thirds of the Jews in the world lived in the united kingdom of Poland-Lithuania (after they were expelled from England, France, most of Italy and Germany, Spain, and Portugal). The kingdom of Poland and Lithuania was then the largest country in Europe, stretching from the Baltic Sea almost to the Black Sea and from the outskirts of Berlin to a short distance from Moscow. This territory eventually became the great reservoir of all of Ashkenazi Jewry in the modern age—spreading from Moscow to Manchuria and Australia and from Tel Aviv to Buenos Aires and Los Angeles. In general, we may say that, in the Polish kingdom, the Jews filled a position of mediation between the Polish nobility and the Polish government in the center of the country and the minorities in the eastern territories, like the vast spaces of Lithuania or the breadbasket of Ukraine. From here, too, they overflowed into neighboring countries like Romania and Hungary, and to the West and overseas. At the end of the eighteenth century, when Poland was divided and devoured by its neighbors—Russia, Prussia, and Austria—large Jewish populations were included in those countries. In Russia, where Jews had previously been forbidden to live and where the majority of the former Polish Jews were now incorporated, they were not allowed to leave the occupied territories and were enclosed within a huge geographical ghetto, the *Pale of Settlement* (the area that is now central Poland, Ukraine, Byelorussia, Lithuania, Latvia, and some Russian cities—all combined). In Prussia (which later became Germany) and in Austria, they moved west, first in a trickle and then—when allowed—in a massive stream, especially into the capital cities of Vienna and Berlin. Thus, the families of Scholem and Schocken came to Berlin from the Posen area (Polish Poznań), and other Berlin Jews came from Silesia; Freud's parents came from the Jewish towns of Brod and Tysmienitz in eastern Galicia, and other Viennese Jews came from Galicia or Hungary.

In the nineteenth century, there was an enormous increase in the Jewish population in Eastern Europe and poverty intensified. In 1800 there were 2.2 million Jews in the world and in 1880, 7.5 million;[23] in Eastern Europe the numbers grew from 1 million to 4.25 million in just eighty years!—most of them crammed in the Pale of Settlement (only a privileged few were allowed in Russia proper). Their mediating place within the triangle *Polish landowner–Jew–Ukrainian peasant* was emptied of its content when the Polish head of the triangle was lopped off. Economically, the *shtetl* remained on the back roads of capitalist development and became a trap for its fast-multiplying inhabitants. Most Jews did not live among those who spoke the language of the ruling nation but among linguistic minorities: Ukrainians in Poland; Poles, Byelorussians, and Ukrainians in Russia; Czechs, Hungarians, and Poles in Austria; and so on. This also helped separate them linguistically and culturally since they looked up to the culture of the center or the dominant power rather than to that of their neighbors. In the Pale of Settlement, the Jews were a very large minority; they were not simply scattered around the country but lived in compact towns and city quarters where they composed the bulk of the population, while the majority of non-Jews lived in villages, town suburbs, and big cities. In what is now the republic of Byelorussia, in the beginning of the twentieth century almost 70% of the population of all the cities and towns was Jewish (see Szmeruk 1961).

When such Jews were allowed to move and enter in masses the national centers and the capitals—Warsaw, Vienna, Berlin, Moscow, Kiev, New York—they were conspicuous in their cultural and linguistic foreignness, their strange accents and behavior. Thus the vicious antisemitism that arose in Vienna (on which Hitler grew up) and in other capitals can ultimately be seen as a by-product of the dissolution of the large feudal state of Poland without a solution to the problem of the Jews who lived there. Suddenly, at the end of the nineteenth and the beginning of the twentieth century, this problem exploded, and millions of Jews with foreign accents filled the big cities that opened up, and competed for positions in the expanding new culture and economy.

On this background came the shock of the pogroms of 1881–82 in the Russian Pale of Settlement. The pogroms themselves look rather innocent in terms we have since come to know (in 1881, only forty Jews were killed in all of Russia; in 1882 the numbers were much higher but still far from the figures of 1919). Furthermore, in popular consciousness, there was nothing new about pogroms in Ukraine: popular folklore and Jewish folk songs recalled the seventeenth-century "Khmyel" (Bogdan Khmelnitski) and the eighteenth-century Gonta as if they had killed Jews only yesterday and were still around today. The shock was felt as such among enlightened Jews, a thin layer of Hebrew writers who believed in Russian culture (and didn't read Dostoevsky carefully!). Just a few weeks before the pogroms, the influential secular Hebrew writer Moshe-Leyb Lilienblum

23. At the eve of World War II, the world Jewish population was close to 17 million.

(1843–1910) wrote that such a thing could not happen in Russia. Indeed, with the wave of pogroms, the *Haskala*[24] (Enlightenment) was exposed as bankrupt. The shock around the Jewish world was enormous and led to radical conclusions about the possibilities of Jewish existence in Russia, and perhaps in the Diaspora as a whole. One reason for this was that, by that time, new strata of the young intelligentsia arose who studied Russian and German culture (if they were not allowed into the schools, they studied as "externs") and absorbed European concepts of culture, consciousness, pride, beauty, ideology, and action in history. As Jonathan Frankel shows, the representatives of the young intelligentsia took over the leadership of politics and communications in Jewish society during the period of confusion in 1882. The second reason for the shock is that the same masses who always knew the situation instinctively, now—under the influence of the new trends hovering in the air and the future-oriented ideologies—awoke from their lethargy and their surrender to the ahistorical Jewish fate. They voted first of all "with their feet," by emigrating, and later by joining the emerging political movements. Between 1881 and 1914 more than 2.5 million Jews migrated from Eastern Europe to the West, but their population in Eastern Europe increased too.

Every textbook in the history of Hebrew and Yiddish literature claims that, in 1881–82, the *Haskala* died. Indeed, as a specific trend of Hebrew and Yiddish literature, the *Haskala* did come to an end. But the death day of the *Haskala* in literature (among small groups of Hebrew-reading intellectuals) was a day of its victory in the life of the people. Millions accepted and realized its principles. Perhaps there was no longer a naive belief in learning and self-improvement as a key to equality, but the drive to learning was merely enhanced: the disappointment with the Russian regime or with the generosity of the Austrians did not prevent thousands of young people from trying to assimilate into the Russian and German language, education, and culture, enter the universities, contribute to the new culture, and dissociate themselves from their former coreligionists with their foreign accents and from the culture of the past. All the central notions of the *Haskala*—*learning, beauty, self-realization*—became common property. And these were accompanied by more specific principles: *productivization, aestheticization,* admiration of *nature,* purification of *language,* expression of *private sensibility,* legitimation of sensuous *love,* equality of *women.*

Take the principle of learning. First, we must note that the Jews in medieval Europe—and into the twentieth century—were the only people who maintained mandatory education (at least for males) for many years of a person's life; reading

---

24. The *Haskala* was a literary and cultural movement among Jews (1772–1882), initiated by Moses Mendelssohn, promoting European culture, secular values, and aesthetic forms of behavior and writing. It created a literature in Hebrew and Yiddish. The Hebrew term itself is a translation of the German *Aufklärung,* connoting wisdom and rationality, but came to mean "education" in modern Hebrew.

some texts was a daily business even for simple people (at least for prayer). Most of them had a multilingual and multicultural perspective. Spoken Yiddish itself included distinguishable elements of at least three different language groups: German, Slavic, the Semitic Holy Tongue (i.e., Hebrew with Aramaic), and was an open language: its speakers, if they wished, could go out in the direction of any one of its components and absorb Slavic nature terminology, or produce a more Germanic or Hebraic and more "learned" discourse.[25] A Yiddish speaker was by definition a speaker of one or more other languages and was aware of the relativism of their structures (even if his knowledge was rudimentary). Belonging to the Jewish religion in a Christian world also meant constant awareness of the relativism of the two opposing systems of faith and popular semiotics, breeding cultural perspectivism and irony. All this is not yet intelligence and knowledge; many Jews were as boorish as can be imagined; but it creates a perspectival network of several open language systems that may be filled with new knowledge when the time comes. Though one of the ways the revolution was expressed was in contempt for traditional religious education, the habit of study and the appreciation of study per se continued to operate, and were reinforced by the new ideals of the general, non-Jewish "culture" and "education."

Second, the Jews were the only people without an official class structure. Naturally, there were poor and rich, powerful and weak in each community; but there were no permanent, "caste" divisions from birth as in the class structure of European Christian societies. A poor yeshiva scholar, who was an *iluy* (a genius), would marry a rich bride and rise in society. For the purposes of joining general society, all Jews were one "class," the barriers they had to overcome were not class boundaries but national and religious ones. And in a nominally secular society, where religion was ostensibly abandoned or relegated to the private domain, what was needed to join a national society was to master its language and literature. Indeed, joining general society was easier on the cultural level. There, what an individual learned by dint of his own intellectual ability and personal perseverance put him on an intellectual plane equal to that of others (social acceptance was another matter, of course). Learning gave the individual intellectual power to master the foreign culture—and culture knew no discrimination, as actual society did. Similar attitudes can be seen in the Jewish tradesman or store owner—an individual in a fluid marketplace.

In his book about Jewish immigrants in New York, *World of Our Fathers* (Howe 1976), Irving Howe describes the New York Yiddish poets of the Young Generation, who "dreamed of being pure poets" while they were also poverty-stricken poor immigrants: Mani Leyb a shoemaker, Zisho Landoy a housepainter, H. Leyvik a paperhanger, Moyshe-Leyb Halpern a jack-of-all-trades. "Imagine in any other literature the turn to impressionism or symbolism being undertaken by

---

25. See my book, *The Meaning of Yiddish* (Harshav 1990a).

a shoemaker and a house painter, the dismissal of the social muse by men laboring in factories!" (Howe 1976:432). Indeed, what proletariat translates Rimbaud or Japanese poems—into Yiddish? The point, however, is that this was not essentially a proletariat. To be a shoemaker was a livelihood in a time of need. In their consciousness, they were a fallen spiritual aristocracy and not a proletariat by birth. (Jewish folklore reflects the unique blend of an aristocracy of the mind fallen from greatness and indulging in learning, on the one hand, and the vulgarity of a lower socioeconomic class from Eastern Europe, on the other.)

Indeed, it was not only a thin layer of the intelligentsia but an entire nation constituting one "class" that tried to penetrate the general system of learning and science; the obstacles in its path only intensified the selection of quality and reinforced the myth of the "smart Jew." A German writer of Jewish origin, like Franz Kafka, did not have to be—and was not—a personal friend of writers of Christian origin, especially since, at the time of his rise in literature, publishers and readers of Jewish origin also emerged. And they were the ones who recognized his value. (In fact, to a large extent, Kafka's acceptance as a major figure in German literature came after the Holocaust, after his strong reception in Paris and New York—that is, over the heads of the Germans.)

The slogan of *aestheticization* referred not only to external appearance (changing their garb, shaving their beards, cleaning up their streets) but also to the appreciation of beauty, love, nature, art, literature, and beautiful forms within literature (e.g., the reverred sonnet). And the ideal of *self-realization* was common to all directions and trends: the self-realization (*hagshama*) of the youngsters of the Second Aliya (the "Palestinocentrists" inside labor Zionism); the obligation of Zionist self-realization by immigration to a kibbutz in Eretz-Israel, required of all members of labor Zionist youth movements, such as *Ha-Shomer Ha-Tsayir*, in the Diaspora; the Communist realization in the Russian Revolution or in the Spanish Civil War; or Chagall's self-realization as an artist, coming from a people that had no tradition in high art.

Personal self-realization had roots in traditional Jewish society. Two social ideals in popular semiotics were study and trade: the Yiddish proverb combines them in a rhyme: "*Toyre* iz di beste *skhoyre*," "Learning is the best merchandise." In both, the individual's personal talent, activity, and initiative are what determine success. Jews almost never worked in large collectives, in fields or factories. It is the individual merchant or peddler who connected the Jewish and the general economy or two areas of the marketplace—between village, town, and overseas. And certainly achievements in learning (the popular ideal that your son would be a rabbi or a doctor) were fully dependent on the individual's talents and success. On this base of habits and ideals, internalized in behavior and popular consciousness, appears the assimilated individual who drastically abandons the consolidated Jewish society, its norms and conventions—that is, embodies social individuality as a mode of life—and fights for a place in general society as an individual who has to prove his talents and adapt his behavior to newly adopted norms. The ideal of self-realization is demonstrated in the names of several books, emerging from all directions: by the Israeli novelist Moshe Shamir, *With His Own Hands*; Norman Podhoretz (editor of *Commentary*), *Making It*; or Jerry Rubin (the rebel of the days of the Vietnam War), *Do It*.

No doubt, all these tendencies were quite fluid, intersected with each other in various ways, sometimes materialized and sometimes didn't, contradicted one another, and fitted into general social trends. What is interesting here is that such tendencies were predominant in Jewish society in transition, acceptable to people of various ideological trends, and absorbed in popular consciousness.

The basic paradox of the Jewish responses and Jewish destiny in the nineteenth and twentieth centuries lies in the clash between two grand semiotic trends, or—to use a suggestive metaphor—between two mental temperaments of European society: liberalism and enlightenment on the one hand, and radicalism and totalitarian ideology on the other. The utopian ideals shared by all kinds of Jewish responses were fueled by the first trend, but the reality into which they were thrown was already the reality of the radical century. Furthermore, their own impetus in implementing their personal and public agendas was part of the new, radical age. Both the tragedies and the successes stem from this clash.

We may end this chapter with an anecdote. A former Berlin Jew living in New York said that the only difference between the Jews and the Gentiles in Berlin in the twenties was that the Jews did not go to synagogue and the Gentiles did not go to church. But the fact of "not going" is a powerful force in a person's psyche, and all overcoming of the past in this generation included the "overcoming" itself and that "overcome" past with a minus sign too.

THIRTEEN

Politics and Literature

The changes described above did not take place all at once. The pogroms that symbolized the momentum of the changes and launched the great immigration occurred in 1881–82. The consolidation of political responses, however, came a generation later. In 1897, several events symbolic of the period of the revolution took place: 1) Dr. Theodor Herzl's World Zionist Organization was founded in Basel, Switzerland; 2) the Jewish Socialist party, *Bund*, was founded in Vilna, the symbolic center of religious learning called "Jerusalem of Lithuania," then in the Russian Pale of Settlement; 3) the Yiddish newspaper *Forverts* (*The Daily Forward*) appeared in New York, combining Socialism (the paper's motto was: "Workers of all the countries unite!") and serious literature with kitsch and melodrama for the masses; with time, it attained a wide circulation (250,000) and served both to Americanize the Jewish immigrants and to consolidate their national consciousness; 4) the Hebrew journal, *Ha-Shiloah*, was founded in Odessa; edited by the ideologue of Spiritual Zionism, Ahad Ha-Am, it became the prestigious periodical of the new Hebrew thought and literature; 5) the first of the *Letters on Old and New Judaism*, which formulated the theory of Jewish Autonomism, was published by Simon Dubnov; 6) Sigmund Freud joined the Viennese chapter of Bnei Brith, thus openly accepting his link to Judaism. Ominously, in the same year, the first programmatically antisemitic mayor was elected in Vienna, the city of Hitler's youth.

Thus, an entire generation—about sixteen years—passed from the shock of 1881–82 to the formation of political and institutional instruments in 1897. The generation stunned by the pogroms was in a panic and did not know how to respond. Its immediate reaction was flight, mass emigration. Only in small, though historically significant, circles of young people—the Zionist *Bilu* (actually founded before the pogroms) and the America-oriented *Am Olam* (meaning both "World Nation" and "Eternal Nation")—did some kind of ideological response take shape. Sixteen years after the pogroms, a new generation arose, of people who were children during the events, had grown up in the new reality, and could react with a formulated and organized political response. What happened between 1881 and 1897? The new Jewish literature burst onto center stage: first poetry, fiction, and essays in Russian; toward the end of the eighties, the new prose in Yiddish; at the beginning of the nineties, the new Hebrew poetry of Bialik and his followers. (All genres existed in all languages, but these were the prominent achievements.) This new literature created a fictional image of the world, which served as a vivid base for the nation's and the individual's self-awareness; it was mostly a critical picture, but written from the inside. Only on the basis of that self-image were the political ideologies formulated. Without understanding the rise of literature and its role in the formation of the new intrinsic polysystem, we cannot understand how these ideologies suddenly blossomed.

Incidentally, in a different time, after the anti-Jewish massacres of 1648–49 in Ukraine, sixteen years also passed before the quasi-political mass response of the Shabtai Tsvi movement exploded in 1665–66. (And sixteen years also passed between the end of the Holocaust in World War II and the Eichmann trial, which signaled acceptance of the Holocaust as part of the Israeli experience.) We can point to other parallels as well: Yosef Karo (1488–1575) was born in Spain a few years before the expulsion of 1492 and moved at the age of 48 to Tsfat (Safed) in Eretz-Israel, where he wrote his mature and classic book, the *Shulḥan Arukh*, codifying the world of Jewish religious behavior; Ḥayim Naḥman Bialik (1873–1934) was born a few years before the pogroms in Russia and moved at the age of 48 to Eretz-Israel, where he promoted the idea of "ingathering" the treasures of Jewish culture. The classical conception of culture in both cases came about forty years after the disaster, was formulated by persons who perhaps knew it as a veiled childhood trauma but did not experience it directly at a mature age, and was oriented toward the "third generation." (Compare the interest in and reassessment of the Holocaust shown by young people in Israel and the United States in the 1980s, forty years after the event.)

Although the three areas of the new intrinsic establishment—literature, ideology, and the social and cultural network—were interdependent and nourished one another, their rise was not monolithic and the social emphasis often shifted from one area to another, from literature to history to politics and back, and from one genre or ideology to another.

It is no accident that the great prose at the end of the nineteenth century was in Yiddish and the great poetry in Hebrew. The prose of Mendele, Sholem Aleichem, and Peretz raised a critical perception of Jewish life, though it raised it from the inside, as self-examination, thus blunting the critical edge. Urban, secular Jews did not yet have a distinguishable Jewish identity. Painting, when confronting Jewish topics, is constrained by the iconography of the figure of the religious Jew, for the secular Jew has no distinguishing appearance; thus, Max Weber, the early American Cubist, resorts to Jewish religious types when responding to the news about the Holocaust in 1940. Similarly, literature had to resort to the world of the *shtetl* as a social and semiotic space, symbolic of the nature and fate of the nation. Y. L. Peretz located his humanistic themes in the milieu of simple "people" or of Hasidic mores and beliefs, which seemed authentically "Jewish." This was so despite the fact that writers and readers no longer lived in primitive *Kasrilevke*[26] or believed in Hasidic Rebbes.

However, the European genre of the novel was not suited to the world of the *shtetl*, whose prototypes did not even kill anyone or carry on sophisticated love affairs, and where social pressures ruled out any individual personality (even the crazy person filled the slot of the "town *mishugener*"). The *shtetl* was depicted in that literature from within, through its authentic semiotic material: the profuse and associative speech of typical—though exaggerated—characters who leap from subject to subject and steep every subject in a pan-historic Jewish consciousness and popular metaphysics, relying on proverbs and quotations from the library of traditional texts. This double-directed dialogue—between every person and every other person, and between the present and a world of texts—produced the episodic, associatively structured novel that did not need a narrative backbone. It could be realistically presented only in the authentic language of dialogue of the protagonists, Yiddish. Mendele, who later "translated" or recast his fictional worlds into a Hebrew mold, inventing an artificial "spoken language," thus created the beginnings of great Hebrew prose (see Alter 1988).

On the contrary, the concept of poetry in the 1890s was influenced primarily by Russian poetry (and through it, by German Romanticism). What was central to this poetry was not social or critical realism but the image of the poet, an original individual creating from a supernatural inspiration and evoking the worlds of nature, childhood, feelings, love, personal suffering, and quasi-religious experience. It is no accident that such Hebrew poets as Bialik and Tshernikhovski were born or spent their childhood in villages rather than *shtetls* ("in the lap of nature," as the Hebrew idiom says) and made it into a key issue in presenting their spiritual growth as emanating from childhood experiences in healthy, open, pure, and mysterious *nature*. Such a poet, turning to society, is seen in the image of a prophet, and his social message comes from the irrational source of deep childhood experiences, direct contact with uncontaminated nature, as well as emotional suffering. A high language of prophetic poetry was available only in Hebrew. Bialik, while still in a Lithuanian yeshiva, was influenced by the Russian poetry of Shimon Frug (1860–1916), a Jew who wrote Yiddish poetry as well, and, later, by Pushkin. But, if Pushkin, in his poem "The Prophet," drew on the language of the Bible, the language of the Bible was more available to Bialik, it

---

26. In a later generation, modern Jews too were depicted in literature, but in order to express some Jewish aspect, the characters had to confront it themselves, evoke the past, talk about it and endeavor to understand it; hence the verbosity, or the verbal level of represented reality (supported by modern trends in the poetics of fiction) in novels by such different writers as Kafka, Brener, Agnon, I. B. Singer, and Bellow.

was ingrained in the very language of Hebrew poetry. Thus, the image of the poet as a prophet, as perceived in German Romanticism, was naturally flourishing in Hebrew poetry. Then came Tshernikhovski, Zalman Shneur (1886–1959), Yaakov Fikhman (1881–1958), Yaakov Shteynberg (1887–1947), and others, who expanded the scope of themes and genres of Hebrew poetry until they covered the principal areas of European verse. In the immigration, however, in London and America, where Yiddish reigned, a new poetry in Yiddish emerged. It was not given to lyrical imagination and subtleties of language but promoted political rhetoric in the precise meters of Russian verse.

Soon after the first round of the formation of literary and political institutions came the second cycle: at the beginning of the twentieth century, the great Yiddish prose of Mendele, Sholem Aleichem, and Peretz was celebrated as classical literature and received wide distribution and public pride. The same holds for the Hebrew poetry of Bialik and Tshernikhovski. Dr. Yosef Klauzner's taking over the editorship of *Ha-Shiloah* from Aḥad Ha-Am in 1903 symbolized the shift from cultural ideology to aesthetic literature. And again, after the failure of the Russian Revolution of 1905, there emerged a whole rainbow of factions of various Jewish parties that became defined and institutionalized in a more refined and sophisticated manner than in 1897. It is well known that after the failure of the 1905 Revolution, the Russian intelligentsia and literature fell into a politically "defeatist" or inward mood, out of which the most interesting period in all the arts in Russia emerged. Young Jews were influenced by that mood, but their sensibility was enhanced by the experience of the pogroms: many turned again from ideology to literature, and from the general, Russian domain to the Jewish world. A new literature, individualistic and broadly "decadent"—as opposed to the social fiction of the classics—took center stage; in Hebrew we may mention Brener, Gnesin, Yaakov Shteynberg, Fikhman, Avraham Ben-Yitzhak (1883–1950); and in Yiddish, the fiction of Dovid Bergelson (1884–1952) and Der Nister (1884–1950) and the poetry of Dovid Aynhorn (1886–1973), Leyb Naydus (1890–1918), and "The Young Generation" ("Di Yunge") in New York: Mani Leyb (1883–1953), Zisho Landoy (1889–1937), Y. Rolnik (1879–1955), Moyshe-Leyb Halpern (1886–1932), and H. Leyvik (1888–1962). Many of these writers, though originating in Russia, actually moved to study or live in the West. Some of them were born in Galicia and influenced by contemporary German poetry, but they too joined the general mood and poetics.

Original Hebrew prose on a high level arose only in this individualistic literature after 1905. An internal monologue by a subtle, drifting intellectual could be written in the socially detached language, Hebrew. Indeed, Gnesin's protagonist in "Eytzel" ("On the Margins") writes Hebrew fiction, the girls surrounding him attend "courses" in the city and speak Russian, and both are alienated from their parents who, "perhaps," still live in some distant *shtetl* and speak Yiddish.

For a while, the nationalist awakening fed Hebrew literature and Zionism, but in a very short time the tide had turned toward Yiddish and the Bund. The Bund too became more nationalistic (as Plekhanov said: they were "Zionists afraid of seasickness") and it appealed to the masses in their own language, Yiddish, and with a more realistic program than emigration to a backward Turkish province. Berl Katznelson remembered that time:

> In 1905 began a flight from Hebrew literature, a total despair of Hebrew took over, Hebrew books stopped being published. And then began the short and very beautiful blossoming of Yiddish literature. Almost all young writers of that time either transferred to Yiddish (like Peretz Hirshbeyn) or were about to do so. And as I was highly skeptical in matters of Zionism, I was also full of doubts about Hebrew, whether Hebrew has any function in the life of the people. (B. Katznelson 1947b: 76)

After 1905, it was hard to publish books in Hebrew, and Brener's tiny magazine *Ha-Meorer* ("Reveille"), printed in London's Whitechapel in 1906, seemed like a herald of a new Hebrew literature. But writers do not easily change their language after two or three years, they continue writing even without an audience; hence Hebrew literature was so receptive to decadent trends of the time (who could be lonelier than a Hebrew poet, writing in a "dead" language with no audience?), and hence it was so strongly critical when confronting social and cultural issues. (Similar swift changes occurred later in Yiddish literature, when it felt the ground swept away from under its feet.)

FOURTEEN

Consolidation

World War I with its millions of victims and millions of Jews uprooted from their homes, the two Russian revolutions and the Balfour Declaration of 1917, the Civil War in Russia (1918–1922) and the terrifying pogroms of 1919 in Ukraine—all that shook the picture again. Modernist poetry in Yiddish—screaming, absurd, grotesque, visionary, utopian—carried the day; Yiddish avant-garde journals appeared in the early 1920s in Warsaw, Lodz, Berlin, Kiev, Moscow, Paris, and New York. The wave was over around 1924, though its fruits continued to feed Yiddish literature. By 1928, Modernism also rose to the center of Hebrew poetry, which was now concentrating in Eretz-Israel.

Masses of Jews in the Diaspora, especially the young generation streaming out of the disintegrating *shtetl*, now embraced the conquests of the Jewish revolution: the new parties and the new culture were no longer confined to narrow circles of the intelligentsia. Within the relative freedom for national organization of minorities allowed for a while in liberated Russia and in the newly established nation-States after Versailles (Poland, Lithuania, Latvia), this movement gave rise to a new and ramified cultural establishment. Only now did large networks of secular schools in both languages arise, especially in Poland, Lithuania, Eretz-Israel (only in Hebrew), and the Soviet Union (only in Yiddish). In 1925, a Hebrew University was founded in Jerusalem and a Yiddish Scientific Institute (YIVO) in Vilna, with parallel academic institutions in the Soviet Union. A mass journalism thrived in Yiddish (Hebrew journalism folded in the Diaspora and struck root in Eretz-Israel), and alongside it sprouted a literary establishment, publishing activity, mass political parties, professional associations, and so on.

For some time, Hebrew literature still wavered between Eretz-Israel and the Diaspora, where, between the two world wars, Bialik, Tschernikhovski, Agnon, Uri-Tsvi Grinberg, Fogel, Shneur, Halkin, Shofman, and others resided for various periods.[27] But by the mid-1920s, the center of Hebrew culture had no other place to go; it retreated to Eretz-Israel, where it found a Hebrew-speaking social base, and separated from world Yiddish literature.

In the 1920s, in fact, all the achievements of the Jewish revolution were consolidated. Intrinsically, a full-fledged Jewish secular polysystem emerged in the reborn Poland with its three million Jews; a truncated system in the Soviet Union; a consociational political and social entity in Eretz-Israel; and partial implementations in other countries. Extrinsically, this was the time of the amazing rise of Jews to the centers of German, Russian, Polish, and other cultures; their flocking to European universities and United States colleges; and their prominent role in the Soviet establishment and the international Communist and leftist movements. A Jew could be President of the Soviet Union (Yakov Sverdlov), its Minister of War (Leon Trotsky), Secretary of the Communist International (Grigory Zinoviev), German Foreign Minister (Walter Rathenau), or French Prime Minister (Leon Blum). It seemed that the ideologies of all the trends were vindicated: assimilation and integration in European societies was a stunning success; the Yiddish "jargon" produced a great literature and a full-fledged social polysystem; the "dead" and "clerical" Hebrew language became the unifying force of a young, secular, Zionist society in Israel.

27. Immigrants from Russia, who came from Odessa to Jaffa on the famous ship "Ruslan" in 1921, including an important group of Hebrew writers released from Soviet Russia after Gorky's intervention with Lenin on their behalf, even then went to Europe soon after they arrived in Eretz-Israel; Bialik founded his "Dvir" publishing house in Berlin.

FIFTEEN

Two Endings to One Revolution

Today, it is clear that the multifaceted Jewish revolution is over. The unsettled and colorful generation that carried out the radical transitions is gone. Some achievements were wiped out, some settled into a new status quo.

The ideologies and parties that had engulfed Jewish society at the beginning of the century exhausted their debates and disappeared in the Diaspora, and their survivors blended into the puzzle of political and pragmatic parties vying for power in the State of Israel. The imaginative efforts to establish a Secular Jewish Polysystem without a territorial power base did not last: Yiddish and Hebrew died out in the Diaspora as base languages of a society, and with them went their literatures and cultures. Their assumption that an autonomous Jewish secular culture in Diaspora was possible did not transfer to English or other languages.

Indeed, the multilingual Jewish creativity left a powerful literature expressing this period of transition. Unfortunately, it is a literature not easily accessible to those who are not "native speakers" of the languages and of their unique cultural intersections. Even the Hebrew literature of this period is not truly accessible to most Hebrew readers in Israel. The reason for that lies precisely in the nature of the strength of that literature, which is twofold: a) It was a literature constantly and profoundly conscious of its recently conquered language and of the "language of literature," a consciousness enhanced by the general interest in language in modern literature and philosophy of culture. It played with its language in the multilingual and transhistorical perspectives in which it was born; and it played with the language of literature in the telescoped perspective between Realism and Modernism in which it discovered the European world. Even when translated, such multiple layering cannot possibly be conveyed in another language, and even less so can one translate the allusions and horizons of meaning effected by the sheer situatedness in a multidirectional linguistic and cultural context. b) Thematically, Jewish literature could not represent any unique physical or psychological world, different from what European fiction evoked, for its protagonists did not have one. Hence, its strength consisted in representing the world of transition itself, which was immensely enriched by the transhistorical and transtextual consciousness of the characters and the narrators. Thus, to enjoy this literature truly, a reader has to empathize with this state of transition, including its transhistorical perspectives.

The Nazi Holocaust and Soviet antisemitism put an end to the forms of Jewish culture in Europe. But even before that, assimilation worked at full blast: in terms of personal commitment, the attachment of any individual to Hebrew or Yiddish literature or to the intrinsic Jewish establishment was a matter of one generation, two at most. Typically, most secular Yiddish and Hebrew writers and readers were still born into religious families and their children moved on to other languages (or to the Hebrew society in Israel); and that process repeated itself for several generations with ever new protagonists.

With the desiccation of the source—in the religious world of Eastern Europe—of this secularizing move, Yiddish literature has almost come to an end. And so has "Jewish" literature in Hebrew, whose great blossoming in the work of Shmuel-Yosef Agnon (1888–1970) was still grounded in Diaspora characters and language. It was a literature written by persons whose mother tongue was not Hebrew but who were nourished by a world of Hebrew texts in the Religious Polysystem and harnessed them to their writing at a time of secular rebellion; those conditions have disappeared. The new Hebrew language and literature was nourished, on the one hand, on the "Holy Tongue" of the religious library and, on the other hand, on the connotative wealth of Yiddish; but it matured by becoming independent of both. Today, Hebrew literature is the literature of a young, Hebrew-speaking society in Israel and no longer fills the role of a "State in the making"; it is merely literature. The Russian poetics that dominated Hebrew poetry from Y. L. Gordon (1830–1892), through Bialik, Tshernikhovski, Shlonski, Alterman, and Abba Kovner (1918–1989), is no longer perceived as a value, or even understood. The fictional world of Hebrew literature, located in Eastern Europe before the Holocaust, is an incomprehensible lost continent.

The heyday of "a Jewish strain" in European or American literature written by Jews is also over. Yiddish literature was carried by first-generation immigrants (to the big city or to America and other countries); because of the continuous waves of that migration, Yiddish literature flourished for several generations. Famous Jewish painters, of the School of Paris or of American Modernism, were first-generation immigrants too. But, with a few exceptions (the famous case of Conrad), to master a language of high literature one has to be born and educated in it: Saul Bellow's parents were Yiddish-speaking, and so were Franz Kafka's and Sigmund Freud's mothers, but the new language of books (if not the slang of the street) was theirs. Several immigrants wrote books in English, but those have mainly a documentary value. Important literature—to the extent that it was "Jewish" (i.e., having some Jewish aspects)—was created by brilliant writers of the second generation who mastered Russian, German, Polish, English, French, or Spanish literature at their most exquisite, Modernist moment and, with that discourse in hand, could look back at the experience of transition. More correctly, it was the second generation's experience, that is, the experience of a first generation of a new cultural race. Some of them were still conscious of having been "Jewish," however radically separated from their parents, for their "Jewishness" meant existential neurosis more than cultural content. It is doubtful whether writers even farther removed from a Jewish cultural milieu will have sufficiently concrete "Jewish" material in their personal experiences to create any "Jewish" substance in fiction.

The integration of assimilated Jews into general culture is also completed, and the negative side effects of the first general wave, which brought an outlandish semiotics of discourse to clash with the proprieties of Western society, have almost disappeared. To be sure, the professional and class distribution of Jews in general society all over the world is again as slanted as ever. Yet there is no more revolutionary trend of upward mobility particular to Jews, and if children of Jewish academics become academics themselves—or become carpenters—they are probably no different, even statistically, from any others.

In terms of the wandering centers of Jewish history, too, a relative equilibrium seems to have been reached, with two major centers in Israel and the United States (and smaller concentrations in France, Britain, and elsewhere) supplanting the earlier centers in Poland, Russia, and Germany. The tremors of change have subsided and, both in Israel and the United States, young Jews feel as if the present situation had always been there. The Zionist analysis of Jewish history envisions the liquidation of Diaspora and the eventual ingathering of all dispersions in the Hebrew State; and, in the meantime, Israel is supposed to be the spiritual center, with other Jewish centers assuming a mere passive role (as the Israeli writer Amos Oz put it, Israel is the "stage" and the Diaspora is a mere observing "gallery"). Yet now, as all the waves subsided, the alternative, Dubnovian interpretation seems to be more appropriate: Israel itself, however important culturally it may be, can be seen as one of the two new major centers of a "world nation."

The period of the Jewish revolution opened with a wave of pogroms. How did it end? As befits a Modernist narrative, we must complete the story with two endings: one tragic and one "happy" ending.

The period was very short, the developments dizzying. The intrinsic establishment reached its full flourishing between the two world wars, particularly in Poland (where three and a half million Jews lived in 1939) and in the Hebrew *Yishuv* in Eretz-Israel (which numbered half a million Jews in 1945). World War II broke out on September 1, 1939; Poland was dismantled and ghettos were established for the Jews in its major cities. On June 22, 1941, the German army invaded Soviet Russia, where five million Jews lived at that time, and began a mass liquidation of the Jewish population. As in other cities, the Jews of Riga, the capital of Latvia, were enclosed in a ghetto; among them was Simon Dubnov, the distinguished 81-year-old historian, who had stood at the cradle of the whole period. According to one account, on the night of December 7/8, 1941, during a major German *aktsia*, Dubnov was pushing a wheelbarrow with his manuscripts, when a German soldier ordered him to run. But dignity was a central motto of all the trends of that period; Dubnov walked erect, and the German soldier shot and killed him on the spot. According to another story, the German who killed Dubnov had been his student in Berlin. Just four days earlier, on December 3, 1941, and without knowing of each other's lot, Dubnov's son-in-law Henryk Erlich was arrested in the Soviet Union on Stalin's orders. Erlich had been a Socialist member of the Petrograd Soviet in 1917, left Bolshevik Russia for Poland where he became a leader of the Bund, had been arrested by the Soviets in 1939, and had recently been released from jail as a Polish citizen; now he was arrested again and—in the very days the Red Army stopped the Germans at the gates of Moscow—accused of spreading defeatist propaganda and executed (along with his colleague, Bundist leader Victor Alter). Such was the symbolic end of two ideological solutions: Autonomism and Jewish Socialism.

A year earlier, on August 3, 1940, the ideologue of the Zionist radical right, Ze'ev (Vladimir) Jabotinsky, died of a heart attack in New York, helpless as his prewar cry for "catastrophic emigration" from Europe ended in nothing and the Holocaust highlighted the correctness of his position. A fortnight later, on August 21, 1940, Leon Trotsky, founder of the Red Army and symbol of the prominence of Jews and intellectuals in the Russian Revolution, was murdered in Mexico by Stalin's agents.

The eve of the war was no less ominous. Vicious antisemitism threatened the lives of Jews in Poland, Romania, and elsewhere. The conspicuous role Jews played in German culture was brought to an end with Hitler's ascent to power. The purges of Trotskyites left the Politburo with not a single Jew in 1926; and the Stalinist purges of 1937–38 put an end to the Communist dream and eliminated most of the Jews from positions of power in the USSR. The Arab "riots" (or "revolt") in 1936–1939 against the Zionist presence in Palestine made it difficult for Jews to move safely between towns and villages, or between streets in Jerusalem, and exposed their minority status even in their "National Home." The British White Paper of 1939 blocked every expansion of the *Yishuv* and closed the land and the gates of immigration for Jews, sealing their minority status in Eretz-Israel. Abba Kovner, a young leader of *Ha-Shomer Ha-Tsayir* in Vilna, a movement that believed both in Zionist Utopia and in the Bolshevik Revolution, told of the mute despair that came upon them when hearing the news from both utopias; that was the mood the heroes of the Resistance to the Holocaust imbibed on its eve.

The situation may be illustrated by the following anecdote, told by Dov Sadan: in 1939, one of the founders of the Vilna YIVO, Zelig Kalmanovitsh, visited Jerusalem and was taken by Rachel Yanayit, a leader of women pioneers, to see the Hebrew University library. YIVO and the Hebrew University were the two academic institutions founded in 1925 and representing the two cultural options, Yiddish and Hebrew. Needless to say, both interlocuters knew both languages. Kalmanovitsh admired the library and said: if only that we could save it and ship it to Vilna! To which Yanayit responded: if only we could save the YIVO library and bring it to Jerusalem! Four years later, Kalmanovitsh, the sage of the Vilna Ghetto, was liquidated by the Germans; parts of the YIVO library were shipped to Germany for Rosenberg's "Institute for the Study of Judaism without Jews"; and were saved after the war and shipped to YIVO in New York. Rachel Yanayit was the wife of Yitzhak Ben-Tsvi, who became the second President of Israel.[28]

Thus on the threshold of World War II, all political solutions seemed blocked or defeated. Everybody's pessimism has been proven correct. The Zionists seemed to be right that assimilation of the Jews is impossible, and the "Jewish Question" will emerge even under Communism. Both Assimilationists and Zionists were right in assuming that cultural autonomy without territorial power cannot survive. The Bundists seemed to be right in claiming that Zionism is unrealistic in an Arab world and provides no solution for the millions of Jews. On August 26, 1939, Chaim Weizmann tearfully adjourned the last prewar Zionist Congress, held in neutral Switzerland, with the words: "I have no prayer but this: that we will all meet again alive." The Holocaust, which came soon after, wiped out both the nation with its intrinsic institutions developed in Europe and the amazing achievements of assimilated Jews as well.

I doubt whether all these tragic outcomes could have been envisioned realistically in the 1920s, or even in 1930, when German and Russian Jewry were thriving and Yiddish culture prospered in Europe and America. Jews were always attuned to the precariousness of existence and tried all imaginable possibilities for alternative solutions; those alternatives that survived gave rise to the new historical centers of the nation, as Israel and the United States are today. Yet I wonder if one can "prove" that these solutions were the only "correct" solutions from the beginning, or if it was a gamble that won out in the lottery of history. Would two and a half million Jews have been saved in Russia if the People's Commissar for Transportation, Lazar Kaganovitsh, had not provided trains for their evacuation to the east in the midst of the Red Army's debacle, when the German armies advanced in the summer of 1941? Would Israel exist today if, by chance or luck, the Germans had not been stopped in El-Alamein by the British army, which was prepared to retreat as far as Iraq? The *Yishuv* did not rebel when the benevolent Mandatory authorities arrested its leaders in 1946, and it is hard to see how it could have stood up against the conquering German tanks. At any rate, because of the perversions of history, and in light of the demise of other solutions and the

28. Professor Shalom Lurie, Kalmanovitsh's son in Israel, does not believe the story. Nevertheless, the fearful atmosphere of the late thirties and the unpredictable games of history are there.

repeated enlistment of Diaspora Jewry for the Zionist cause, and thanks too to the help of the nations of the world at the decisive moment—but most especially thanks to the obstinacy of the new Hebrew culture and society, their supreme sacrifice and collective will—the Hebrew revolution was eventually consolidated in Israel and became a State.

And here, as in a modern novel, attached to the story is an opposite ending, this time a happy one, though coming only after the tragic ending was complete. The State of Israel arose and stood in the War of Independence of 1948, aided by survivors of the Holocaust and by world public opinion influenced by it. Assimilation, which failed in the totalitarian regimes of Europe, now achieved a splendid success in the United States and in other Western nations. This time, participation in the general polysystem is possible in conjunction with—at least nominal—Jewish identity. It seems that both their awareness of the heroic Jewish State and of the Holocaust have contributed to a new consciousness of Jews in the West.

Thus, the ideologies of Jewish secular culture, Zionism, and assimilation were all vindicated after all. International recognition came for the trilingual Jewish literature created during the period of revolution: Nobel Prizes were awarded to Shmuel-Yosef Agnon (Hebrew literature) in 1966, to Isaac Bashevis Singer (Yiddish literature) in 1978, and to Nelly Sachs and Saul Bellow (Jewish literature in German and English) in 1966 and 1976 respectively. Thus, recognized by the world, the trilingual Jewish literature of the period of migrations came to an end.

SIXTEEN

The Age of Modernism

I began this essay by hinting at parallels between the Jewish revolution and the age of Modernism in literature and the arts, and I shall end with a comment on that.

Modernism impressed all of Jewish culture and literature and, vice versa, many who were active in general Modernism were Jews. Joining general culture was especially convenient at a point where the whole previous tradition (not shared by Jews) seemed to be overthrown. The radical impetus that freed the individual Jew from his community ties was an asset for any avant-garde.

But the more profound issue lies in the similarity of central phenomena and the historic roots of these two simultaneous movements. Like the Jewish revolution, Modernism emerged at the end of the nineteenth century, thrived after 1905, erupted to center stage after World War I, completed its achievements by the end of the 1920s, and became respectable again in the 1960s. In Modernism, artists and means of expression from the periphery came to the center: in art, in society, and in politics. And this is also true of the Jews who entered general culture from the place of an "anti-society." The period of Modernism in Europe was the same period that allowed the flourishing of a radically new Jewish culture, the rise of Jews in general society, as well as the rise of the fanatic ideologies and totalitarian regimes that turned against the Jews and against Modernist art as well.

Parallel to Modernism, the revival of language and the awareness of language and its problematic nature were central to the Jewish revolution. As in Modernism, this revolution is characterized by a negation, or reevaluation, of all the traditional values of two thousand years of culture and the mapping of a new set of values, from which a new reconstruction of history emerged. Indeed, by 1930, the period of conquest of all basic new possibilities was completed in both domains, and in the 1950s and 1960s their classic formulation was accomplished: the display window of Modernism in the Museum of Modern Art in New York and the display window of the State of Israel highlighted their acceptance in the center of general culture.

In the last generation, it has become fashionable to talk about "post-Modernism" in literature, art, and architecture. And in the Jewish realm as well, we may talk about the "postrevolutionary" period. The era of a proud "Hebrew" revival in Israel is over: once again Israelis identify themselves as "Jews." Since the mid-sixties we can observe in Israel too the popularity of the stock market (once a contemptible symbol of Diaspora speculators and "Menakhem-Mendels"); the international trade based in Israel (notably, of merchandise created by the revolution: weapons and agricultural products); a traumatic awareness of the Holocaust (including the relation of the majority of nations to Israel in what seems to be an eternal pattern of antisemitism); the return to a transhistorical religious awareness, both in the form of an ultra-Orthodox religious revival and of fundamentalist symbolism; and the loss of confidence in secular and cultural values—all these are signs of the "counterrevolution" and will certainly demand new kinds of balance. The "third generation," both in Israel and the Diaspora, is trying to look back—to the Holocaust, and to the "prerevolutionary," perhaps religious past, though with little concrete personal experience. To the fourth generation, all this may seem too ephemeral to be of general interest.

Nevertheless, Modernism can be overcome but not entirely disregarded. Similarly, it is hard to imagine a Jewish State or Jewish literature without the achievements of the revolutionary secular period; as it is hard to imagine Jews in the West abandoning their integration into general culture—whether they preserve their separate identity or melt into general society as did the Huguenots in Berlin, who are Germans with French names.

The hundred years described here have no parallel in history in the dizzying, exuberant multitude of intersecting trends, personalities, changes, creativity, achievements, and defeats. Whether—and how—either of the two new options may survive for another hundred years is a matter of speculation.

PART II: THE REVIVAL OF THE HEBREW LANGUAGE

Anatomy of a Social Revolution

SEVENTEEN

The Miracle of the Revival of Hebrew

The unprecedented revival of the ancient Hebrew language and the creation of a new society on its base was perceived as a miraculous event. As we shall see, there was an intricate combination of social and historical factors, of collective willpower and accidents of history, that brought it about. The importance of this renaissance is not just in the miracle of language and all that a language means to its users; beyond that, it created the base on which a new, secular-type Jewish society and culture could emerge again and give life to that burnt phoenix, that "fossil" of history (as Toynbee saw them), the Jews. It gave its users a vehicle for expressing a totality of twentieth-century experience in a language of their own, and a new social identity, irrespective of their various countries of origin and political views.

Another possible base for such a new Jewish national society was the revived Yiddish language and culture—and for several dozen years that, indeed, was the larger movement around the globe and seemed the more viable option. After the emergence of the large nation-States in Europe, the smaller ethnic groups also developed nationalist movements striving toward national identity based on a common language, literature, and cultural heritage. The idea that ethnic cultural autonomy within larger States was desirable and possible was raised in the multi-national Austro-Hungarian empire, and from the Austro-Marxists it was taken over and modified by Stalin (in his pamphlet, "Marxism and the National Question," 1913), who determined the nationalities policies in the Soviet Union almost from the beginning. Alas, as history showed, that idea did not work: today, in the territories of the old Austro-Hungarian and Russian Empires, even the smallest ethnic groups, identified by a separate language or religion, demand political independence and territorial sovereignty. In other words, the American solution, imposing one national mythology and one language of government and education on various ethnic groups, won over the Yugoslav or Soviet models (of course, former ethnic groups in the United States do not live in continuous areas in their ancestral territories, as they do in Europe). In view of that general lesson, it is doubtful whether a Jewish secular society without a majority population in any territory and with doors open for its participants to other, coterritorial and major-ity cultures could have survived in the long run. But this was precisely what was attempted with Yiddish cultural autonomy, and the hypothetical question of whether it would have lasted became irrelevant when the social base of Yiddish was wiped out by the two totalitarian empires, Nazism and Stalinism.

Stalin claimed that the Jews are not a nation because they lack two indispensa-ble attributes of a nation: a territory and a common language. The Zionists, influenced by similar theories, held similar views but set out to remedy the situation by actively trying to supply the lacking attributes. They denounced the present in favor of a future that would restore the deep past, including territory, language, and political independence. Indeed, they implemented the "American" rather than the "Yugoslav" solution to the national problem, enforcing Hebrew and a whole new conceptual world in Hebrew on immigrants from all countries and languages. And they believed in national power and sovereignty rather than mere cultural autonomy.

From the outside, a return to an almost mythological past after two thousand years may have seemed a quixotic enterprise, something like the return of all Germanic tribes to Iran or India. But subjectively, in their own mythology and literature, the Jews had never abandoned their ties to that land and had never neglected the Hebrew language. Therefore, when thoroughly squeezed in their European existence and revived by their nationalistic aspirations, some of them moved with the trends of this radical century and, after countless defeats and sacrifices, achieved the dreamed-of return to the land and the language. Theodor Herzl said: "If you will, it is not a dream," and there was a small number of people who showed enough willpower to make the dream come true.

The advantage of Hebrew over Yiddish—apart from the good fortune of having escaped that Holocaust—was its inherent link to a territory and to a classical, private, and also internationally sanctified, literature: the Bible. Indeed, the Jews called themselves "the People of the Book": it was not that the "Book of Books" belonged to them but rather that they belonged to the Book. They called Palestine by the old name "Eretz-Israel" (i.e., the land of the Jews); and the Hebrew language was enshrined as the language of that land. But unlike other ancient civilizations that were modernized and gained independence at about the same time in their own traditional space, Hebrew came back to its ancestral land from a long absence, from the outside, and from the world of Europe and modernity. It was not an ancient language of a great ancient civilization, stagnant for hundreds of years (as Arabic or Indian cultures were), that is now gradually growing into the twentieth century; but rather a new language, recreated in the very heart of the transitions of modernity, in the context of the intellectual ferments in Russia, which itself underwent an earthquake, trying to embrace abstract, idealized forms of the culture of the modern West. In that general spiritual wave, Hebrew grew as a language of modern sensibilities, fiction, politics, and ideology, while roaming in a library of texts written over a period of several thousand years. That depth and that link to a land were missing in Yiddish.

On the eve of this revival the Hebrew language was a very one-sided vehicle indeed. It focused on a limited range of religious topics and neglected many other areas, even those that had been alive in the past. The vocabulary of the Bible is rather small, often an accidental selection, bound by the texts included in the canon and confined to the literary language appropriate to the genres of that book, characterized by its sparse and succinct language. The vast Talmudic litera-ture includes names of *realia*, such as tools, plants, or animals, but those are mostly incidental to other topics and scattered in multiple contexts, and many lost their specific denotations for the readers, as the objects they denoted were no longer in sight; also, throughout the ages, the students of those texts were interested in the universally valid law and not in concrete objects mentioned in passing. As a result, Hebrew lacked the simplest words in many domains of life, not just of the modern world but of the basic domestic and surrounding objects: Jews either paid no attention to concrete nature or else used words from other languages. In a multilingual culture, that was no problem; it could be left either to the spoken language or to the language of the majority population. Hebrew dictionaries, even in the second half of the nineteenth century, translated the most basic names of plants and birds from other languages into Hebrew with: "a kind of tree" or "a kind of bird." Whenever such terms were needed, foreign names were simply embedded in the Hebrew text (which is how the twelfth-century Hebrew commentator Rashi preserved many old French words and Bohe-mian commentators preserved old Czech), and protocols of Rabbinical trials often quoted witnesses in Yiddish. One of the efforts of the language revival went into research, identifying and classifying such words mentioned in the sources, that is, "Biblical Zoology," "flora and fauna in the Talmud," and so on. And many of them were restored or adapted to modern use. For example, "potatoes" are *bulby* in Ukrainian and *bulbes* (plural) in Yiddish. Now, there is a word *bolbos* or *bulbus* (vowels undecided) in the singular, in the Mishna; it is clearly the Greek word *bolbos* (or the Latin *bulbus*), a kind of onion bulb, spelled in Hebrew letters (even then Hebrew was poor in words for *realia*, but the Hebrew spelling made it a "Hebrew" word); Mendele, hearing the sound of the Yiddish word in an authentic Hebrew word from the "sources," appropriated it for "potatoes," and gave it an Aramaic plural: *bulbusin*. Israeli Hebrew, however, discarded it (it sounded too Yiddish) and opted for *tapukhey adama* (from the French *pomme de terre*).

The legendary figure of the language revival was Eliezer Ben-Yehuda (1858–1922). He was hailed as the ideologue and pioneer of reviving Hebrew as a spoken language and the person who sacrificed his own family for the sake of raising the first Hebrew family and the first Hebrew-speaking child after two thousand years of exile from the language. Streets were named after him in every

Israeli city and a whole hagiographic literature was written.[29] Indeed, Eliezer Ben-Yehuda began propagandizing the idea (though still vaguely) in his first article "A Burning Question," published in the Hebrew journal *Ha-Shahar* in Vienna in 1879, and devoted his life to it, immigrating to the backward, Ottoman-ruled Palestine in 1881. He edited Hebrew newspapers in Jerusalem, cofounded societies, invented over two hundred new Hebrew words, and copied with his own hand about half a million quotations from the historical library of Hebrew texts for his great (OED-type) Hebrew dictionary, which was posthumously edited and published in seventeen volumes. He became the symbol of the possibility of mastering Hebrew as a spoken language, the embodiment of the idea, hailed in Hebrew education around the world, especially after his death. But, as a matter of fact, in spite of his pathetic figure and life, Ben-Yehuda had no real influence on the revival itself, which began to strike roots about twenty-five years after his arrival in Eretz-Israel, in the milieu created by the Second Aliya. In his thorough study of Ben-Yehuda's life, Jack Fellman (1973) shows that in six of his seven goals (i.e., except for his newspaper *Ha-Tsvi*) he actually achieved no influence.[30]

In 1989, celebrations in Israel and around the world commemorated "One Hundred Years of the Revival of the Hebrew Language," on what was proclaimed to be the centenary of the foundation of the "Language Committee" that eventually became the Hebrew Language Academy in the State of Israel; stamps were printed and books published on the occasion. But this was surely an exaggerated claim. Indeed, in 1889, the "Precise[31] Language" ("*safa brura*") Society was founded in Jerusalem by three Sephardi and two Ashkenazi Jews (including Ben-Yehuda). Their stated goal was to fight the "jargons" of the Ashkenazim and Sephardim (i.e., Yiddish, Ladino, and other spoken dialects) which enhance the animosity between the multiple Jewish ethnic groups sojourning in Jerusalem, and promote one Hebrew pronunciation. Eventually, this coterie appointed a "Language Committee," consisting of four scholars, including Ben-Yehuda. But that Language Committee existed only in name for only half a year and left no results or documents. Fifteen years later, in 1904, the newly founded Teachers' Association set up a new "Language Committee" with the same name, but this Committee too was dormant. The new Language Committee actually showed its first modest results only in 1911—thirty years after Ben-Yehuda's arrival in Palestine—in a little pamphlet of Do's and Don'ts in the use of some words (see Fellman 1973: 92), and wrote the first brief account of its reconstructed history in the first issue of the *Memoirs of the Language Committee*, 1912 (see Academy 1970:27–35). That modest activity, however, was not the force that revived the language: it occurred

---

29. Including Robert St.-John's book in English, *Tongue of the Prophets: The Life Story of Eliezer Ben-Yehuda* (1952).

30. See also the summary of this issue in the review of Felman's book: Nahir 1977.

31. It may also mean: "Select," "Clear," or "Precisely Articulated," i.e., pronounced in the Sephardi accent that was its main goal.

when the social base for the language revival had already been conquered by the generation of the Second Aliya, when both Tel Aviv (founded in 1909) and the labor movement (since 1906) conducted the frame of their lives in Hebrew. The work of the new Language Committee consisted primarily of coining words and promoting the Sephardi accent,[32] and was again interrupted during World War I. It is only after the world war, that is, under the orderly British Mandatory rule that recognized Hebrew as one of the three official languages in Palestine, that the Language Committee published a journal *Leshonenu: Our Language: a Journal for the Improvement of the Hebrew Language*, and seriously launched its standardizing activities. Indeed, the glory of the earlier Language Committee can only be understood as a back-projection from the present-day prestigious Academy of the Hebrew Language (which had turned *Leshonenu* into a journal of research rather than "improvement").

At any rate, although the significance of Eliezer Ben-Yehuda and the Hebrew Language Committee in the revival of the language is not in question—they provided some prestige to the effort and coined many words—it was not they who created the new Hebrew culture, the living Hebrew language, and the *Hebrew society* that was later transformed into the State of Israel.

The revival of the Hebrew language has no single birthday; it occurred—asymmetrically—both much earlier and much later than the centenary date of 1889 would suggest. On the one hand, without the multifaceted and imaginative renaissance of the Hebrew language *in writing*, it is impossible to understand its sudden flourishing as a spoken language. The fruit of this renaissance can be seen at least from the middle of the nineteenth century in Russia: in Abraham Mapu's (1808–1867) novel, *Ahavas Tsiyon* ("Love in Zion" or "The Love of Zion," 1853; the word "love" itself was revolutionary!); in the novels translated by Kalman Shulman (1819–1899) into Hebrew (notably Eugene Sue's *Les mystères de Paris*, Vilna, 1859); or in the first Hebrew newspaper explicitly devoted to science and technology, *Ha-Tsfira*, founded in Warsaw in 1862; and, especially, in the appearance of Bialik's poetry in the early 1890s; Mendele's translation of his own *Travels of Benjamin the Third* from Yiddish into Hebrew, published in 1896; the founding of the periodical *Ha-Shiloah*, edited by Aḥad Ha-Am, in 1897; and in the flourishing of Hebrew literature and writing ever since. On the other hand, *social cells*, using the Hebrew language in oral communication, arose in Eretz-Israel only in the Second Aliya (especially between 1906 and 1913), as part of the radical ideological package, realized by those devoted and fanatic pioneers (the Hebrew term is *meshuga le-davar*, "crazy for one thing," or "single-mindedly

---

32. I have preserved the accepted translation "accent" for *havara*. Indeed, the Ashkenazi, Sephardi, Yemenite, and other readings of Hebrew are not full-fledged dialects because we are not dealing with living languages but with ways of orally performing the same canonized written texts; on the other hand, the differences in pronunciation sound much greater than between many normal dialects or even cognate languages.

crazy")[33] who built the two wings of the Hebrew *Yishuv*: the labor movement and the first Hebrew city.

The revival of the Hebrew language was not a simple matter, even for its heroes. The Israeli writer Natan Shaḥam tells in his memoirs (*Sefer Hatum*, 35) of his father's meetings with Bialik. His father, the writer Eliezer Shteynman (1892–1970), knew the Traditional Hebrew Library inside out and was a key figure of revolutionary Modernism in Hebrew literature; Bialik was the accepted "National Poet" of the "Renaissance Period," who transplanted Talmudic legend into modern Hebrew literature, edited Hebrew poets from Medieval Spain, and worked for the "ingathering" of Hebrew writings of all the ages; between them, the two writers mastered all the treasures of the Hebrew language—and yet they would stroll in the First Hebrew City, in the early 1930s, speaking Yiddish. One of the anecdotes about Bialik attributes to him the saying: "*Yiddish redt zikh, hebreyish darf man reydn*" ("Yiddish speaks itself, Hebrew has to be spoken"). And Gershom Scholem (1897–1982) tells of coming to Bialik's house on a traditional Friday-night gathering, where the spoken language was Yiddish: when Scholem entered, Bialik would say: "*Der yeke iz gekumen, m'darf reydn loshn koydesh*" ("The 'Yekke' [German Jew] has come, we've got to speak the Holy Tongue") (Scholem 1982:188).

In a lecture to the "Brigade of the Defenders of the Language," in Tel Aviv in 1929, Professor Dr. Yosef Klauzner tells that he was in mourning for his mother and wanted to read, as is customary, from the Book of Job but he had a problem: "Instead of *reading* the Book of Job, I had to *study* it." He took a French translation of Job and no longer needed explanations: "the *language* was simple and intelligible, so that I could direct my thinking to the *idea*, admire the lofty arguments, and find solace in my grief" (Klauzner 1956:362; emphasis in the original; see translation of the essay in this volume). Professor Dr. (as he insisted on signing all his publications) Yosef Klauzner, a leading propagandist for the revival of the "Hebrew Tongue" in Russia, editor of the central journal of Hebrew literature, *Ha-Shiloaḥ*, the first ever Professor of Hebrew Literature at the new Hebrew University in Jerusalem, whose mother tongue was Yiddish, whose cultural language was Russian, whose doctorate was in German—this man required a *French* translation of the Hebrew book of Job to console himself for his mother's death!

In his autobiography, "A Dream Come True," Eliezer Ben-Yehuda confessed

---

33. The metaphor of craziness appears throughout the period. Nekhama Feinstein-Pukhatshevski of Rishon Le-Tsiyon (= "The First [settlement"] of Zion) tells how David Yudelevitsh, the fanatic Hebrew teacher, would persecute any child who did not talk Hebrew in his presence. When a girl, lying in bed with a high fever, called to Nekhama in Russian, he screamed: "Hebrew, Hebrew!" The girl too began screaming, until Dr. Mazie hushed him: "Crazy is the man of spirit," "*meshuga ish ha-ruaḥ*" (Academy 1970:26).

that there were two things he regretted all his life: that he was not born in Eretz-Israel and that his first mumblings were not in Hebrew. In accordance with the romantic conception of the irrational connection of a human being with his roots in his homeland, he admits: "I will never be able to feel for the ancestral land that deep affection a person feels for the place where he was born and spent his childhood." (What did he have in mind: the gray autumn of his native Lithuania?) The same is true for language:

> I speak Hebrew, only Hebrew, not only with the members of my family but also with every man and woman who I know understands Hebrew, more or less; and I do not trouble with courtesy or respect for women, and behave very coarsely, a coarseness that has caused a lot of hatred and opposition to me in Eretz-Israel. [. . .] And I think in Hebrew day and night, awake and in dreams, in sickness and in health, and even when I am tormented by harsh physical pain. And yet, I must admit again: sometimes, when my mind is steeped in thought, especially of days gone by, days of childhood and youth, and it frees itself for a moment, without my sensing it, from the Hebrew yoke I have forcibly imposed on it for so many years—I suddenly realize that I was thinking for a moment not in Hebrew, that, from under my thought in Hebrew words, surfaced a few foreign words, in Ashkenazic [= Yiddish[34]] and also in Russian and French! (Ben-Yehuda 1986:57)

Popular mythology feeds on the image of the hero who embodies an ideal, the individual whose personal life-story, easily understood and empathized with, and especially the suffering and sacrifice in his life, symbolize a lofty goal. Thus Theodor Herzl is constructed as a legendary Jewish King (despite the fact that he was preceded by the Russian movement of "The Lovers of Zion," *Hibbat Tsiyon*); Hayim Nahman Bialik as a poet-prophet, who "paid with his own blood and marrow" (as he himself confessed in a poem) for the spark in his verse that ignited a fire among the people (despite the fact that, during the Period of Revival, there were also other excellent poets, like Shaul Tshernikhovski or Yakov Shteynberg); Yosef Trumpeldor (1880–1920), killed in the defense of Tel Hai (Galilee), as the "One-Armed Hero" (despite the fact that he lost his arm defending Russia from the Japanese in 1905); Yosef-Hayim Brener as the carrier of the torch of *af-al-pi-khen*, "in-spite-of-everything" (as if his death at the hands of Arab rioters in Jaffa in 1921 justified the despair and determination in his writings); and Eliezer Ben-Yehuda as the father of the revival of the language, who sacrificed his family on its altar. These figures assumed superhuman dimensions between the two world wars, when Hebrew education, Hebrew schools, and Zionist youth movements emerged and spread through Eretz-Israel and around the world, when it

---

34. A staunch Hebraist would never mention Yiddish by its name but would refer to it as "Jewish-German" or "Ashkenazic."

was imperative "to win souls" for the Zionist cause.[35] In a society built on dogmatic propaganda, such figures are fostered; today we have gained sufficient distance to delve more deeply into the facts and the real historical forces that shaped history.

But before we narrate the historical story, a clarification of some theoretical issues is in order. We shall do so in the next two, brief chapters.

35. Bar-Adon (1988:117) recounts Bialik's virulent attack on the Zionist activist from Odessa M. Usishkin (1863–1941), for pronouncing Ben-Yehuda "father of the revival of Hebrew speech," and Agnon's objection to calling Ben-Yehuda the "reviver of the Hebrew language." In an interview with Bar-Adon, Agnon said that Usishkin admitted to him that it wasn't Ben-Yehuda who revived the language, "but the people seek a hero, and we give them the hero..."

EIGHTEEN

The Social Existence of Language

The importance of the revival of the Hebrew language is not simply, as it was often put by patriots and writers, a matter of emotions about the *Language* itself, as a personification of a beloved body-of-words ("language" is feminine in Hebrew) borne by the nation throughout its exile. Nor is it simply a case of a "dead" language that was resurrected, thus symbolizing the "resurrection" of the nation; a Holy Tongue that became a secular language, symbolizing the secularization of the nation; or a written language that began to be a privileged, *spoken* language and to be used to talk about everyday nonsense, a language children bicker in, as Ben-Yehuda dreamed, that is, a language not of learning alone but of family and daily life, competing with the Yiddish of Diaspora.

The genuine achievement of the Hebrew revival includes all these; but its essence lies in the creation *ex nihilo* and the instant establishment of two interrelated instruments, each dependent on the existence of the other:

1. *A base language of the individual*, which is not necessarily his first or only language, but provides the foundation for his language activities.[36] On its basis he can take off, whenever desired, into more specialized or historical areas of the language and professional idiolects, as well as into other languages.
2. *A base language of the society*, that is, a "natural language" (in the precise sense of the term), with a basic vocabulary and syntax, which serves as *a spoken language for the society* and as *the language of its oral and written informational networks*.

36. Most Hebrew writers throughout history, including in the modern period, were not born speaking Hebrew. Though today there are many Israeli-born writers, such poets as Natan Zach, Yehuda Amichai, Meir Wieseltier, Amir Gilboa, Avot Yeshurun, and Dan Pagis were born in Europe. All presidents of the Hebrew Writers Union, till this day, were born in Diaspora. And so were most ministers in the Israeli governments, including Yitzhak Shamir, Moshe Arens, and David Levy.

Relying on the base language of a society, special or professional "*secondary languages*" in various areas are developed. A society consists of a large network of interrelated systems: the legal system, administration and politics, social organizations and parties, literature and theater, education and mass media, agriculture and commerce, army and military discipline, children's games and labor relations. Some of these systems are formal and specialized, shared by small groups of people (e.g., the sciences), some are quite free and become part of the general base language, and often there is a fuzzy transitional area between the two (compare, for example, the popular names of trees and plants with scientific Botany, or the function of political institutions with Constitutional Law). All together they constitute the *polysystem of culture and society*.

Each of these social systems active in society has its own "secondary language"—encompassing a domain of formulated laws, accepted "rules of the game," and typical discourse. All those "secondary languages" rely on the syntax and basic vocabulary of the given natural language, repeatedly taking off from and returning to its expressions. Thus members of a society, mastering its base language, can freely move from one social or cultural system to another, from work to home, from one topic to the next, and back.

The base language serves also as a common ground for all the social, ethnic, and immigrant groups composing a nation. Such groups, too, may form their own "secondary languages," or fragments of such, but those are deviations from and anchored in the common base language. This was, eventually, an extremely important factor in the revival of one Israeli nation from tribes arriving after two thousand years of separation, who attached their particular "accents" or idiolects to the common base. The base language may also accommodate foreign languages, embedded in it to various degrees, for example, in pop music (where you can hear English on Hebrew or Dutch radio), science teaching, computer software, or technical manuals—a common feature of the cultures of small nations in this "American age."

Thus the base language is the "lifeblood" of the entire ramified network of social and cultural systems that constitute a living nation: the rules of such systems are formulated in this language and fall apart when it is lacking; the base language is shared by society as a whole; and the easy transition from one system to another goes through it. The various systems are interconnected and interdependent in two ways:

a. *In the social network*, where the various systems appear side by side, form hierarchies, support one another, influence and compete with one another. The theater, for example, is connected with literature, is dependent on the cultural and ideological level of the audience, is supported by foundations or the Ministry of Education, requires translators, relates to theater in other countries, and so on—and each of these has its own, autonomous system. All such systems are open-ended and interdependent with others.

b. *In the personal junction* of each individual, where various manifestations of several heterogeneous systems intersect in his life and consciousness. Every individual is a participant in some systems and a consumer of others: he reads a certain newspaper, works in a school, drives a car, goes to the theater, breaks the law, votes for a particular party, watches television, and so on. Every individual has his own *junction*, his particular combination of (parts of) systems selected from the general network and changing throughout his life.

The mutual dependence between the base language of the society and that of its individuals relies on the reciprocal relationship between the social *network* of cultural systems and the personal *junctions* of many individuals. Moreover, the base language of both serves also as the vessel for absorbing aspects of other cultures and building new secondary languages—ranging from world literature to electronics—which the society or a group of its individuals are willing to adopt or are interested in.

A personal example of the possibility of realizing a new, *Hebrew base language of the individual* was provided by Ben-Yehuda in the education of his children. But, practically, he had no broader success because a matching Hebrew base language of society was lacking. The necessary connection between these two was understood by the pioneer Hebrew teacher David Yudelevitsh (1863–1943); in an address to an assembly of eight Hebrew teachers in Palestine, held in the first Zionist settlement of Rishon Le-Tsiyon in 1892, he said:

> The idea that is rising now in the House of Israel and took roots in the hearts of many of our people, to revive the ancient Hebrew language and make it into a spoken language, should be examined more carefully. Right now, the nation of Israel has no Hebrew courthouses, community or government centers, marketplace or stock market, no country and no commercial place on the face of the earth we can point to: here we shall employ and develop and persist in speaking Hebrew so we can get used to it, and it will become a language spoken in our mouths. None of that do we have, and we have no place where we can speak in our language about daily experience. Just one corner, one small place is left us, where there is hope, where all our faith lies that the language will emerge from there and be spoken by the sons and daughters of Israel who will then be able to bring it to the marketplace, to commerce, to community centers, to all walks of life—and that place is the school... (Karmi 1986:80–81)

A base language of a Hebrew society began to be created, at least in principle and in isolated islands, only during the time of the Second Aliya (especially between 1906 and 1913), and became the framework for the life of the *Yishuv* throughout the country from the Third Aliya (1919–1923) on, as part of a comprehensive ideological and institutional system that evolved in Mandatory Palestine. Without *the revival of Hebrew in this sense, as a base language of a widely ramified society,* including most of the areas of life and civilization, the *Yishuv* would not have become a national entity and the State of Israel would not have existed, and speaking it would have remained as much a curiosity as speaking Esperanto. No innovations of words would have been effective without a social and semiotic system in which those words might be used. If Hebrew had few names of flowers, the invention or recovery of such names from old texts was not enough; it took root when Botany teachers guided groups of school children in learning to know nature and distinguish between the various kinds of flowers; and vice versa: those distinctions could be made only with such names in hand. In other words, *the social process of expanding a semiotic field went hand in hand with the linguistic process of expanding a subfield of the language*. This circularity is what made it so difficult to break through in the revival of Hebrew. And it could not be done in an isolated domain alone: teaching the names of flowers also required the establishment of Hebrew schools and youth movements, the writing of textbooks, the existence of publishers and distribution of books, a cult of nature, the establishment of Jewish villages—and all those involved further social and cultural systems. Thus, the whole entangled network of social systems and subsystems had to be implemented at one and the same time, along with the revival of the language. It was achieved through a purposeful ideological effort to create a full-fledged nation on a new continent, all at once. And that is why the process of reviving the spoken language was not gradual but sprang suddenly like Athena from Zeus's forehead. Once such a ramified network was established, however, filling it in with new words or adding an entirely new domain was less of a problem.

In sum, the revival of the Hebrew language was not just the revival of a nice accent or of words "that can already be said in Hebrew." It was a revival not only of the Hebrew *language* but also of Hebrew *culture* and a Hebrew *society*. Moreover, the process was circular: the revival of Hebrew culture and of an ideological society brought about the revival of the language; and, reciprocally, the revival of the language enabled the growth of the culture and the new society. In other words, it was not only that *Hebrew was established by the young Yishuv, but Hebrew also established the Yishuv itself*. The relationship between a *framework* and its *product* was reversed. The reversal succeeded so well that, now, the language is as automatic and obvious to most inhabitants of Israel as the ground under their feet.

NINETEEN

Theory of Twin Systems

The base language of the individual and the base language of society can be described as *twin systems* "mirroring" each other. The fact that Ben-Yehuda's understanding of the problem was located primarily in inventing words for objects reflects the old theory of *res et verba*, which assumes a one-to-one correspondence between individual words and things. The ideal of speaking the language too was perceived merely as a matter of daring to provide an oral correlative to the written language.

Structural linguists discuss language not as a collection of words but as a system; but it is usually seen as an independent and closed system. Yet, as the revival of Hebrew shows, a language is anything but independent of a host of nonlinguistic aspects. All this requires a reformulation of our understanding of language as a social system. We will suggest here some basic notions for such a conception.

The strength of the social existence of language lies not in its being an independent, axiomatic, or "arbitrary" system of signs but, on the contrary, in its "life," in the sense of an ever-changing, responding and unstable, open system. When we use words for things, we do not simply convey meaning inscribed in the language system but send our interlocutor to the outside world, to frames of reference in "reality" or in other texts, to extract information from them. Thus, in the simple example used above, the names of flowers are mere indexes, pointing to the colorful, fragrant, many-petaled, beautiful or ugly, flowers themselves. Hence there is an interdependence between our knowledge of the field of flowers, that is, the external frame of reference, and the semantic field of flower names in the language. Such interdependencies are multiple; indeed, language can be described as a cluster of several *twins* participating in *intertwined systems*.

Intertwined systems, or *twin systems*, are two autonomous systems, interdependent and interacting in many ways, which exhibit two basic relations: *mirroring* and *asymmetry*. "Mirroring" here is a general term for imitation, copying, approximating, modeling, reflecting, excerpting, that is, any kind of representation of elements of one twin by the other; and "asymmetry" indicates the fact that one twin has parts and aspects not mirrored in the other, and vice versa. Language is a cluster of such twins, some of which have their counterpart inside the language itself and some outside of it. Language advances, changes, grows richer, precisely because parts of it interact with twin systems, respond to the asymmetry, and try to mirror the asymmetrical counterparts.

Such intertwined systems are, for example:

1. The base language of the individual and the base language of society (as discussed above). On the one hand, no individual mirrors the whole base language of society, and his mirroring may have individual shades and connotations; the individual develops by enlarging his share of elements mirrored from the social base language; parts of the social base language that are not used by any individuals in the present are "dead" or "historical" layers. On the other hand, in the base language of the individual, meanings of words may be much richer in specificity than what is excerpted in the social base language; also, features developed by several individuals may enter and enrich the social base language or part of it.

2. The oral and written language. Structuralist Phonology saw the written as mirroring the spoken language; but the phonetic and connotational specificity and richness of the spoken language cannot be reproduced fully in its written twin. We know of reverse phenomena, when, with mass literacy, spelling has influenced pronunciation; and Derrida argued, more comprehensibly, for the primacy of the written over the spoken language. The expansion of the written language and the libraries of knowledge stored in it was again partially mirrored in the spoken language, which often includes fragments of written systems of discourse.

3. The language as a modeling system and the Fields of Reference (in the "real" world, in worlds of knowledge, or in various hypothetical "possible worlds")[37] to which it relates (such as the flowers and their names, mentioned above). Language imposes its modeling on our perception of such Fields of Reference; at the same time, the expansion of such Fields of Reference influences the expansion of language. The rich language of literature of the modern age, especially in French, Russian, and English, drew on the rich differentiation of observations in civilization, society, and psychology; and this language of literature expanded the natural language immensely.

We cannot discuss language as an autonomous system with fixed rules of grammar without understanding its permanent expansion and shifting through interaction

---

37. This is based on my theory of the literary text and of "Integrational Semantics" (see Harshav 1982, 1984).

with its twins: literature, philosophy, and "reality." Thus, language is not simply a system to describe the "world" but a system that sends us to the external world to get information from it not provided in language but supplementing and qualifying it.

The same twin structure applies to numerous more specific areas that can be carved out as autonomous systems, such as: the language of a science and the knowledge developing in that science; the contemporary, active (or "living") language and its dormant historical layers; the language systems of two closely related individuals; or the two languages involved in a translation.

In all such intertwined systems, the twins are interdependent, one cannot be fully explained without relation to the other, and an essential circularity obtains. Of course, both *mirroring* and *asymmetry* take on different forms in different twins. Asymmetry here is a key feature because only as a result of the asymmetry can each part influence the growth of the other. And the same process is fruitful in the growing interpretations of works of literature in which the text may be related to various twin systems: to the "Internal Field of Reference" (the "fictional world") or to several External Fields of Reference: a historical situation, an ideology, the author's biography, the literary system. Each relation of this kind is circular because "mirroring" is never identical and the interpretation of one twin influences the interpretation of the other twin.

Hence we cannot fully learn a language as an independent system; we have to consider the twins of the system in several directions: while learning from a written text, we have to learn its oral twin as well, its twin in the external Fields of Reference, its twin in the author's world, and so on. French education abroad always understood it when it taught not just the French language but "French Civilization."

After this theoretical excursus, we can see that the revival of the Hebrew language involved breaking into several circular situations and building up simultaneously both parts of such twin systems: the written and the oral language; a person's adult and childhood language; the base language of the individual and of society; Hebrew terms and their counterparts in other languages; language as a modeling system and the "world" it models. In the last category, the expansion of the new Hebrew vocabulary was interrelated with the expansion of the modeled "world," both in knowledge and in actual reality: to put it simply, nature, agriculture, defense, government, secular education, and so on, had to be reinvented for the Jews. Hence, building a full-fledged social polysystem and a complex and pluralistic society, including many kinds of vegetables, kindergartens, sciences, literary genres, architectural varieties, and so on, was a twin counterpart to the expansion of the language.

An important role was played by the process of translation (taken in the broadest sense): the social system and the system of general knowledge were not built *ex nihilo* but rather translated and adapted from other languages. Thus, the

classification of flowers and of political ideologies was based on such classifica-
tions in other languages and then provided with Hebrew names, but also selected
through the filter of the Hebrew language and of the observable flowers in the
Hebrew semiotic field (i.e., both in immediate nature and in literature).

The new Hebrew language in any given domain established twin relationships
in several directions simultaneously. For example, the language of nature mirrored
the developing nature in the country, the language of nature in European languages and fiction, the international science of nature, and the nature vocabulary
in old Hebrew texts, as well as the general perceptions of grammar and word-
formation in modern Hebrew. Those twin relationships were mutually limiting,
and the development of each twin system influenced the others.

TWENTY

Language as a Unifying Force

Now we can approach the social role of language from the side of Jewish history.

As some scholars have indicated, various aspects of the revival of Hebrew are "in principle" similar to linguistic phenomena in other societies; but the revival itself, its force and the force of the changes it produced in the consciousness of the individual and the society, and especially its amazing success, are unprecedented in history. Yet, the revival of the Hebrew language cannot be understood outside the context of the *Modern Jewish Revolution*, which is also unprecedented in history. This revolution has been described in detail in Part One of this book and we shall not repeat it here. Let us only point out that it consisted in a massive and centrifugal move of Jews out of the old, Jewish Religious Polysystem and into two kinds of secular polysystems, intrinsic and extrinsic.

The new intrinsic Jewish Secular Polysystem was erected in a short period of time in 2 + 1 languages—Hebrew, Yiddish, and the language of the respective States where Jews lived. It consisted of three interrelated areas—literature, ideology, and a sociocultural network of institutions—which offered the individual emerging from the world of the *shtetl* a spectrum of options for self-enrichment and expression and intellectual and cultural integration. But in the same territory, he was also offered options in the languages and cultures of other nations, that is, in an extrinsic Secular Polysystem. Despite antisemitism and alienation caused by his strange accent and others' stereotypes, he could turn to that culture, where the wealth of literary experience and the height of educational opportunities seemed incomparably higher. Even those individuals who stayed in the intrinsic field participated, to varying degrees, in the institutions of both the new Jewish Polysystem and those of other nations. For example, such pure Hebraists as the poet Shaul Tshernikhovski and the literary critic Yosef Klauzner, both of whom were Zionists, wrote almost exclusively Hebrew, created Hebrew literature, contributed to Hebrew journals, and refrained from writing in Yiddish or other languages, as most of their contemporaries did—even they also were steeped in

Russian literature, read world literature in Russian and German, and both wrote doctoral dissertations in German at the University of Heidelberg. In the personal junctions of their intellectual worlds, the two cultures coexisted; indeed, the extrinsic culture influenced their creative work: Klauzner transferred the methods of German literary science of the late nineteenth century (notably, Wilhelm Scherer's theory of literary history) to the study of Hebrew literature;[38] and Tschernikhovski emulated European poetic genres and translated world literature from Russian, German, and Greek into Hebrew (see above, chapter 6).

The Jewish Secular Polysystem that arose in Eastern Europe had the character of an almost-State (minus a government and physical power). Indeed, in the crowded Jewish communities or city quarters, the population lived within such a Jewish quasi-State (with a Gentile mayor and police force); but when the Jewish population moved from the *shtetl* to the big city and scattered overseas, there was nothing to hold the package tightly together in the territory of other languages and nations. When Tshernikhovski wrote Hebrew poetry in Heidelberg or in Swinemünde, he may have had German lovers and patients for his medical practice but hardly any Hebrew cultural environment. His collected works were lavishly published in Leipzig and Charlottenburg, as late as 1935, and he himself was a Hebrew poet and could not help but continue writing Hebrew poetry, but there was no hope for a next Hebrew generation in Swinemünde. Jewish affiliation and "identity" were no longer automatic as they were for a member of a "normal" ethnic group (even a subjugated group like the Czechs or the Poles before independence) for whom dwelling in his own land and affiliation with a linguistic and religious entity are self-evident.

Under these conditions—without a State, a political framework, or an exclusive and continuous territorial base—decisive importance was accorded to *unifying forces* that would motivate the individual to take part more than casually in various institutions of the intrinsic polysystem. Ideologies provided a unifying model to explain various aspects of existence and suggest a horizon for a better future. Political parties, youth movements, and professional associations also filled a unifying role, providing an immediate social framework for ideological solidarity; they usually organized social life as well, including educational activities, sport, parties, summer camps, and so on. Youth movements fostered ideological debate and love for Jewish and world literature, as well as love for nature, discipline, human pride, and personal, intellectual, and physical development.

But for such an intrinsic polysystem to exist fully, one stream must flow through the entire network, a unifying language force. A political party can assemble people who all think alike, but a language can offer a neutral interparty arena of debate—and for secular Jews especially, ideas did not exist without argument

---

38. Scherer's dictum that a literary historian has to account for what a writer has "inherited, studied, and experienced" ("das Ererbte, Erlernte, Erlebte") determined the structure of Klauzner's tripartite biographies of writers in his multivolume *History of Modern Hebrew Literature*.

and debate. Language is ideologically neutral and also provides a convenient stage for shifting from the abstract to the concrete: from ideology to literature, cultural activity, education, and so on. The two Jewish languages that permeated all those activities provided a sense of national entity and identity. The development of Yiddish from a popular spoken language to the language of a modern society served such a purpose for its adherents; even extensive Zionist activity was carried on in Yiddish. Indeed, Yiddishist ideologues spoke of *Yiddishland*, where "the world language," Yiddish, served in lieu of a State. In 1908, the *Czernowitz Conference*, attended by prominent writers and activists, proclaimed Yiddish as a Jewish national language (though not *the* national language, as some radical Yiddishists demanded). The Conference granted cultural prestige to Yiddish literature and led to an intensification of the "war of languages" between Hebrew and Yiddish. The Hebrew response came in a Conference in Vienna in 1913, though its echo was weaker and was hushed by World War I. All this happened during the time of the Second Aliya, and the choice of a base language for the new society was of paramount importance.

During the brief time of the Modern Jewish Revolution, and particularly in the first third of the twentieth century, Yiddish produced a unique prose, excellent modern poetry, translations from world literature, grammar, linguistics, textbooks in natural science, terminology for plants and birds, schools and academies, journalism, and a language for politics and urban civilization. Its vocabulary grew beyond recognition in every direction, and significant quantities of "international words" were accepted into it or parallel ones were invented; orthography, vocabulary, and terminology were codified by academies. The language was now supple enough to support impressionistic prose, expressionistic poetry, and precise studies in economics and phonology. The revival of Hebrew mirrored this process, was parallel to and in competition with it, with one cardinal difference: the new idiolects of education, politics, journalism, botany, literary criticism, linguistics, and science in Yiddish had an existing common *base language of a society* in the form of a language spoken at home and in the street, and used in newspapers and other media of information and entertainment and flowing from the "lowest" to the most cultured layers of society. Perhaps it was still a modest language intellectually, but it was felt to be expressive ("juicy"), emotive, and idiomatic. Equally important, it was a flexible language, wide open to its component languages—German, Russian, and Hebrew—and, through the first two, to the general international vocabulary; one could easily tap any of those languages for the enlargement of the language resources of Yiddish.[39]

For Hebrew culture and Hebrew literature similarly to flourish, such a social base language was needed, which would serve as the ground for a full-fledged secular polysystem: organizations, ideologies, science, journalism, and everyday

---

39. See *Meaning of Yiddish* (Harshav 1990a).

life. Indeed, Eliezer Ben-Yehuda's first reason for moving to Eretz-Israel (he coura-geously undertook it even before the first wave of Zionist immigrants and before the pogroms in Russia) and reviving Hebrew as a spoken language was not for the sake of the language itself but rather to rescue what he saw as the expiring Hebrew literature (in the last days of the *Haskala*), to provide literature with the base of a nation speaking its own language in everyday circumstances. He also aspired to create a "mother tongue," a language in which a mother would talk to her infant from the day it was born—in clear competition with the concept of *Mame loshn*, the common nickname for Yiddish. But what was needed was much more than a mother tongue. For literature to flourish, Hebrew had to be revived in two interrelated modes: the basic spoken language of society and language as the dominant vehicle for a sophisticated and ramified written network of information. For literature must draw both on the intonations and turns of the spoken language and on its connotations and socially developed hierarchies of meanings, as well as on a rich and multifarious "world" against which to build its literary fictions.

Hebrew literature, as it was, could exist in Diaspora as long as it was embedded in a society with two base languages: Yiddish—for internal community and family matters, as well as for the basic network of information; and the language of the State—for institutions of government and all the lacking political, technical, and scientific knowledge. And even so, it could barely survive—because of the compe-tition of Yiddish and because of the weak defenses of Yiddish itself. It was only in Eretz-Israel that Hebrew could ever hope to become the sole base language of an entire society, a base on which several conflicting ideologies could coexist, along with the entire social and educational establishment, Hebrew literature and culture, kitsch and the marketplace, the ideologically motivated person and the indifferent one. The revival of the Hebrew language in Eretz-Israel was a historical challenge—indispensable for the emergence of a new Jewish Secular Polysystem.

TWENTY-ONE

The Pitfalls of Scholarship

In the last generation, there has been a great deal of research to clarify the precise course of the revival of the language: the activity and thought of Eliezer Ben-Yehuda, the education in the agricultural settlements, the role of the teachers, the problems of vocabulary, and so on. (A selection of these studies are listed in the References.) A great many quotations from various sources have been gathered, and we have a general picture of the situation. Yet it is not quite clear how a lame process of about twenty-five (or even forty) years suddenly had a stunning success. It is not clear, first, because there is in the various statements of the period a confusion between desires and wishful thinking of the contemporaries and their actual implementation. Second, our information is extremely vague about the facts of spoken Hebrew in this brief and decisive period: contemporaries did not see fit to state the facts precisely, and it is hard to know exactly what they meant when they said "they spoke Hebrew." For example, according to some vague accounts, Hebrew was "spoken" in Jerusalem and Jaffa back in the middle of the nineteenth century, particularly in the marketplace, in conversations between Ashkenazim and Sephardim. How many words did they say? Did they mix them up with Arabic and Yiddish? How was it different from using a French or Arabic name of an item?

Or, how are we to understand such an informed witness account as: "Ten families in all Eretz-Israel spoke Hebrew in 1904"? Is "ten" a precise or a vague number? How did they speak? How much did they speak? Did they speak all the time? Only with one another? Only Hebrew? Or was it just that they could and occasionally did speak it? In what social cells was Hebrew spoken? Only in formal gatherings or also during arguments? People did not document such issues except accidentally or tendentiously: either the recording was not important to them or they did not dare say they did not speak Hebrew when this was the ruling ideology; and perhaps it seemed to them that they were speaking Hebrew since, after all, they were supposed to speak Hebrew, and they spoke it better than they had in the past and felt the elation of the achievement. Furthermore, many of the accounts are reconstructions made dozens of years later, when everyone wanted to show that he was among the first, and still remembered the effort and the achievement of the breakthrough; and also, perhaps, the later reality and ideology overshadowed the actual past in his own memory.[40] Usually, those who labored hard for the advancement of the language saw every small step as a miracle, while outsiders observed the ridiculous limits of the achievement. Hence many witnesses from the First Aliya and its teachers certainly exaggerate in their claims, while the first immigrants of the Second Aliya recognized almost no spoken Hebrew, no professional teacher, and no school worthy of that name.

An interesting example of the problematic reliability of such evidence can be deduced from a different source: Sigmund Freud tells of his father that he "spoke the holy language as well as German or better" (Gay 1988:600). Can it be that Jacob Freud actually *spoke* Hebrew in the nineteenth century, when no one spoke Hebrew? And even spoke it well? What Sigmund Freud meant, perhaps, is that his father could *use* the language, that is, that he could *read and write* Hebrew better than German; or perhaps he meant Yiddish, which was not nice to mention. And this is the testimony of a scientist who was normally precise in his language!

Another example: the history books keep repeating that "the First Hebrew School" was established in Rishon Le-Tsiyon in 1886 (*Rishon Le-Tsiyon* means "The First [settlement] in Zion"). The Rishon Le-Tsiyon school was, indeed, established in 1886, but "Hebrew" it became much later. The adjective "Hebrew" here is a back-projection from a later period and is extremely dubious, unless it means they tried to teach "Hebrew in Hebrew" (the Berlitz method brought from Istanbul to Jerusalem by Nisim Bechar [1848–1931], a progressive Hebrew teacher with experience in French schools of the *Alliance Israèlite* [see Haramati 1978]), that is, Hebrew as a foreign language and, in fact, *Hebrew as a third language* (after Yiddish and French). Many witness accounts make us doubt the contention that it was a Hebrew school from the beginning. For example, in 1888, Ben-Yehuda's newspaper *Ha-Tsvi* in Jerusalem reported enthusiastically on the achievement of the first "Hebrew" school in Rishon Le-Tsiyon: "How lovely is the sight, on Saturday the children gather and play children's games like 'Odds and Evens' and such. And play and quarrel and fool around—and all in the Hebrew language." But right after that, the level of their Hebrew knowledge becomes clear: "During

---

40. A personal recollection: when I began teaching at the Hebrew University, in the mid-fifties, Lea Goldberg (1911–1970), Hebrew poet and Professor of Literature, denied that her friend Abraham Shlonski, poet of the pioneers, ever knew or wrote in Ashkenazi Hebrew (which was, of course, taboo and smacked of Diaspora mentality). When I insisted, she asked Shlonski, who did not like the idea at all. But the undeniable fact is that his first books of poetry, up to 1928, are composed in precise meters in the Ashkenazi dialect, for this was the norm of Hebrew poetry, even though he himself studied in Gimnasya Hertseliya in Tel-Aviv and was a member of a kibbutz where Hebrew was spoken in the Sephardi dialect! Even for Shlonski, the virtuoso metrician, it was convenient to forget it and claim those were avant-garde poems in "free verse."

the outing, the teachers explain to their pupils in the Hebrew language the names of everything their eyes behold: *mountain, valley, river, plain*, and so on" (Haramati 1979:33; my emphasis—B.H.). (This is what country children don't know! And where did they find a river in Rishon? That must have been Ben Yehuda's own imagination: he knew the Jordan River, presumably flowing in his own city Jerusalem, from Mapu's novel, *Love in Zion*, modeled on the Lithuanian Kovna.)

Six years later, in the "Minutes of the Second Assembly" of Hebrew teachers in Eretz-Israel (with all of eight participants), we read the proposal of the teacher Y. Belkind:

> It is also imperative to teach the child all the Hebrew names of all the objects and things he sees around him in school and in his parent's home. For example: *table, bottle, father, son, pen, hand, foot* [sic!], and so on. *And also short oral conversations: Come here, I want to drink*, and similar phrases. (Karmi 1986:70; my emphasis—B.H.)

Fifteen years after the "First Hebrew School" was established, the pioneer Hebrew teacher Yitzhak Epstein (1862–1943) wrote in his textbook *Hebrew in Hebrew* (published not in Palestine but in Warsaw, 1901) that the child should first be taught a small vocabulary of 200–300 words (Fellman 1973:98). No scholar of the revival of Hebrew and Hebrew education ever asked how many French words the same child knew. Yehudit Harari, who was a student in the neighboring Rehovot Hebrew school in 1896, remembers: "We first began learning Hebrew in Hebrew in the Ashkenazi accent; at first, our teachers too had difficulties speaking Hebrew and very often used foreign words. We too spoke Hebrew mixed with Yiddish." (Haramati 1979:24).

Aside from noting such pitfalls, we shall not go into details or examine the specific advances and retreats of the language revival, the propaganda for it, or the problems of the existing research on this topic (which is still influenced by apologetics or not sufficiently analytical in examining its sources). Rather, on the basis of existing research, we shall try to reconstruct the process and understand the determining factors and the essential structure of the language revolution.

TWENTY-TWO

The Beginnings of the Language Revival

The First Aliya (1881–1904) built settlements of private farmers (*moshavot*), spoke Yiddish, and taught their children French so they could be sent to France. In their new settlements, a new kind of secular-type "schools" (rather than the traditional religious *heder*) emerged where, at first, they taught in French (which the children hardly knew) and Yiddish (which they spoke at home and in the community). Even David Yudelevitsh, an idealist teacher devoted to the revival of Hebrew, taught arithmetic in Yiddish—and no one noticed that these were the first Yiddish schools in the world! (Of course, their Yiddish was rather primitive and they had no Yiddish textbooks.)

Most of the farmers in the agricultural settlements supported Herzl's Uganda Plan, to erect a Jewish State in Africa; that is, for them, the Zionist dream of Eretz-Israel was bankrupt. Had Yiddish remained the base language of the *Yishuv*, it would have been the poorest part of the Yiddish-speaking world and the ICA[41]-supported settlements in Eretz-Israel would have been abandoned by the second generation, as were the ICA Jewish settlements in Argentina. The revival of Hebrew as a base language of society was imperative for their staying in this country. But how can that be done even when there is a linguistic consciousness? How do you force people suddenly to speak to their children in a language they don't even know themselves?

The effort to revive the Hebrew language was a central ideological slogan of the period, but it was always part of a larger ideological package, which could justify a mere linguistic goal. Such ideologies required intense but difficult realization in the life of the individual, a realization of a whole cluster of objectives, which involved the entire personality and was effected under extraordinary pressures. The specific cluster itself changed from one trend to another.

---

41. Jewish Colonization Association, founded by Baron Maurice de Hirsch.

Ben-Yehuda, who left Europe in the last days of the *Haskala*, integrated the aspiration for the revival of Hebrew with the major objectives of the *Haskala*: learning, beauty, self-realization (see above, chapter 12). In his account of the revival of the language, "The Dream Come True," Ben-Yehuda tells of sailing with his child bride Dvora on the Danube, on their way to the Holy Land. When the boat passed between two cliffs (water and cliffs, sight and terror = sublime beauty!), he relates: "I was almost frightened by the splendor of the sight and I could not refrain from calling out in Hebrew: 'How beautiful is this place!' The girl replied: 'Indeed, this place is beautiful!' " The girl has rearranged the order of two simple words in a short syntactic frame, but forty years later Ben-Yehuda declares solemnly: "Those were the first words spoken by a woman in our time in a profane conversation in the Hebrew language, as a living, spoken language" (Ben-Yehuda 1986:83–84). To him, the beauty of nature, of his bride, and of the Hebrew language revival, all came together. Describing a later stage, in his praise of the "Oriental pronunciation," which was chosen in Eretz-Israel as the accent for living Hebrew, Ben-Yehuda states: "All those who heard it spoken by the new generation were stunned by its beauty." For him, Hebrew—and in an Oriental accent to boot—embodied beauty, as opposed to the Diaspora ugliness of the "crooked Jewish brain." He harnessed the ideal of *learning* to the goal of reviving the language by scanning Hebrew texts from all ages and collecting about five hundred thousand quotations for his great dictionary. And he embodied the ideal of *self-realization* by immigrating to Eretz-Israel, and by his own life and the life of his family, which were devoted to the revival of the language: when his first wife died, he invited her sister from Russia to marry him and join him in the idealistic effort of raising the first Hebrew family; and gave her the Hebrew name Ḥemda ("bliss").

The cluster of principles promoted by the next generation was more radical and involved a demand for the rejuvenation of the whole human being. Thus, Menakhem Usishkin, sent in 1903 by the Central Committee of the *Lovers of Zion* in Odessa to organize the Teachers' Association in Eretz-Israel, wrote to the teachers:

> There are two main demands which the settlement of the land makes on those to whom the education of the young generation in Israel is entrusted: 1. To educate and *raise a generation full of strength* [. . .] *healthy in body and spirit*, who will know and *love its nation, its land and its language* [. . .] 2. To create in Israel one Hebrew [. . .] nation from all the different groups that are now in the country. (Fellman 1973:101; my emphasis—B.H.)

Ben-Yehuda placed such emphasis on the creation of words that were lacking in the language—a "word factory," as it was mockingly called by the Hebrew writers—that it is not clear whether he himself could speak Hebrew fluently. In the course of the years, he did invent many words, including terms for such common concepts as: *towel, handkerchief, doll, ice cream, bicycle, soldier, brush,* immigration, sympathy, sausage, butterfly, police, restaurant, art, airplane, dictionary, telegram, office, exercise, train, movie, and many more words no Hebrew speaker today suspects are new coinages (see Sivan 1986:24–27; and the classified list in Fellman 1973:67–69). The Hebrew Language Committee, the Israel Defense Forces, politicians, writers and translators—Tshernikhovski and Shlonski being the most prominent—also coined many new words. Some of these words were accepted in general usage and some remained within the context of a single text—and it does not really matter: for the invention itself created the challenge and the vacuum, which could later be filled by another coinage. What is important is not the "existence" of a Hebrew word in the dictionary in some case or other but, first of all, the existence of a Hebrew social base and an idiolect in a given area of life or profession, which can invite such words, absorb them, and integrate them into a usable professional and systematic network; and second, the development of productive grammatical patterns enabling the invention of new words and their orderly integration into both written and oral texts. When Tshernikhovski invented lists of words and included them in his poems (adding footnotes with translations in four languages: Russian, German, English, and the indispensable scientific term in Latin), that was, at the same time, part of the opening of Hebrew poetry toward the topics of nature, botany, physical anatomy, poetry and poetics, that is, part of the whole "package of revival" and the exit from the spiritual "ghetto." Beyond that, it was simply coincidence that "tut sade" that appears in his poetry was accepted as the Hebrew word for "strawberries" and "tut sne" was not accepted for "raspberries" (in Israeli Hebrew: petel).

Yet, of course, the lists of words, the attempts at codification of a standard language, the struggles between the purists and the innovators, and the social consciousness that rejected or accepted innovations—all that played a role in the revival, filled and widened the new language framework; without them, there would not have been such an amazing expansion of the Israeli language and of Israeli culture, universities, technology, and so on.

Ben-Yehuda's social achievement is manifest in the fact that he was a symbol for inexhaustible propaganda for the revival of the Hebrew language. He was not the first, perhaps, or the last, but for a while he was the standard-bearer. Yet, because he was also one of the leading spokesmen for the Uganda Plan (a "traitor" in the eyes of the Second Aliya) and supported "bourgeois" politics, the workers of the Second Aliya were indifferent or hostile to him. One of the saints of the Second Aliya, A. D. Gordon, called him "Mister Ben-Yehuda," and that was offense enough (in an article titled "A Worker's Response to Mister Ben-Yehuda's Appeal to the Workers"). Moreover, Ben-Yehuda was still a man raised in the Haskala, but it was only after he had immigrated to Eretz-Israel that an elitist Hebrew literature arose in Russia, and many of its writers were contemptuous of him, his antiquated Hebrew, and his "word factory." At any rate, although Ben-Yehuda accepted the Sephardi accent, his success in Jerusalem was almost nil. The Hebrew in his house was apparently quite wretched. When Eliezer wanted his wife to pour him a cup of coffee with sugar, he lacked the words for "cup," "saucer," "pour," and "spoon," so he said: *"Take that and do that and bring me that and I'll drink"* (Fellman 1973: 38). According to Yosef Klauzner, who visited him in 1912, Ben-Yehuda communicated with his wife in gestures and signs and most of the time she did not understand the simplest words in Hebrew (most of the time he was steeped in his dictionary anyway).

The First Hebrew Child, Ben-Tsiyon ("the Son of Zion"), was isolated from everyone but his parents, so he would not be contaminated by a foreign language and, for that purpose, Dvora was forbidden to hire a maid and had to do all the household chores by herself. No wonder the child did not speak at all until the age of 4 (Did he ever hear a real conversation?). Everyone in Jerusalem thought he would be retarded or a deaf-mute, until a friend and Hebrew writer, Yehiel Mikhel Pines (1843–1913) (who himself "betrayed" the pact to speak Hebrew he had earlier made with Ben-Yehuda, and educated his own children in Yiddish) suggested to Dvora that she speak to the child in another language. In her husband's absence, she sang Russian songs to the boy, and when Ben-Yehuda found out, there was a quarrel and the First Hebrew Child, in great excitement, interfered by uttering the first Hebrew sentence ever pronounced by a native speaker. For his son's seventh birthday, the father worked secretly at night translating *The Count of Monte Cristo* into Hebrew, but the son said: Thank you, Papa, I have already read it in French. Ben-Tsiyon Ben-Yehuda became the writer Itamar Ben-Avi (1885–1943); he changed his father's proudly invented Hebrew last name to "Ben-Avi," which means both "son of my father" and "son of A.B.Y. [acronym for Eliezer Ben-Yehuda]." He also published in 1934 a Hebrew newspaper in Jerusalem in the Latin alphabet. Eliezer Ben-Yehuda preceded B. F. Skinner by over half a century.

Ben-Yehuda's influence on others was hardly sweeping either. Four families that spoke Hebrew under his influence were the subject of an article entitled "The First Four," which Ben-Yehuda wrote in 1918, almost forty years after the official "beginning" of the revival of the language. They included two Hebrew teachers (Yehuda Grazovski-Gur, later the author of the first modern Hebrew dictionary, and David Yudelevitsh, the teacher of the First Hebrew School in Rishon Le-Tsiyon): both married their students who had studied by the method of "Hebrew in Hebrew"; a third married a Sephardi woman and Hebrew was their only common language; and a fourth married a Russian woman who quarreled with him constantly because she did not know Hebrew and did not want to learn it (Fellman 1973:39). Certainly none of them refused, as did Ben-Yehuda, to talk with other people, that is, inevitably, in other languages.

The myth of Hebrew speech between Ashkenazim and Sephardim in the nineteenth century or in other times is not relevant: throughout history, Jews from distant countries with a genuine knowledge of written Hebrew could exchange a few words or sentences and understand one another. But this did not transform the Hebrew language into the base language of a society.

According to many eyewitness accounts, most settlers of the First Aliya did not speak Hebrew fluently or regularly. In 1893, after a visit in Palestine, Aḥad Ha-Am, the ideologue of Spiritual Zionism, wrote in his essay "The Truth from Eretz-Israel":

> He who hears how the teachers and the students stammer, for lack of words and expressions, will immediately realize that such "speech" cannot evoke in the speaker's or the listener's heart any respect or love for the limited language, and the child's young mind (who learns also French) feels even stronger the artificial chains imposed on him by the Hebrew speech. (Aḥad Ha-Am 1950:33)

And Ze'ev Smilanski (1873–1944), who came to the country in 1891, wrote in the same year:

> Even the few fanatics, who devoted themselves with excitement to the revival of Hebrew speech in the new *Yishuv*, were mostly stammering and speaking with utmost effort. [. . .] Because of the lack of experience in speaking Hebrew, their talk was not natural and fluent, and often, in the middle of a sentence, with lips still moving, one had to stop to think and find the proper word, or it was altogether lost in the speaker's memory. The speech was mostly artificial and to a bystander it often appeared as an attempt to declaim while waving with both arms and beckoning with their eyes. (Haramati 1979:101)

In his book, *First Year*, Shlomo Tsemakh—one of the first to arrive with the Second Aliya (and later, a Hebrew writer and critic)—describes Rishon Le-Tsiyon in 1904, where the women sew dresses on Ḥemda Ben-Yehuda's patterns (published in Ben-Yehuda's Hebrew newspaper) and everyone speaks Russian, French, and Yiddish, except for the teacher Yudelevitsh, who makes solemn speeches in Sephardi Hebrew. Young Tsemakh, who wants to speak in the name of the "Zionists of Zion" minority (those who preferred Eretz-Israel to Uganda) at the general assembly of the "First Hebrew Settlement," sits up all night translating Aḥad Ha-Am's essay "Moses" into Yiddish:

> In Eretz-Israel, in a Jewish settlement, I sit and translate the words of Aḥad Ha-Am into a language I call "Jargon" [i.e., Yiddish] and I boil against it and fight it ["boil against it" is itself a Yiddishism—B.H.]. (Tsemakh 1965:130)

The learning standards of the Hebrew schools in the settlements were miserable. Hebrew teachers were paid less than the teachers of French, and in 1892 there were all of nineteen Hebrew teachers in the whole country. When we read accounts collected in recent studies, for example in Shlomo Haramati's book *The Beginning of Hebrew Education in Eretz-Israel* (1979) or in the protocols of the teachers' assembly (Karmi 1986), we see autodidacts and idealists who are said to have laid the foundations for the instruction of Hebrew in Hebrew, a system imported from French education. There is a lot of excitement about every utterance of spoken Hebrew. But education in the settlements was aimed at the children of peasants (on the Russian model of separating urban and rural schools) who were supposed to study up to the age of 13, at the most, before joining their parents in the field. The ability to say a few sentences in Hebrew did not go beyond what might be expected of the study of a second foreign language in a village school, and was certainly lagging behind French. As late as in the beginning of the twentieth century—twenty years after the "First Hebrew School" was established (as uncritically stated by some historians)—science and other disciplines were still conducted in French; and only after 1907, when Yosef Vitkin (one of the heralds of the Second Aliya) became Principal, the Hebrew character of the Rishon Le-Tsiyon school was implemented. At the same time, Zikhron-Ya'akov (settled by Romanian Jews) was called "Little Paris," and its first kindergarten, opened in 1892, was conducted in French (M. Eliav 1978:404–405).

The general intellectual level of the children was also low; in 1893, Aḥad Ha-Am recommended: "It wouldn't hurt a bit if, as long as the Hebrew language is not fit for it, science, even in Eretz-Israel, were taught in some European language" (Aḥad Ha-Am 1950:33). Even as late as 1913, when the American Yiddish poet Yehoash was impressed by girls of a settlement playing in Hebrew, he asked a girl of about 14 or 15 the names of the flowers in her own garden and she replied: "*Flowers don't have names*" (Yehoash 1917, 2:29; my emphasis—B.H.).

During this period, Hebrew was introduced by a few devoted teachers who often made up their own words and even their own pronunciation; in the Galilee a different Hebrew dialect (closer to the Syrian Arabic pronunciation) was implemented by just two teachers, and spread and survived for a whole generation: peasants in Yavniel called a fly *zbub* rather than *zvuv* (see Bar-Adon 1975, 1988). In 1903, the Teacher's Association was founded; it made efforts to standardize the language, accepted the "Sephardic" accent, but still decided on teaching sciences in a foreign language.

Let us not lump together all kinds of Hebrew knowledge. We must distinguish between a) the study of Hebrew as a foreign language; b) the ability to speak Hebrew on occasion with some measure of fluency; c) the use of Hebrew in daily life; and d) accepting Hebrew as the base language of individuals and of the society. Only the first two were implemented to some degree by a few individuals in the period of the First Aliya. Children in Palestine also studied French, as well as Arabic and Turkish, and it is not clear how Hebrew compared with those. In any case, even students who knew Hebrew well in school did not use it consistently outside of school. And from all the collected evidence it is clear that when Hebrew was used by groups of young people outside of school, it was done only occasionally. In 1904, Shlomo Tsemakh observed: "Many in Eretz-Israel know Hebrew, but very few, almost none, use it for everyday needs, and the question is how to turn those who know Hebrew into Hebrew speakers" (Tsemakh 1965: 122).

The Diaspora played a key role too. Since the 1890s, circles for the revival of Hebrew arose throughout the Jewish world. Intelligent teachers launched a movement of a new type of elementary school under the guise of reformed religious *heders*: the so-called *Heder metukan* or, in Ashkenazi Hebrew, in which it was implemented, *Kheyder mesukn* (which is a pun on "dangerous *ḥeder*"). These schools dared to teach Hebrew grammar as well as some secular subjects, such as mathematics and Russian, and provided good training in Hebrew, though not the spoken language. In Warsaw, Hebrew textbooks written in Eretz-Israel were printed. But suddenly, the situation has changed. The Kishinev Pogrom of 1903 and the Jewish Self-Defense during the pogrom in Homel, crushed by the tsarist police, led to the revival of national consciousness in Diaspora. The failure of the Russian Revolution of 1905 also brought young people and intellectuals into the Hebrew movement (though the great majority went elsewhere). The Conference of "The Socialist Organization Poaley-Tsiyon (Labor Zionists) in America" in December 1905 declared solemnly: "We recognize *Hebrew* as the national language of the Jewish people"[42]—and that happened three years before such a decision was adopted by the same party in Eretz-Israel![43] There was even an attempt to set up a Hebrew theater in New York.[44] After World War I, Zionist youth movements arose in Diaspora along with a network of secular Hebrew schools, gymnasia, and teachers' colleges. All those provided Eretz-Israel with Hebrew speakers and teachers. It is wrong to isolate, as Israeli scholars often do, the history of the language in Eretz-Israel from what was going on in Diaspora when the exponential growth of the *Yishuv* came from there.

The arena of the revival, however, was Eretz-Israel, and the language revolution took place between 1906 and 1913. The Second Aliya (1904–1914) also started out in Yiddish (Ben-Tsvi and Ben-Gurion edited a party newspaper in Yiddish) but quickly, and with a supreme effort, shifted to Hebrew. The *Yishuv* constituted a small minority in the Jewish world, was dependent on that world, and was inextricably tied to it by ideological and family ties. To adapt to physical labor in a forsaken province of the backward and despotic Ottoman Empire, in that desolate and hot land, amid the hostile Arabs, was difficult and required a sharp break with Diaspora: the separation of languages served that purpose. Moreover, the justification for the settlement of the young people from Europe in this place depended on a secular transformation of a historic mythology connecting Zionism with this land, and that was available only in the Hebrew language. Jews had no

---

42. *Der yidisher kemfer*, May 4, 1906.

43. A great deal of material on worldwide Zionist activities at that time can be found in the *Poaley-Tsion* (Labor Zionist) weekly journal published in New York in Yiddish from 1905 to this day, *Der yidisher kemfer* (with the English title *The Jew Militant*). In America, as almost nowhere else, there was a free press that could report events from all over the Jewish world, a source that should be tapped by the historians of Eretz-Israel.

44. See the call for actors written in Hebrew, in *Der yidisher kemfer*, May 24, 1907.

recent history in Palestine and *Hebrew was their first "archaeology"* binding the immigrants to the Bible and to the land of the Bible. Naturally, the ingathering of the exiles from all over the world, emanating from the Zionist ideology, could succeed only in Hebrew.

In 1906, the first ostensibly secondary school ("Gimnasya") was founded in Jaffa with seventeen children. It had only four grades of elementary school and was opposed by many parents for its coeducation and secular character. After several years this school moved to Tel Aviv, was renamed "Gimnasya Hertseliya" and grew to be a high school, but was still opposed even by Aḥad Ha-Am for introducing Bible criticism; by 1913 it had five hundred students. In 1906, the art school *Betsalel* and in 1908 the *Hebrew Gimnasya* were opened in Jerusalem. Those were city high schools with higher academic standards than the elementary village schools of the settlements; they appealed to the new immigrants in the cities who had higher academic ambitions for their children, and even drew students from abroad.

But the schools in the agricultural settlements had also begun gradually to shift instruction in all subjects to Hebrew. This process was first encouraged when Baron Rothschild left the agricultural settlements in 1899 and French waned but no other language could substitute for it. (What language could that be? Turkish, the language of the hostile authorities, when there was no Turkish population around? Yiddish, when there were not yet Yiddish schools in Diaspora?) It is an accepted claim that, by 1908, all the agricultural settlements had shifted to Hebrew instruction, at least nominally (most studies pronounce it a fact, but there is no concrete evidence that this objective was implemented in all disciplines). Yet in the cities, schools in French, German, and English still prevailed.[45] The "Ezra" network of schools (which arose with financial aid from the Berlin *Hilfsverein der Deutschen Juden*) had three thousand students in 1912 (for Yiddish speakers, German is relatively easy to learn). But the great language rebellion of teachers and students in 1913 forced "Ezra" to shift to instruction in Hebrew, even in the Haifa technological institute, the *Technion*.[46] Thus, on the eve of World War I, Hebrew became dominant in the schools of the "New *Yishuv*" (the Zionist immigration) though not in the orthodox "Old *Yishuv*"; and other language schools still operated in the mixed cities.

We must warn against over-optimistic estimates. For example, as the Jerusalem statistician Roberto Bacchi showed, in the census of 1916, about 40% of the Jews declared Hebrew as their main language (see Bacchi 1956a, 1956b). But, as we know, declarations are one thing and reality is something else. There was a *consciousness* of the need to speak Hebrew and pride in it as the great achievement

---

45. A contemporary survey of Jewish schools in Palestine can be found in Bentwich 1912.

46. There is a considerable literature on this issue, which raised spirits around the Jewish world. An interesting contemporary pamphlet in English by Israel Cohen, titled *The German Attack on the Hebrew Schools in Palestine*, was published in London in 1918 (sic!).

of the Zionist entity, hence the respondents identified with Hebrew speech, especially for external, political purposes, and declared as they did. (What language could they declare: Arabic, which would indicate an even larger proportion of Arabs? Russian, the language of the enemy in World War II? The despised Yiddish, connoting Diaspora? The French they hardly knew? Nevertheless, 60% did declare such languages.)

Conceivably, a few of those who knew Hebrew were products of the First Aliya, particularly teachers, writers, and former high-school students; they were eventually integrated into the revival of the language. Now that a spoken language had emerged, they could activate their basic knowledge. But there was no direct continuity: just as Hebrew in the First Aliya was not the continuation of the revival of Hebrew literature in the Diaspora but a separate branch, a parallel line of a new development, so the revival of Hebrew in the Second Aliya was a new beginning, achieved in opposition to the "bankrupt" First Aliya; when it succeeded, it absorbed the remnants of the previous wave within its framework. However, at the end of the First Aliya, two generally accepted principles did remain: it was now *possible* to speak Hebrew and it was clear that *the revival of the language was a condition for the revival of the nation.* Two beginnings of the First Aliya—the Hebrew Language Committee and Hebrew education—materialized with the advent of the Second Aliya, about twenty-five or thirty years after Ben-Yehuda had moved to Eretz-Israel.

TWENTY-THREE

Three Factors in the Revival of the Language

Instead of a detailed examination of the problematic evidence and investigation of every person who spoke or taught Hebrew (the accounts of which are not clear anyway), we will try to analyze the basic phenomenon, the deep structure of the language revolution. Clearly, there was a strongly felt ideology demanding the revival of the language; but that was not enough. The revolution could occur because of *the unique intersection of three complex historical factors in the lives of many individuals*:

1. *The life of Hebrew in Diaspora*: In the Jewish religious polysystem, Hebrew was not an altogether "dead" language but a language "living" in many aspects.
2. *The revival of Hebrew in writing*: In the Jewish secular polysystem, which emerged in the Diaspora in the nineteenth and twentieth centuries, many genres were conquered for the new and free Hebrew writing: in fiction, poetry, essays, journalism, popular science, and translations.
3. The establishment of *new social cells in a "social desert"* (in Eretz-Israel) by groups of young people and children who cut themselves off from the chain of generations and did not assimilate to an existing language base.

Abbreviated, those were: the *religious*, the *secular*, and the *realized Zionist* polysystems.

The revival of the language was carried out by people who personally, in their own biography, linked these three areas. Their unique integration—in one generation and in the lives of those very people—was indispensable for the miracle of the revival of the language. Each contributed its own dimension:

1. The religious world provided a treasury of Hebrew texts, and also *vivid meanings* of many Hebrew phrases and words, as well as habits of analyzing the meanings of words and phrases.

113

2. The secular world of the new Hebrew literature enabled the creation of *new sentences* and *new texts* in Hebrew (i.e., texts that do not constitute commentaries on canonical texts but which discuss new topics) as well as the *absorption of the European world* in the language, including the coinage of many new words, terms, and expressions—even though all of it was only in writing.

3. The Zionist realization supplied *new social cells* of devoted idealists, for whom personal realization was the highest value; and Eretz-Israel/Palestine provided the social desert, abandoned by its people two thousand years ago, where it was possible—and imperative—to build a new society speaking a new language.

The Hebrew writers Brener, Bialik, Berditshevski, A. D. Gordon, Agnon, Shlomo Tsemakh, and many others studied the Talmud in their youth in yeshivas or at home and then read *Haskala* literature in Hebrew on "modern," fictional or "scientific" topics. It was, indeed, not easy to start speaking a new language that is not spoken in society and has no established models to imitate; it was like building a boat under your feet while floating in it. Nevertheless, one could make an effort to resort to the rich vocabulary passively available in the mind of the individual, and put it into practice. For Yosef-Hayim Brener and A. D. Gordon (who were roughly the prototypes of the characters of *Oved Etsot* ["Disoriented"] and *Arye Lapidot* in Brener's story "From Here and From There," 1910), it was natural to speak in the "Holy Tongue" (probably in the Ashkenazi accent) even if no one around them did, and although they never learned to speak through the Berlitz method of "Hebrew in Hebrew." The American Yiddish poet Yehoash, who translated the Bible into Yiddish, immigrated to Eretz-Israel in 1913, after he had lived in Denver, Colorado, and New York for almost thirty years; while still on the ship, he spoke Hebrew. But these were not the children of peasants in the agricultural settlements of the First Aliya who learned their first Hebrew words from a teacher.

Each of those three factors has a complex cluster of features in its own right and requires separate examination.

TWENTY-FOUR

The Life of "Dead" Hebrew

In the Renaissance Period of Hebrew literature, the claim was made that Hebrew was a "dead" language and its books "dead books" (Fayerberg). That was, of course, a "dead" but potent metaphor. The revival of the language was seen primarily as the task of turning Hebrew into a spoken language. We can easily sense here the competition of Yiddish, which was the native language of all advocates of spoken Hebrew, as well as the general atmosphere of populism which assumed that the everyday speech of simple people is an indispensable base for any high culture.

To this day, arguments are made as to whether Hebrew was "dead" or "alive" and how much speech may constitute its revival. The question, however, cannot be intelligently discussed as an either-or issue. What we call "language" is a rather complex cluster of social, mental, and linguistic aspects, and each may be active or passive to different degrees at a given time; and "active" may also mean different things: simply "in use" or expanding and innovating. A language called "English" is spoken in the United States, but is Shakespeare's English "alive"? And to what extent is scientific language "alive"? Isn't it the case that in any language there are layers of the language that are not "alive" in the sense of being used in daily speech, or even in habitual writing? And isn't speech influenced by various genres of writing, as much as the reverse? The fuzzy biological metaphor must be dropped—and is used here only as a convenient label.

Those who founded the new *Yishuv* and set the basic character of the Israeli language came from Eastern Europe where the traditional Jewish society lived in a multilingual situation: the texts that were studied were in the "Holy Tongue" (a generic name for various historical layers of Hebrew and Aramaic in the library of texts);[47] social life, speech, and eduation were in Yiddish; and with non-

---

47. Sometimes, the whole cluster of the "Holy Tongue," with its several historical layers, or "languages," of Hebrew and Aramaic, was called "*Hebrew*." Characteristically, in Yiddish the word "*Hebrew*" means "learning," "knowledge."

Jews and government institutions, European languages were used. The relations between Hebrew and Yiddish, however, were not limited to the difference between a written language and a spoken language—there were many crossover phenomena. Nor was the position of Hebrew similar to the position of Latin vis-à-vis French or English in the Middle Ages, for Hebrew was a language embedded in the daily, multilingual life of the Jews, and was "alive" in many ways:

A. *Jewish existence was based on a library of texts*, including interpretations of classical texts, written predominantly in the Holy Tongue. These books were studied assiduously and were applied to the life of the community and of the individual both in an ideological mode and in daily practice. Every Jewish boy had to study texts in the Holy Tongue for several years, from morning to night, every single day of the week. Hebrew and Aramaic texts were also used for daily prayers, blessings, and holiday readings. Even if many poor people did not go on to advanced studies, every man knew—or was supposed to know—how to read, and Jews habitually did some reading every day.

   Many women too studied Hebrew, usually with private tutors, for there were no religious schools for women until the modern age; and most women learned Yiddish, which is written in the Hebrew alphabet. The text of *Tsene verene*, the popular retelling of the Bible for women (men were supposed to read the original), that saw over three hundred editions since the sixteenth century, and other religious books for women contained many Hebrew words embedded in Yiddish sentences. Yiddish texts were printed in a different typeface (called *vaybertaytsh*, "women's German"), to separate them from the holy, "square letters" of the holy texts (much as women were separated in the synagogue); but the many Hebrew words embedded in the Yiddish text were placed in parentheses (in the middle of the sentence) and flashed out typographically, by the use of the Hebrew typeface. Thus Hebrew was known well in every Jewish community and, at least to some extent, in every family.

B. Education emphasized the *understanding of texts* in two ways:

   i. Children studied Torah in *Ḥeder*, from the age of three or four, in the system of word-for-word translation, read aloud and memorized: a Hebrew word followed by a Yiddish word, another Hebrew word followed by another Yiddish word, and so on.

   ii. In the study of the Talmud (*Gemara*), particularly in the yeshivas, there was a discussion of the texts, consideration of reasons for and against an interpretation or a law. The discussion was in Yiddish, while the fragments of the original arguments were quoted in the original Hebrew and Aramaic.

C. *Interpretation* of texts occupied a central place in the highest, that is, Rabbinic, literature and education, as well as in popular preaching and in social life; that is, there was in society an awareness of the meanings of words and of the parallels between various texts in the Hebrew Library.

D. Unlike the monologue form that molded European thought, the Jewish worldview was shaped by *dialogue*, or, more correctly, *disputation* (for it was no casual dialogue on mundane matters but the raising of theoretical arguments for or against some point or interpretation). The teachings were conveyed in the form of a dialogue between sages and commentators or between positions expressed by authors of various generations. While the living dialogue in religious education was carried on in Yiddish, fragments of the dialogues in the sources were quoted in the original. True, those were mere quotations of ready-made fragments and not free combinations of words; but their gist and special intonation were heard. What was lacking was dialogue in Hebrew between people living in the present.

E. Hebrew functioned (although not exclusively) as *an active written language*; that is, many people could compose texts in writing: religious books, commentaries, Responsa, as well as community records, posters, business and private letters. Such texts used ready-made formulae and appeared as mosaics of "prefabricated" phrases with embedded quotations, and often had features of Yiddish grammar and a Yiddish subtext; but they were nevertheless original texts composed in Hebrew. In the domain of Ashkenaz, that is, in Central and Eastern Europe, Ashkenazi Rabbinic Hebrew developed—a sort of "mixed" language, intermingling collocations from various historical layers of Hebrew, with inserted Aramaic expressions, and grafting meanings from Yiddish onto it. Agnon developed one stylistic trend in this tradition. This language has not been studied much—for the revival of interest in Hebrew had a pro-Biblical and an anti-Ashkenazi bias, and Israeli scholars of Ashkenazi origin would rather study the Yemenite accent—but even a cursory glance reveals that written Hebrew was not altogether "dead."

F. The base language of society, Yiddish, was a fusion language of many components, especially German, Slavic, "Internationalisms," and the "Holy Tongue." Several dictionaries have listed about five thousand words and expressions from Hebrew and Aramaic (or "Chaldaic") which were used in Yiddish. *These Hebrew expressions were part of the spoken and living language.* The meanings of Hebrew words in Yiddish also changed as in any living language. To a large extent, these meanings evolved out of post-Biblical texts, especially prayers, the Passover *Hagada*, or the Talmud; in many cases, the Yiddish meaning of the word came from a ready-made phrase or an idiom, as they were present in consciousness, and not from the dictionary definition of an individual word or its morphological form. For example, "*mekhaye*" in Yiddish is a noun, meaning "pleasure" (though in Hebrew it is a verb meaning "he revives"), deriving from the collocation "*mekhaye nefashot*" (literally: "he revives human souls"). As Bialik said, Yiddish preserved Hebrew throughout history; indeed, no other Jewish dialect carried pieces of Hebrew texts to such an extent in the daily language. Yiddish also integrated various Hebrew grammatical forms in its grammar, covering all components of the language, and hence made them familiar to every child.[48] Naturally, the actual proportion of Hebrew elements in Yiddish discourse changed sharply from one genre to another and from one speaker to another; learned men used it a great deal, and on the Sabbath there were those who actually "spoke" Hebrew, that is, used only Hebrew quotations in an absent Yiddish syntactical frame, indicated by hm . . . hm. . . .

G. Way beyond the relatively stable Hebrew component in the Yiddish dictionary, Yiddish served as a frame language in which phrases, proverbs, and expressions could be *embedded* from all sorts of authentic (i.e., not integrated into Yiddish) Hebrew and Aramaic texts. Religious sermons (e.g., the present-day sermons of the Lubavitsher Rebbe in Brooklyn) may include a high percentage of Hebrew and Aramaic words and phrases—sometimes up to 80–90% of the text—but the framework of discourse and the syntax of the sentences remain Yiddish.

This embedding was not just learned discourse but common practice, as can be seen in the monologues of a simple person, Sholem Aleichem's Tevye the Milkman (even when he distorts the original phrases). Even the Yiddish mass newspapers that emerged at the end of the nineteenth century in the United States and were addressed to the urban proletariat, presumably simple, uneducated laborers, impressed by Socialist or Anarchist ideology, used the Holy Tongue a great deal in headlines and quotations. In such texts, Hebrew sentences and even whole fragments can be quoted, but new phrases in Hebrew cannot be formed.[49]

H. In all of this, the sounds of Hebrew were heard a great deal, as *fragments of an oral language*, even though no one could speak it as a separate language. And it was heard as pronounced in the accents of various Jewish ethnic groups and dialects. In the Ashkenazi community, general rules of Ashkenazi Hebrew obtained—the basic identifying mark is the stress on the penultimate instead of the ultimate syllable of a word; and the Yiddish dialect of every area was superimposed on these rules, realizing the written vowels in different ways. (For example, what is in Israeli Hebrew **baRUKH aTA**, "blessed be you," is pronounced in Lithuania **BOrukh Ato** and in Galicia **BUrikh Atu**.)

---

48. E.g., the plural of *doktor* ("doctor") is *doktoyrim*—with the Hebrew unmarked plural suffix; and many words had the marked feminine plural -*es*: *kale-s* ("brides"), *shmate-s* ("tatters"); see *Meaning of Yiddish* (Harshav 1990a).

49. See the analysis of the "language of scribes" (*leshon ha-sofrim*) in Weinreich 1958.

In spite of all this hovering of Hebrew over the living Jewish discourse, however, it lacked some major aspects of a usable language:

   i. It lacked an active vocabulary in many areas (you could not say *train, pencil, teapot, towel, culture,* etc.);

  ii. New sentences were not normally composed in it orally (although they were in writing);

 iii. No dialogue was normally conducted in the language;

 iv. Children were not raised in this language; it was no person's "mother tongue."

These were lacking because Hebrew was an *embedded language* within two frame languages, Yiddish and the language of the State.[50] Hebrew was not responsible for daily communication or official matters and could rely on the other languages for that. This situation began to change when an autonomous Hebrew literature and culture emerged, with its own journalism and education.

---

50. Thus, it was not simply a case of "diglossia" of two languages as equal partners with divided roles.

TWENTY-FIVE

The Revival of Written Hebrew

Before the revival of spoken Hebrew, a vigorous and multifaceted revival of written Hebrew began in Europe, embracing all areas of modern life. Without a State. Without organized science. Without an Academy, without schools. But with the ambition to make it possible to write in Hebrew about everything, and in competition with the so-called "spoken language," Yiddish—which rapidly became a full-fledged written language and also attempted to encompass all areas of culture in the same period. Take, for example, *The Mysteries of Paris* by Eugène Sue, translated into Hebrew by Kalman Shulman and published in Vilna in 1859 (I have the sixth edition, 1911); the book opens with a preface by the Hebrew poet and grammarian Adam[51] Ha-Cohen Lebenson (1794-1878), still written in the elevated style of the *Haskala* (note: "language" in Hebrew is feminine):

> Who among our people, knowing that the splendor of the language is the splendor of her people and in her honor they too will be honored, will not rejoice to see today that our Holy Tongue—which, since honor was exiled from Israel, suffered the decline of her honor also, and she was exiled from the face of the earth and imprisoned between two covers [of a book], in her few holy books and her few holy places—now God's spirit began to revive her in these generations, by the hand of her writers, few and scattered, that she might return to her past state and, little by little, begin walking on the face of the earth too, and she returned to speak again of all the works of the Lord and all His creations in heaven and on earth.

In short, Sue's Paris underworld is also part of "the works of the Lord," deserving a Hebrew description. And Lebenson continues:

> And her words are issued from the end of the world and come from the four winds of the sky, wherever all the sons of her people are scattered—and she speaks a

---

51. Adam—acronym for Abraham Dov-Ber Mikhaylishker.

parable for thousands, and her poem is for multitudes, *and she speaks about every wisdom [= discipline] and every science and every art*. Ultimately, there was no important matter and no precious object she now found in the hands of her younger sisters [other languages], who prevailed on the earth in honor and splendor at the time of her poverty and suffering, that she would not hurry, shaking the dust off her body, to emulate in these few days, so that this miracle would give hope to the hearts of her writers that *they will soon see her a language spoken by the sons of her people*, as in ancient times. (Shulman 1911:3; my emphasis—B.H.)

This is followed by "A Hymn" to the Hebrew language and its Lithuanian masters, composed in meter and rhyme by Adam Ha-Cohen's 19-year-old son, the Hebrew poet Mikhal (Mikha Yosef Lebenson, 1828–1852). It begins with the words:

Wake up, Oh awake, Hebrew Language,
 From the graves of Zion, from the caves of the wasteland,
 You widow of writers, abandoned by your sons!

Thus, the motif of reviving the language was not invented by Ben-Yehuda but was a lingering sentiment in Lithuanian *Haskala* circles (the head of Ben-Yehuda's yeshiva risked his position while clandestinely teaching him Hebrew grammar, considered a heresy, yet showing the deep love for the language).

Then, after several more poems and introductions, we finally get to the novel, opening in a Paris dive where murderers and robbers drink their wine; the concept of such a dive is explained by the translator in the text itself—for his dear readers had presumably never seen one.

During the Enlightenment, those were scattered but persistent efforts, and gradually, or in spurts, the trend was broadened. In terms of the revival of the language, we encounter several important achievements here:

 i. Opening Hebrew texts to *new thematic domains* of knowledge and imagination not directly related to the lives of its readers;
 ii. Mastery of *new genres* in literature, journalism, and thought;
 iii. Writing of *new texts* in Hebrew (i.e., texts that are not direct exegesis of or commentary on canonical texts);
 iv. Formulation of *new sentences* in Hebrew (i.e., a new, free "Hebrew speech" in writing);
 v. Gradual release of the *individual word* from the bonds of ready-made collocations and phrases in classical texts; this was enhanced by the rapid invention of many new, individual[52] words and terms;

---

52. That too was a problem, since the first impulse was to invent a new term in the tradition of florid circumlocutions. Thus, a "teapot" was first called in Hebrew: "Pot-to-cook-petals-from-China," until the twentieth-century *kumkum* was invented (*kumkum* is a Talmudic word, from the Greek *koukkoumion*). Many neologisms imitated European terms, thus the "telegraph" was called *dilug-rav*, which sounds similar and means: "long leap"; "protocol" became *pirtey-kol*, i.e., "the details of everything."

    vi. Subordinating Hebrew words and sentences in poetry to European *poetic meters*, thus upsetting the inherited order of the words in traditional texts;

    vii. Submitting the language to the constraints of *a text translated* from another language, its world, terminology, and word order;

    viii. Opening the Hebrew language to terms and words borrowed from the common European vocabulary;

    ix. And, subsuming all that, the intentional and vigorous *creation of a new and modern Hebrew language*, European in spirit and purpose, or in Adam Ha-Cohen Lebinson's words: a language that "speaks about every wisdom and every science and every art."

The entire complex was called "Hebrew literature" and was published in the same periodicals, but it actually included also journalism, news, essays, criticism, philosophy, popular science, and translations. Someone who wanted to express himself in Hebrew in writing—in poetry or prose, in fiction or memoirs—had the ground prepared for him. Toward the end of the nineteenth century, Hebrew newspapers emerged and in them the relation between literature and politics was inverted and literature became embedded in the general journalism. The great expansion of original imaginative literature in Hebrew—the so-called "Renaissance Period" of Hebrew literature (1882–1914)—occurred in Russia when the *Haskala* broke down, that is, *after* Ben-Yehuda had gone off to the remote Ottoman province of Palestine. Hence, even though he invented many words and classified old words by the thousands, his writings seemed antiquated and rhetorical, his newspapers old-fashioned, and his speech sounded like babbling to his visitors who had experienced the revival of Hebrew literature in Europe. The Renaissance Period of Hebrew literature began with the writings of Aḥad Ha-Am and Bialik (1889, 1892) and dominated Hebrew literature until about 1920; yet the cracks of Modernism had been appearing in it since about 1906, with the writings of Brener, Gnesin, and Avraham Ben-Yitzhak. The immigrants of the Second Aliya came to Eretz-Israel with the pride of the literary achievement, including its modernist cracks, in their hearts and on their pens.

    In their youth, most writers of the Renaissance Period received a traditional religious education in the canonical texts orally translated and explained in Yiddish. Even studying Hebrew grammar was considered a heresy and could lead to secular culture and atheism, as Ben-Yehuda tells in his autobiography. But they achieved freedom of expression in Hebrew by breaking out of the religious fold and joining Hebrew literature, that is, by the very act of writing in the European genres that were emulated by Hebrew literature and journalism. They drew on the Hebrew textual treasures of the past, pouring them into new molds, new sentences and clauses, based on Russian and Western models.[53] In poetry, the prestigious genre, the discipline of the accentual-syllabic meters forced them

---

53. See Itamar Even-Zohar's (1985) study on Russian models in the prose of A. N. Gnesin.

to break the habitual word-combinations and throw the old words into new, imaginative alliances.

During the revival of the language, its propagandists were particularly concerned with what was lacking in the vocabulary and with the necessary innovation of words; but an equally radical, though less conscious, revolution took place in the area of syntax, rarely observed by the practitioners themselves: some typical markers of Biblical syntax were abandoned and the construction of complex sentences with subordinate clauses, modeled on European languages, opened the Hebrew text to general, modern thought and culture. Henceforth, *in principle, it was possible to write in Hebrew whatever could be expressed in European literatures*—and if words were lacking, substitutes could be found, borrowed, or coined in Hebrew. If today some of these writings may look simple-minded and old-fashioned or, on the contrary, difficult and esoteric, this is because of the amazing dynamism that characterized the changes in the vocabulary and in the forms of expression of the Hebrew language in recent generations.

Let us now indicate some major characteristics of this Modern Hebrew, still only a *written* language in the Renaissance Period:

A. Fusion of Various Historical Layers

As late as 1929 in Tel-Aviv, Y. Klauzner (1956) argued that Hebrew is not one language but at least four different languages—Biblical, Mishnaic, Tibbonite[54] (Medieval), and Modern Hebrew—and the speakers of each language could not understand the speakers of another. This list can easily be increased to six or eight Hebrew languages, as distinct from one another at least as Ukrainian is from Russian or even Italian from Portuguese. Yet, there is also a unity to the overall "Hebrew language" (the "Eternal Language"), which is expressed not only in social consciousness (as Rabin 1988a assumes), in the continuity of the generations who thought they were using one and the same language, but also in the basic morphology (including alternative variants); in the basic texts (Bible, Mishna) that were assumed as the foundation of the language and used in all periods; and in the unity of the Hebrew Library and education, which incorporated all of these layers. The uniqueness of the modern language among all these historical languages consists in the fact that it was not yet another monolithic layer but the all-embracing receptacle and crucible of materials from all the layers that preceded it, turning the diachronic and "multilingual" library into a synchronic, fused text.

To be sure, Klauzner was not born into spoken Hebrew, he acquired the language from texts. Therefore, his personal Hebrew base (i.e., the mode in which he and his contemporaries absorbed the language) included texts in what look like—and had to be studied as—several separate languages: Torah, Prophets,

---

54. Four generations of the Tibbon family in the twelfth and thirteenth centuries translated scholarly and philosophical works from Arabic into Hebrew and created an Arab-influenced style of Hebrew thought and science.

Mishna, Midrash, Talmud, medieval philosophy, medieval poetry. In his consciousness, every modern Hebrew text was filtered through that prism and broke
down into the mosaic of its historical colors. Hebrew dictionaries to this day
indicate from which historical layer (or "language") each word derives. For the
Hebrew reader today, however, his personal base is Israeli Hebrew, which looks
like one monolithic language, with no source-markers to each word, and, for him,
on the contrary, the search for sources looks like linguistic nitpicking.

The nostalgia for the land of the Bible was bound up with admiration for the
beauty of the language and poetry of the Bible, which was also sanctioned by
such non-Jewish authorities as Herder. But the Hebrew literature that brought
the pioneers to the land of the Bible was not written in the Biblical style. The
quasi-Biblical style of the Hebrew Enlightenment, which aspired to a "pure" Hebrew language, suited the idealist taste of the German Romantic tradition and
reflected the hatred of Gentiles and Maskilim for the Talmud and for the "ungram-
matical" distortions of Rabbinic Hebrew, and the contempt of educated Jews for
the perverse "hodgepodge" of Yiddish. The admiration for the "pure" Biblical style
was the legacy of the Enlightenment, which was certainly not a Zionist movement.
Paradoxically, the revival of Zionism broke through that fence, since its essence
was modernization, and Hebrew literature of the Renaissance Period written in a
"synthetic" style was its inspiration. It is hard to imagine alert and flexible thinking—in the forms of the philosophy, science, or political debate of Europe—within the limitations of the Biblical style and paratactic syntax; and it is
hard to see in it a vivid and variegated dialogue or internal monologue of a
complex human consciousness in the civilization of the twentieth century. That
was clear to both modern Hebrew literature and the pioneers of the language
revival.

The problem was not one of language alone but one of creating a literature
that would not just spin a narrative yarn but confront the "real world" in a text
that is simultaneously realistic and symbolic. The understanding of that "real
world" would ideally match the norms of both depth and concreteness developed
in European literature, combined with the new, critical reassessment of the place
of the Jews in history. For that purpose, opening the treasures of four, or more,
Hebrew languages of the past was a powerful move, but what use was made of
them was decisive. We have various studies on the linguistic source-components
of Mendele and other writers, but very little on the linguistic challenges posed by
their genres and fictional worlds. That link between language and representation
was explored in a pathbreaking little book by Robert Alter. He states:

> Even the most ardent loyalty to the language as a repository of distinctive values
> could not conceal the awkwardness and the artificiality of classical Hebrew as a
> medium for representation of modern realities, whether social, historical, relational,
> or psychological. What was needed to make Hebrew transcend these inadequacies
> was the bold intervention of genius, which would find ways to make the old lan-
> guage answer to a radically new world. (Alter 1988:14)

Thus, paradoxically, the return to the Land of the Bible, coming out of love and admiration for the Bible, was accomplished in a consciously non-Biblical Hebrew, fitting the political and literary discourses of the revivalists. In literature, it was achieved in two stages: the first, almost single-handedly created by Mendele Moykher Sforim, and the second, splitting in two directions, represented by Brener and Gnesin.

The first language revolution in this sense was made by Mendele Moykher Sforim, master of the Hebrew "Style" ("*nusakh*," as Bialik dubbed it). At first, Mendele too wrote prose in the naive, quasi-Biblical style (the novel *Fathers and Sons*). But when he began writing major, sophisticated and cynical fictional works in Yiddish, he developed the principle of the controlled balance of components of the Yiddish language—a balance between Hebrew, Slavic, and German elements in the garb of popular, spoken Yiddish—which established the play of mutual metaphorization between the components, laced with tensions and ironies. Thus Mendele, in fact, created the modern literary language in Yiddish which was *a new and synthetic language*.[55] When Mendele reworked his Yiddish books into Hebrew, he applied similar principles and found such a *new and synthetic* language for Hebrew as well—except that the synchronic layers of the language (in Yiddish) were replaced by diachronic layers (in the Holy Tongue): rather than interacting source languages we now have a play between several historical components of Hebrew and Aramaic.

The license to fuse historical layers of the language also passed into journalism and oral discussion. The Hebrew journalism of the *Haskala* was Biblical in style, that is, archaizing, and, as discourse intended to convey information, almost ridiculous to the modern reader. Hebrew journalism underwent a veritable revolution, influenced by the modern political and intellectual tone of Yiddish newspapers and by the political, cosmopolitan discourse of the ideologically oriented immigrants of the Second and Third Aliyot. It was primarily Hebrew journalism that boldly formulated the style of modern spoken Hebrew.

Henceforth, the gates of absorption were open: 1) The absorption of all historical layers of Hebrew within one synchronic framework had opened all at once a broad potential treasure of words and expressions, synonyms and stylistic variants, which may be reunderstood and activated for the new purposes. 2) The intellectual and political, "international" vocabulary was introduced with the new paradigms of thought from Yiddish, Russian, or German and, later, English.

The Hebrew writers emerging after Mendele—Gnesin, Brener, Agnon, Hazaz—mark different directions of this "synthetic" Hebrew prose. They all made a second step, of reaching out to the international culture, at that time massively translated into Yiddish and Hebrew, but also read original and translated literature in Russian and German. Gnesin went out—to the psychological Russian and

---

55. Mendele had some predecessors in this matter, notably Mendl Lefin, but he is the one who placed it in the center of the literature in a major and influential body of writing.

Scandinavian literature of the beginning of the century—and came back to the unspoken Hebrew language, unspoken even by his fictional characters themselves: "Gnesin's literary transformation of the classical language made it a lifelike vehicle for the ebb and flow of consciousness of his hypersensitive, self-subverting, Russian-speaking intellectuals" (Alter 1988:67). And Brener went out to the world of journalism and Yiddish (which he wrote before he turned to Hebrew fiction) and returned to Hebrew, combining Dostoevskian ideologically tortured characters with the most topical "*publitsistika*" (essayistic and political journalism) of the Yiddish-speaking ideological world (Zionist and non-Zionist) of the beginning of the century. Robert Alter described it in a bold and suggestive construct:

> If one can entertain the hypothesis of an international language—call it *novelistic*—with characteristic patterns of presentation of data and analysis, then Brener is thinking novelistic (say, Dostoevski, Zola, George Eliot) while writing Hebrew— unlike the *nusakh* writers [i.e., those using Mendele's "style"], who often think Mishnaic-Midrashic-liturgic while writing novels in Hebrew. (Alter 1988:50)

This is precisely the issue: *Thinking novelistic [or: thinking European] while writing Hebrew*. In other words, after the first step, that of creating a synthetic Hebrew language, came the second: thinking in terms of the representations of a European world and reaching out for means of expression in the treasures of pan-historical Hebrew. All this was still accomplished in an unspoken language, by writers who absorbed large quantities of Hebrew texts from the historical layers in their childhood.

We may distinguish three ways of integrating the historical layers in a Hebrew text:

i. *Embedded discourse*, as in the Talmud, which is constructed as a well-controlled mosaic of an Aramaic frame and Hebrew and Aramaic quotations from the Bible and the discussions of the sages, with well-defined boundaries between the various kinds of fragments.

ii. *"Synthetic" style*, which includes the "Style" of Mendele and the styles of Brener and Agnon, and in which fragments from all the layers of the language may be intermingled in one sentence, but still recognizable: Biblical Hebrew, Mishnaic Hebrew, Rabbinic Hebrew, Aramaic (just as it is possible to perceive the components within Yiddish).

iii. Fused style—the social base language of Israeli Hebrew, in which the choice of most specific words or stylistic variants is decided and the historical source or the age of a word is hardly recognized by the speakers, as is the case in contemporary English. The only words that stand out as a different stratum in Israeli Hebrew are loanwords from the international component: they are visibly different in their morphology, sound structure, and the place of the stress in the word, as well as in the bridge they build to international culture. From this fused base language of society, a writer can take off for particular purposes toward a Biblical or some other historical Hebrew style, thereby achieving a special stylistic effect.

In 1929, in the article cited above, Klauzner wrote: "Our language today is not a language at all but a Biblical patch on a Mishnaic patch and, on top of that—a Tibbonite patch" (Klauzner 1956:42). But today, just sixty years later, all those patches have fused into one surface, which has to be upturned to discover the original layers. Mendele made the breakthrough and opened all the treasures of the historical language, but his style is not the Israeli style, for in his "synthetic" style there is an interplay of layers while contemporary Hebrew is almost completely fused. The decisive influence on the Israeli spoken language seems to have come from journalism, which constitutes a triple bridge: from the Hebrew literature of the Renaissance Period to the living Israeli language; from Yiddish journalism to the new Hebrew society; and from the universe of international information to Hebrew vocabulary. Newspapers, and the mass media that grew out of them (especially radio), were, perhaps, the major force that disseminated and unified Modern Hebrew (while the schools were too much bogged down by normative concerns and antiquated texts).

Yet the fusion of Israeli Hebrew is by no means "democratic"; not all layers are equally represented in it. Aramaic words and collocations, which were used profusely by Mendele or Brener, as quotations within a Hebrew sentence frame, were either Hebraized or disappeared. Words and roots were adapted from all layers, including Hebraized Arabic words, and given modern meanings, but mostly as individual words with no layer markings. A large part of the vocabulary is newly coined. Morphology and lower syntactic relations are mostly Biblical; however, the larger syntactic patterns and much of the semantics are general European. Naturally, there are considerable differences between the spoken, daily language, the language of popular newspapers, the language of intellectual periodicals, the language of poetry, and the language of fiction. Thus, though it inherited the principle of fusion, Israeli Hebrew does not at all look like Mendele's synthetic style; most words would not even have been understood by Mendele himself.

B. Hebrew as a Base Language of the Text

Above we introduced the two related concepts of the *base language of the individual*, which permits him to go off to special idiolects or other languages, and the *base language of the society*, which permits also the performance of an English drama on the one hand and a Bible quiz on the other. We can now introduce a third category: the *base language of the text*, which makes it possible for a text to have a unified foundation while absorbing new words, expressions, and quotations from other languages and other layers of Hebrew.

A conspicuous debate in the revival of the language, which has continued to the present, is whether to use only words that look "Hebrew," saying with them only what can be said with them;[56] or to write a text whose grammar and framework are Hebrew but which can absorb foreign words, idioms, and syntactic patterns at will. The development of rich languages occurred in the second way and intertwined with the openness of their cultures to cultural and scientific borrowing from the outside. English is a rich language largely because, at various times, it was wide open to Latin, to French and Italian literature, to Yiddish and black slang, or to Structuralist terminology from Paris. Russian made gigantic strides in the nineteenth century when it absorbed the philosophy, fiction, poetry, and culture of Western Europe, including their terminologies (which only in part were replaced by words made of Slavic roots). The great Leo Tolstoy was accused in his time of writing French in Russian words; his syntax and even his prepositions followed French (which was the predominant language of the education of Russian aristocrats from an early age); but this very style became a classical example of literary Russian. Yiddish also evolved with considerable speed in the twentieth century because it unabashedly absorbed hundreds of concepts, words, and means of expression from all European languages: the base of every text remained Yiddish, but Slavic, German, Hebrew, and "International" elements (the property of many languages in the modern cultural alliance) were embedded in it. Hence, the crusade of the Hebrew purists either ghettoized and damaged the culture or remained a lost cause.

True, it was more difficult for Hebrew to absorb an international vocabulary, since it is generally not appropriate for the patterns of Hebrew morphology (although it is possible in many cases to force foreign words into a Hebrew mold: *le-argen* [with the Hebraized root ARG, "to organize"]; *le-talpen* [with the root TLP, "to telephone"]; *le-rafrer* [with the root RFR, "to refer"]). Indeed, in Russian and German too, international words deviate, phonetically and otherwise, from the rest of the language; but those languages do not have to fit the new root into the molds of morphology as Hebrew must do in order to enable the grammatical use of words in a sentence. Nevertheless, various solutions emerged for a massive introduction of such international vocabulary into Hebrew.[57]

Those who wanted Hebrew not as a private curiosity in a backward province but as an alternative to European culture imitated the Yiddish model in this respect. This was natural for anyone who shifted from writing in Yiddish to

56. This includes, however, words from foreign languages, like *dugma* ("example"), which Hebrew absorbed from Greek in the past, and Hebraized forms of words deriving from Arabic or Aramaic.

57. Sometimes, nouns were introduced that could not be transformed into verbs (as most Hebrew nouns can be) and had to be used with auxiliary verbs in a predicate position (an English equivalent would be "to do a telephone" rather than "to phone"), or the matching verb came from a different root than the respective noun (as in English "to call" or in Hebrew "le-tsaltsel").

writing in Hebrew. The stories of Brener, the poems of Uri-Tsvi Grinberg, the speeches of Ben-Gurion, and Hebrew journalism for decades, are replete with words from European languages, as well as from Aramaic and Yiddish. The prominent journal of the Second Aliya, *Ha-Poel Ha-Tsayir* ("The Young Laborer"), generously used international words—according to one study, 14% of the vocabulary of the text (see Fellman 1973:59). The tacit declaration was: *We shall write in Hebrew about everything, without waiting for the lexicographers.* Indeed, a good sprinkling of any Hebrew text with foreign words is always welcome in Hebrew culture; it indicates to the reader the connection to world culture, to the semiotics of the contemporary world, and to world information with which the text is concerned. Even sensational newspapers for mass readership excel in it—and, above all, the snobbish art-and-gossip mass weeklies of Tel-Aviv and Jerusalem, *Ha-'ir* and *Kol ha-'ir*. However, exaggerated proportions of "foreign" words signal alienation and snobbery. And the proportion itself is a matter of genre.

In the final analysis, the dialectics of the struggle between the Westernizers and the purists was a blessing for the Hebrew language: many foreign terms were replaced with neologisms from a Hebrew (or Semitic-looking) root: *kultura* ("culture") became *tarbut*, *communikatsia* ("communications") became *tikshoret* (yet "telefon" did not become the proposed *sakhrakhok*, like the German "Fernsprecher"); but in place of the Hebraized terms, new "foreign" words and concepts were introduced, within the proportions of good taste allowed in a given genre. This was—and is—the *cosmpolitan openness* (as well as the Yiddish and Russian background) of modern Hebrew. It was this openness that constructed a modern State with universities, literature, and an air force.

C. Dialogue

Before the revival of Hebrew speech, a Hebrew writer could already quite freely produce new Hebrew sentences in writing. But what about written dialogues? Another major achievement of Mendele Moykher Sforim was that he translated colloquial dialogues from Yiddish into Hebrew. This was because his major Hebrew books were translations from Yiddish and the bulk of his Yiddish novels was taken up by dialogues; the translation had to provide Hebrew substitutes for what his heroes said in Yiddish. Since then, insofar as there were dialogues in Hebrew literature that reflected vivid, everyday conversations, they were imitations of conversations in Yiddish or some other language. Nevertheless, the tendency to monologues—ideological (Brener) or exegetical (Agnon)—was still strong in Hebrew prose. (Conceivably, even in real life, Brener's prototypes lectured excitedly or stammered, like their models in Yiddish or Russian, though they did it in languages other than Hebrew.) Thus, Hebrew prose reported and invented living dialogue in a language in which no one conversed and internal monologues (Gnesin) in a language in which no one ruminated.

D. Freedom of the Word

When the slogan of free love was popular after the Bolshevik Revolution, Avraham Shlonski—the first prominent poet educated in the first Hebrew secondary school, Gymnasya Hertseliya (who spent, however, the years of war and Revolution in Russia)—demanded: "Free love between words, without the canopy and marriage vows of the holy text." "Words in Freedom" was a key slogan of Italian and Russian Futurism, but in Eretz-Israel it assumed a special meaning. For a language laden with texts, especially the central holy text (the Bible!) memorized by all speakers—for such a language to be a living language, there must be a free lexicon, releasing the words from automatic Biblical associations. For a young literature of young people, getting rid of the burden of classical texts also signaled getting free of the burden of history and the responsibilities or constraints of tradition. A living language means *a language that enables its speakers to say something new* and to make free combinations of separate and precise words with their own, autonomous meanings. If a writer wants deliberate allusions, he must provide us with more specific material for them in the text, but every expression in a living language need not lead us to the episodes of Abraham or Esau, as many literary critics will happily point out.

Shlonski's declaration was part of his iconoclastic manifesto against Bialik's "Holy Tongue" style. But Bialik and all the other writers of the Renaissance Period since the 1890s also attempted to break the bonds of the "mosaic style" and the fixed collocations that characterized the rhetoric of the Hebrew Enlightenment. True, the language was not spoken, the mind of the writer was inhabited less by individual words than by texts he knew by heart. Yet, an important activity of de-automatization of the use of sources was already accomplished in the Revival literature. First, the constraints of the precise, syllabic meter, adopted by Bialik from Russian poetry, forced the poet to break up the original phrases still reverberating in his head; and the patterns of rhyme led him astray from the continuity of some preestablished Biblical source. Second, even while poetry did use the language of various sources, it created in each poem a new, *ad hoc* fictional world, a unity of image and situation, rather than the continuity of one Biblical subtext. As a result, de-automatization of "dead" idioms and ready-made collocations was accomplished through the unraveling of their images and unexpected meanings in the new fictional situation created in the poem and absent in the source.

Let us take, for example, Bialik's poem "Davar" ("The [prophet's] Word" or "The Message"), a poem whose starting point was influenced by Pushkin's "The Prophet," which identifies the poet as prophet in the Schellingian tradition. Both poems draw on chapter 6 of Isaiah and are "prophetic" in tone and language. In a literal translation, Bialik's poem begins thus:

> The live coal of fire from your altar—throw it away, prophet,
> Leave it to the scoundrels—
> Leave it for them, to roast their meat on it and to heat their pot
> And to warm their hands.

The first Biblical allusion is to Isaiah 6:6–7:

> Then flew one of the seraphims unto me, having a live coal in his hand, which he
> had taken with the tongs off the altar: And he laid it upon my mouth, and said, Lo,
> this hath touched thy lips; and thine iniquity is taken away, and thy sin purged.

The first line in Bialik's poem is mainly from this Biblical source with a change
of word order, that is, achieving syntactical freedom.[58] But Bialik adds the word
"fire," which is not in the source, that is, he extrapolates a connotation of the
word "live coal" (*ritspa*). From the second line on, there is also semantic independence: the "fire" comes out of the collocation and out of its symbolic meaning,
turns into a real fire, which may then be employed for domestic, profane use,
in a new context created in this poem. Tshernikhovski, Shlonski, Bat-Miriam
(1901–1980), Avot Yeshurun, (1904–1992), and other poets went far in this
direction; and in the Israeli poetry of the 1960s generation, the fusion language
is so successful that there is even a return to deliberate allusions as a conspicuous
device distinct from the rest of the text, which is written in Israeli Hebrew.

E. Cultivation of the Sounds of the Language

Hebrew was supposedly a "dead" language; but, as mentioned above, there
were many opportunities to hear its sounds. Poets who studied in a yeshiva, as
Bialik did—where studies were conducted by reciting the text aloud by pairs of
students—heard and pronounced it constantly in their youth. They could now
harness those sounds to create a rich musical texture in poetry. But beforehand,
they had to imbibe the musicality of metrical verse, either in Russian or in Yiddish.
The impact of Russian meters was especially pervasive because they did not know
Russian well and could just attend to the magic of verse, especially cherished in
the Symbolist period. Through this filter, they "purified" the coarse intonations
and long-winded periods of Talmudic chanting and fell back to the Bible, which
had compact versets and beautiful symmetries, more easily employable in sym-
metrical verse. For this and other reasons, the base language of poetry was Biblical
Hebrew—far from the synthetic style of prose. Yet, with a few exceptions, the
meter of Biblical poetry was not employed in the two-thousand-year history of
Hebrew verse, and even now the Biblical language was harnessed to the Russian
accentual-syllabic meters.

Unfortunately, the resulting meters and the intentionally profuse musicality of
Hebrew poetry in the Renaissance Period were lost when their Ashkenazi language
was abolished in favor of the Israeli—so-called "Sephardi"—pronunciation. It is
clear, nevertheless, that a poet who took pains with every syllable and vowel and
employed rhymes as pronounced in his own accent and specific dialect—such a

---

58. In this poem, there is no regular syllabic meter, but the convention of breaking up the source
phrase has already become a norm in Bialik's poetics.

poet must have *heard* the words in his inner ear as the poem was written.[59] And so did his readers.

In view of all this, we may ask: What was lacking to turn Hebrew into a living language? The major absences were:

  i. The automatic habit of articulation and speaking aloud, that native speakers have;
 ii. The automatic and fluent formulation of sentences without prior reflection;
iii. The composition of new sentences and responses in a living dialogue situation;
 iv. the exchange of the personal base language for a new base language (an extremely difficult feat!); that is, that a person speaking Hebrew would not translate it from, or base it on, another language.
  v. the creation of a social base language with one, unified, basic vocabulary to be used by all speakers, rather than the library of heterogeneous texts with undecided variants;
 vi. the inclusion of all areas of life and knowledge, not just those that have been expanded in the literature; so as to rely neither on another Jewish frame language nor on the language of the State for such wider areas covered by them.

All the above-described phenomena developed in the evolution of Hebrew literature in its written form; an arsenal of tools was prepared. And now a revolutionary situation emerged. In this atmosphere, the extremely rapid spread of Hebrew speech among those who had known the written language before indicates that speaking Hebrew was possible even without having to give up the wealth of the language, without starting from scratch; it could be entered directly from a high cultural level—and perhaps only thus.

---

59. Bialik himself wrote a series of quasi–folk songs, using the motifs of Yiddish folk songs but harnessing them to Russian meters. He wrote about it: "I am now enamored of the genre of folk poetry. The Hebrew language never tried it and there is in it a special flavor: folk songs in a language that is not spoken [in 1910! That is what the greatest Hebrew poet thought of the "revival" of spoken Hebrew—B.H.]; it is only regrettable that our reading [in the Ashkenazi accent] is distorted, which brings about a poetic meter strange to the ears of the reader and grammarian. This fault will prevent the poems from spreading in Eretz-Israel and becoming full-fledged folk songs, sung aloud [that is what he thought of their intellectual level]" (Bialik 1990:447).

TWENTY-SIX

New Cells of Society in a Social Desert

The third, and decisive, factor that contributed to the revival of the Hebrew language as a base language of society was *the creation of new social cells* in a new land perceived by the immigrants as a "*social wasteland.*" The experiment could be successfully conducted only in a small, controlled laboratory, not in the traditional territory of the millions who spoke another language or the hundreds of thousands who integrated in the language of the State. From the Second Aliya (1904–1914) on, almost every new entity created in Eretz-Israel and formulating itself as new and cut off from the past, tried to impose the Hebrew language in its framework. The revolution took place in three complementary ways: from above, from around, and from within. From above, the schools imposed the language on their students, at least while they were at school. From around, frameworks of life in the city, especially in the "First Hebrew City," Tel Aviv, began to be carried out in Hebrew. From within, groups of laborers created cells of Hebrew speakers. Combining those influences, high-school students also created cells of Hebrew speakers and many families internalized the frame language of the city and the language of their children.

The ideological core of the Second Aliya were the idealist workers. Those were young intellectuals whose imagination was caught by the new secular trends in Diaspora; they never before did any physical work, nor did their "grandmothers" (as the Yiddish saying goes), and they never had any attachment to the soil. The turn to physical work on the land was an ideological decision of self-realization in an effort toward the productivization of the Jews, reclaiming the ancestral homeland, and reclaiming their own character. It was an attempt to create a Jewish proletarian class, as a "normal" nation should have, which would then provide the base for a socialist society.

It was also a movement of conscious, almost proud despair, fed by the failure of the Russian Revolution of 1905, the pogroms of 1903–1905, the helplessness of the self-defense (in which many of them participated) vis-à-vis the tsarist police, and the disintegration of any relevant Jewish response. Many young people left Russia for Western universities or for Berlin, London, and the United States. Among the young Zionists, there was a perception that "everything" was lost, and they embraced Brener's slogan: "In-spite-of-everything!" (*af-al-pi-khen*). The labor leader and ideologue Berl Katznelson summarized the situation in retrospect:

> And at a time when any widespread hope in Zionism was lost, dissipated, when all the Jewish youth began to retreat from this camp, when all the elements of the idea of Organic Zionism—love for the Land, revival of the language, working the soil—began to disappear, at that very moment, by some miracle, a small residue was found in the camp, small and weak, and it too standing on the edge of an abyss; and this handful found in their own souls a strange courage—not belief and hope but courage emanating from the thought that perhaps we are the last ones, and, if history issued a verdict that we have no future or any revival, let us be the last ones, but we shall not leave the battlefield. The torch ignited on the banks of the Thames by Yosef-Hayim Brener[60]—ostensibly the bearer of national heresy—with his call: "We shall be the last ones on the ramparts!"—achieved its mission. Disgust arose—disgust with the desolation in Eretz-Israel, disgust with the weakness of will in the Zionist movement. A revolt arose—not against the oppressing governments. Not against the despotism of the House of Romanov [the Russian Tsar], even not against the social order in general, but against the very movement in which this generation was born, against the Zionist movement, the Jewish intelligentsia, Hebrew literature—a comprehensive, immense revolt in all domains of life. [. . .]
>
> In this situation of terrible isolation within Judaism—that Judaism which, after [the pogroms of] Kishinev and Homel and [the failed Revolution of] 1905, with all the increase of national pain, was totally helpless or saw its way only in abandoning the Zionist dream; isolation among our comrades in party and ideology; and isolation and estrangement within the *Yishuv* in Eretz-Israel—in this situation, the Second Aliya had to continue its work, not always out of faith and satisfaction but often out of ultimate despair; not because we recognized the beauty in faith but because we sensed the ugliness in betrayal, weakness, and impotence; out of an internal imperative to overcome and not abandon the struggle. (B. Katznelson 1947a:12)

In the year of pogroms, summer 1905–summer 1906, about two hundred thousand Jews emigrated from Russia and only thirty-five hundred came to Palestine (Ben-Sasson 1976:861), many of whom left after a short while. Berl Katznelson was aware of the irrationality of this move:

> It was rational to be against Eretz-Israel (to go to Eretz-Israel meant to go to the country of Abd El-Hamid [the Turkish Sultan]. We, who are fighting here [in Russia] against the power of a monarchy, are going to a country ruled by Abd El-

---

60. The Hebrew writer Yosef-Hayim Brener was at the time in London, where he published a little magazine *Ha-Meorer* ("Reveille" or "The Waking Call")—an allusion to an earlier Russian immigrant, Alexandr Herzen, who published in London a Russian revolutionary journal, *Kolokol* ("The Tocsin"). Out of total despair about the future of a Jewish nation, *Ha-Meorer* launched the beginnings of Modernism in Hebrew literature.

Hamid?... The same holds for Hebrew: it was rational to say that the masses don't need Hebrew, have no opportunity to know and study Hebrew. But I did not yet want to close that account. (B. Katznelson 1947b:76)

The workers tried to get work (the so-called "conquest of Hebrew Work") with private Jewish farmers in the settlements of the First Aliya, but that was not always successful because of competition from cheaper Arab labor and the fear those Jewish peasants had of the over-intellectualized socialist newcomers (who might even influence their own daughters). The farmers seemed to the young socialists to be exploiters, "*Boazim*" (from *Boaz*, the Biblical rich farmer). The workers could not survive individually and organized themselves into two parties: *The Party of Hebrew Social-Democratic Workers in Eretz-Israel Poaley-Tsiyon* ("Workers of Zion"), deriving from the Marxist Zionist Labor party *Poaley Tsiyon* that emerged in Europe and America; and the new, non-Marxist party, *Ha-Poel Ha-Tsayir* ("the Young Worker"). Though both were Socialist Zionist and both demanded not just ideology but personal self-realization, there was an ongoing dispute between them almost imperative for ideological expression in a Jewish society. *Poaley Tsiyon* was the more ideological party, whereas *Ha-Poel Ha-Tsayir* was in favor of an "evolutionary revolution" (Shapiro 1967:15) and emphasized the principle of self-realization of the individual who redeems his own freedom through his "sweat and bleeding heart." In its programmatic statement against *Poaley Tsiyon*, it declared that Social-Democracy "hangs in the air, without *any* base in this country lacking industrial development," hence "damaging to the realization of Zionism"; but it admitted that, because of "the highly developed predilection of some of our young generation toward abstract thought," that party too may exist here.

The numbers were extremely small: in 1906, there were 90 members of *Ha-Poel Ha-Tsayir* and 60 in *Poaley Tsiyon*. Even in 1912, at the height of the Second Aliya immigration, and after a six-year struggle for the "conquest of work," there were altogether 522 workers in Judea and 240 in the distant Galilee. It is estimated that no more than three thousand workers immigrated to the country during the period 1904–1914 (i.e., about 10% of the growth of the *Yishuv*) (M. Eliav 1978: 335). The conditions were difficult, the utopian future remote, many suffered physically or mentally, many despaired, and most of the newcomers left the country (according to one of them, David Ben-Gurion, about 90% of the Second Aliya eventually left [1947:17]); but they were the founders of much that was creative in the *Yishuv*, including the agricultural collective settlements, the labor movement, and the Hebrew-speaking culture. As Berl Katznelson put it: "The Second Aliya [. . .] came under a special star; it was *the tragic mode* that accompanied it, which crystallized it and *made in into a force in the nation*" (B. Katznelson 1947a:11; my emphasis—B.H.).

The slogan of *Ha-Poel Ha-Tsayir* was: "Our world stands on three things: on *Hebrew land*, on *Hebrew work*, and on the *Hebrew language*" (emphasis mine—B.H.). Clearly, the word "Hebrew" was a label for the whole revolutionary package, as opposed to the nature of the Diaspora "Jew." Thus, on October 1, 1906, the ideologue and optimist David Ben-Gurion (a member of the other party) wrote from the settlement Petah Tikva to his father in Poland (to whom he had to prove that his decision to leave home made sense):

> The Hebrew Renaissance, here it is! Hebrew signs on every store, Hebrew speech in the streets, stores, and restaurants, the buds of revival! No. Here you cannot doubt. You cannot disbelieve! [. . .] Here is a Hebrew boy riding with assurance on a galloping donkey, a Hebrew girl, eight years old, rides on a donkey loaded with freight—These are the visions of revival! (Ben-Gurion 1972:75)

"Hebrew" here is not just a language but an omnibus positive label for a new kind of Jewish existence. The image of the cavalry of a galloping donkey may signal daring, a return to nature, or the uninhibited behavior of a free child, but not quite a sign of the revival of the language.

The laborers lived in poverty and alienation, the physical mastery of work was a Herculean task. They had no property, no land, no houses. They were not welcome by the Turkish authorities, the Arabs, the Orthodox Jews in Jerusalem, or the Jewish farmers of the First Aliya. Their existence in Eretz-Israel was justified only by the total ideological commitment that filled the entire lives of those stubborn youngsters. The commitment was built on a series of binary oppositions: freedom versus exile, Eretz-Israel versus Diaspora, Hebrew versus Yiddish, Sephardi versus Ashkenazi accent, life in nature versus the imaginary ghetto walls of the *shtetl*, physical labor versus a life of idleness and commerce, the young generation versus Jewry of the past, realization of a program versus empty Zionist speeches, and—above all—personal self-realization versus passive suffering in history. It took character and "a tragic mode" to do all that. Young Tsemakh attributes to Mrs. Pukhatshevski (1869–1934), a pro-Hebrew farmer and writer of the First Aliya, the thought that perhaps "there may be some truth in the rumors about those boys that began to arrive in Eretz-Israel, that they are inquisitive, despondent, nothing will satisfy them, and everything is flawed in their eyes as if all that was built [by the First Aliya] is irreparable." And Ben-Gurion described their personal qualities as "fanaticism, perseverance, and above all—rootedness" (1947:18).

The isolation of the few workers, the need for repeated clarification and reinforcement of their ideological motivation, and the very age of those young people without a world of parents—all intensified group life. Aside from work, most of them spent their time together, debating, organizing and splitting parties, as well as singing, dancing, and sharing meals. As soon as these frameworks were conducted in Hebrew, when Hebrew was imposed as the public language, its future was guaranteed.

This was the source of rural and urban labor collectives and, ultimately, of the small communal settlement, *kvutza* and the larger *kibbutz*. In terms of ideas, this was a democratic society, every individual participated in the public debates and decisions. They had no preconceived or inherited norms—hence the debates themselves were central to their lives—and the debates were about the justification of their very existence here. As a historian of the Eretz-Israeli labor movement wrote, "the constraints of existence forced the worker to accept socialization, collective ownership, mutual responsibility, and the creation of instruments for that" (Braslavski 1955:100). And historian Mordekhai Eliav draws a picture of their lives:

> An abyss opened [between the workers and the farmers] and the new immigrants felt total loneliness, on top of the natural loneliness characteristic of any new immigrant, especially in the areas of ideology, society, and spirit. The immigrants tried to alleviate their loneliness by molding a collective life and a special life-style, nourishing a national-romantic mood, and in heated ideological arguments, while persisting in their goal. Of special importance were the clubs that emerged in the various settlements and served as a focus for cultural and social meetings, parties, and dances, and even as centers of influence on the youth of the settlements. The periodicals of the parties, as well as books and pamphlets, alleviated their psychic needs, strengthened the spirit and tightened the ranks. (M. Eliav 1978:352)

The workers were young people, most were male but there were a few women too, most were unmarried and probably had a negligible or nonexistent sex life, outside of the few steady couples. They were isolated in a difficult land, under the corrupt and oppressive Ottoman regime. Instead of the Jewish Diaspora society, constructed vertically, in large family clans of several generations, here *groups of horizontal sections* were formed, people of a single age without previous ties of blood, without parents or grandparents; and also without children to be educated (in French, perhaps?). The cell of life was not the family but the age group sharing a common ideology and reading the new Hebrew journalism. Theirs was a consciousness of the end of all previous history: the end of two thousand years of exile and the end of thousands of years of class warfare—in the name of a new beginning for man and Jew. Deliberately cut off from the world of their parents, from mother's tenderness, from grandmother's tales, from the customs and superstitions of generations, from the language and the food of their childhood, and, in fact, from the disgusting life of the *shtetl* and its dead-end existence—they tried to create a new world based on the self-education of the individual: to eat the strange and bitter olives, to work the land with a *turiya* (a hoe), and to speak Hebrew.

The social frameworks that arose in the labor movement—the political parties, the "Agricultural Federation," the worker collectives on the outskirts of the *moshavot*, the communes—all aspired to conduct their lives in Hebrew, written and oral. The *Ha-Poel Ha-Tsayir* party accepted the principle of Hebrew in 1906. *Poaley Tsiyon* was attached to its party in Europe where Yiddish was on the rise as a cultural force and the working masses (who knew little Hebrew) could not be attracted by opposing Yiddish (see Yitzhak Ben-Tsvi's recollection, quoted in

Shapiro 1967:21). Ben-Gurion quotes a comrade who told him: "I am for Hebrew like you, but I don't know how to prove it by 'Historical Materialism,' " that is, by Marxist doctrine (Shapiro 1967:21). Indeed, Ben-Gurion and Ben-Tsvi even edited a journal in Yiddish, *Onfang* ("The Beginning"), but there was opposition to Yiddish and it closed after two issues. In 1908, this party too decided to switch to Hebrew.

Nevertheless, the breakthrough was extremely difficult both for the individual and for the group. Many workers spoke and loved Yiddish and opposed the artificial imposition of the difficult and poor Hebrew language by their intellectual leadership. The dominant ideology was Hebrew and no documents were left of that struggle, except for indirect accounts. Thus, in the third general assembly of *Ha-Poel Ha-Tsayir* on Passover 1907, the workers voted against conducting the meeting in Hebrew, and the chairman, Yosef Aronovich, had to resign. Even in 1910, when David Ben-Gurion lectured in Hebrew at a conference of *Poaley Tsiyon*, the entire audience left the hall in protest, except for his friend (the future President of Israel) Yitzhak Ben-Tsvi and Ben-Tsvi's girlfriend Rachel Yanayit. But, in just a few years, Hebrew frameworks were imposed. A major factor that reinforced the implementation of Hebrew was party journalism, which supplied ideological and literary nourishment to this word-hungry society, as well as news, when Yiddish newspapers from abroad were not available. In addition, there was a virtual ban on all public activity (including theater) in Yiddish. The same assembly of *Ha-Poel Ha-Tsayir* that voted down a proposal to conduct the assembly in Hebrew, also decided: "No branch of our organization has the right to perform plays, conduct dances, or arrange public readings in *jargon* [= Yiddish]," as, apparently, they had done before (Greenzweig 1985:207). In 1914, the Fourth Conference of all workers of Judea was already conducted, at least nominally, in Hebrew. Only one faction, the *Left Poaley Tsiyon*, continued to promote Yiddish up to the beginning of the State of Israel.

Shlomo Lavi, later one of the founders of Kibbutz Eyn Harod, wrote:

> It cannot be appreciated how much it costs a man to go from speaking one language to another and especially to a language that is not yet a spoken language. How much breaking of the will it takes. And how many torments of the soul that wants to speak and has something to say—and is mute and stammering. (Greenzweig 1985: 207)

The difficulty here is in changing the individual's base language to a language that is not yet the base language of any society. And "breaking of the will" did not refer to language alone. Even the intellectual Berl Katznelson reminisced:

> In the first days, I had a hard time with Hebrew. I had never spoken Hebrew in my life. As a matter of fact, I saw Hebrew speech as something unnatural, so much so that [in Byelorussia] I had a teacher, a man who was very dear to me—and I caused him great grief. He spoke to me in Hebrew and I spoke to him in Yiddish because I thought Hebrew was not a spoken language. When I came to Eretz-Israel, I couldn't

make a natural sentence in Hebrew and I didn't want to talk a foreign language. I decided I wouldn't utter a foreign word. And for ten days, I didn't speak at all; when I was forced to answer—I would reply with some Biblical verse close to the issue. (B. Katznelson 1947b:85).

We see here, on the one hand, the difficulty of connecting words into sentences other than ready-made phrases; and, on the other hand, the stubborn decision to speak only Hebrew. And that was a spiritual leader of the generation who became a prolific writer and developed a personal Hebrew style within a few years.

There were differences in the human quality of the various waves of immigration. Most of the immigrants of the First Aliya did not have much education. But the workers of the Second Aliya included some who absorbed the intensive academic education of the Russian gymnasium (most of them studied as "externs" or with private tutors) and read a great deal in Hebrew, Yiddish, and Russian. Berl Katznelson, for example, grew up in an enlightened home and never went to any school; his father told him: You'll learn Russian when you know Hebrew well, which he did by the age of ten, then plunging into Russian literature, and from there to Yiddish; in their home, *Midrash rabba*, Dobrolyubov, Pushkin, and Mendele (i.e., religious Hebrew, Russian, and Yiddish books) were lying around on the table, and he himself wrote a paper comparing the Hebrew poet (and convert to Christianity) Abba Konstantin Shapiro with the Russian poet Lermontov (B. Katznelson 1947b:70). Whether they completed their studies or not, there was an "intelligentsia," in the Russian sense of the term, in the Second Aliya: that is, not necessarily members of the "liberal professions" but those who read profusely and ask critical questions about everything and elevate every issue to an ideological level. This essential distinction—between the education, the level of consciousness, the ideological commitment, and the cosmopolitan horizons of the immigrants who came after the failure of the Russian Revolution of 1905 and that of the immigrants of the 1880s—was similarly evident in Jewish New York and in the Yiddish literature created there.

Given this background, motivation was of paramount importance. Motivation bridged the rationality of the conceptual argument and the irrationality of the passion for personal realization. In an article titled "Language Insomnia" (or "Wanderings of Language," 1918; see translation in this book), Rachel Katznelson (future literary critic and wife of Israeli President Zalman Shazar) tells of the soul-searching torments between the emotional connection to Yiddish literature and the choice of Hebrew. "In the Kineret commune, there were discussions of the crisis in Socialism" (R. Katznelson 1946:9)—they were fourteen women workers, barely holding on to the land in the extremely hot Jordan Valley, with no other worry than the crisis of Socialism in Europe! (How similar this is to the sects in the Dead Sea desert, just a hundred miles down the river and two thousand years earlier!) And in this context, "I realized the revolutionary nature of Hebrew literature as opposed to Yiddish" (1946:9). "*We had to betray Yiddish, even though we paid for this as for any betrayal*" (10). "The revolution, *the revolt of our generation against itself—we found it in Hebrew literature*" (12) (my emphasis—B.H.). She admits that Yiddish literature "is more national than Hebrew" (14), but "after the failure of the Russian Revolution of 1905, when the situation of our nation was extremely tense, there was something tranquilizing in the best writing in Yiddish" (15); and she proceeds:

> But that was not what we needed then, on the verge of the Second Aliya. For if we had had only the possibility of seeing and thinking revealed in Yiddish, we could not have thought our nation was still one of the great nations. (R. Katznelson 1946: 15)

Hebrew literature "restored our self-respect"—and the issue "did not depend on talent, but on the *free Man* with which Hebrew literature and its language captivated us. We yearned for Man" (15). Only Hebrew literature lacked the "censorship" that was felt even in the radical trends of Yiddish. "Here, people allowed themselves to think about the Hebrew nation out of freedom" (16). A similar distinction between the two literatures was made by Yitzhak Tabenkin:

> Exposure of the revolutionary truth of the naked Jewish reality, Brener's strong, open-eyed, critical, and analytical attitude—that is what Hebrew literature taught us. And it was this literature of that period, along with the ancient Bible, that educated the individual for his immigration to Eretz-Israel. (Tabenkin 1947:29; see the translation in this volume)

And Rachel Katznelson continues:

> The creation of the spoken language began in Hebrew at the same time that the danger to its existence appeared [. . .] The transition of Hebrew from a reading language to a spoken language was done in literature. [. . .] The language created by Mendele and Bialik will save us from the dominion of foreign languages, and the New Hebrew Man will speak the language of Brener and Gnesin. (R. Katznelson 1946:21)

Brener returned the compliment. He saw the great wave of emigration from the Pale of Settlement in 1905–6, only splinters of which went to Palestine, and he describes them from the perspective of 1920:

> The splinters did not become waves. Many ricocheted back to the ghettos of New York, London, Paris, etc. Only their vestiges are with us today, until a new, Third Aliya comes.
>
> Yet those few who remained—remained. Adapted to the reality of Eretz-Israel, bought quinine instead of bread, were eaten by all kinds of plagues and insects, went up and down, down and up, and became one body, insofar as several hundred Jewish youngsters are capable of forming one body. The ideological differences disappeared—actually, became ridiculous. Marxism, if it ever was there, evaporated in the hard struggle of life, and the national idealism of their opponents became light in their own eyes, in their struggle for the existence of the worker as a worker.

Now this small, remaining camp is unanimous in its opinion that the redemption of the people of Israel and of the Land of Israel will come not by prophets and not by high politics, not by orange-grove owners and not by a spiritual proletariat, but by collectives of new working people who will arrive as a powerful force and in streams, directed by an organized collective-national arm toward the goal of settlements, in the form of *kvutsot* (communes) or *moshavey ovdim* (collectives of individual farmers).

The main problem is: the problem of human resources . . . (Brener 1947:23)

Such was the human aspect, the "new cells of society" that emerged in Eretz-Israel in the Second Aliya. The other side of the coin was the context of the country itself. In other countries of immigration, Jews also established a Jewish culture, at least for one generation: in Venice in the early sixteenth century, Yiddish literature lived among the Ashkenazi immigrants from Germany; and in New York, from 1882 to 1960, among Eastern European immigrants. For the individual, this was a transitional culture, lasting only one generation: most Yiddish writers in the modern age studied in a religious *heder* in their childhood, left that world and built a secular culture in Yiddish; and their children already lived in another language (English, Russian, Polish, or Hebrew). Unintentionally, secular Jewish culture served as a hothouse for a generation of immigrants from which they and their children emerged into the respective dominant cultures. This also happened to Hebrew writers and Zionists during the Enlightenment (the children of Mendelssohn, Mendele, Peretz, Slonimsky, Tsederbaum, and Herzl converted or assimilated).

In only one period did the Yiddish language succeed in surviving for a long time, passing from one generation to another: in Eastern Europe from the sixteenth to the twentieth century. The major causes were: a) the establishment of crowded Jewish town settlements or city quarters, spots of Jewish territory scattered over the area of other nations; b) the fact that most Jews lived among various linguistic minorities and not among the speakers of the ruling language (for example, among Byelorussians, Lithuanians, Poles, Latvians, and Ukrainians, under Russian rule); the peasants seemed lower than the Jews in social class and education, theirs was not a written culture, and, apart from picking up daily conversation, the Jews did not find it necessary to assimilate to them; the few representatives of power, such as the Polish landed aristocrats and bishops or the Russian administrative authorities, did not socialize with Jews and were too few to assimilate to; and the centers of the ruling culture were far and unreachable; c) the existence of a densely filled, comprehensive Jewish polysystem and a separate semiotics of discourse, couched in three Jewish languages and sanctioned by an official religious boundary, which gave cohesion to a separate Jewish nation.

Essentially similar conditions prevailed in Eretz-Israel at the beginning of the twentieth century: scattered spots of separate Jewish settlements were established; the rulers of Palestine, the Turks, were distant; the local Arabs were a subjugated and backward minority; and those two languages were remote from the world of the immigrants from Russia, who claimed a higher level of culture. There were attempts to adjust: Ben-Yehuda became "Ottomanized" and proudly received his changed Hebrew name officially from the Turkish authorities; Ben-Gurion, Ben-Tsvi, and Moshe Sharet studied in Istanbul; Moshe Sharet (later: Israel's Foreign and Prime Minister) was an officer in the Turkish army. But it was not long before the government of Palestine changed, and the ruling language with it. The English language of the Mandatory government was also completely foreign to the world of Eastern European immigrants; neither was it the language of the surrounding population but of a distant power, which did not intend to stay there for good—nevertheless, the process of assimilating to English culture visibly began in the thirties, especially among the second generation and the German Jews who fled from Hitler and considered English a cognate "higher culture" and antidote to the Eastern European mentality of the Hebrew speakers. Still, the official Mandatory power recognized a separate Jewish political entity and thus preserved the Jewish monopoly inside that society, including the Hebrew nature of the affairs in Jewish towns, self-rule in education and other public domains, and a strong measure of internally imposed discipline.

The positive factor, however, was ideological: the existence of the new Hebrew society had nothing but an ideological justification; and that ideology saw Eretz-Israel as an embryo Jewish State belonging to the immigrants and sanctioned as a Jewish "homeland" by the League of Nations. With a few exceptions, they were almost blind to any national ambitions of the local Arabs. More precisely, the view of the Arabs was divided: in terms of fears, the Arabs were all around, and Hebrew literature was attuned to it; but, intellectually, this was not perceived as an Arab land, it was rather a "social wasteland" ready to fulfill the British Zionist Israel Zangwill's slogan: "*A land without a people—for a people without a land.*" Hence, there was no culture in Eretz-Israel into which the immigrants could or would assimilate. In this vacuum, they established their own, secular polysystem and created *a Hebrew frame language* to absorb it. That is, public life and public affairs, journalism and education, were conducted, at least in principle, in Hebrew. But that was in the twenties and thirties.

Let us return to the Second Aliya. The title of honor, "Second Aliya," is generally bestowed on the founders of the labor movement; but most immigrants, even before World War I, went to the city, especially to Jaffa and Tel Aviv. The First Hebrew City, Tel Aviv, founded in 1909, arose out of the dissociation from the past and opposition to the world of the past, and a second opposition to the world of Jaffa. The *framework* imposed on life in the city was Hebrew from the start. The proudly pronounced adjective "Hebrew" in expressions like "Hebrew work," "Hebrew land," "Hebrew Federation of Labor," a "New Hebrew Man," and the "First Hebrew City" indicated an opposition to the discredited, Diaspora name, "Jewish."[61] But, this "Hebrew" quality was also self-evidently connected with the Hebrew *language*. Thus, a *Hebrew* city had to *speak* Hebrew, as part of the same revival package. The council of Tel Aviv planted trees (return to nature and concern for beauty), forbade the selling of alcoholic beverages, organized guard duty, and imposed the Hebrew language. On July 31, 1906, Akiva Arie Weiss, one of the first to promote the idea of a Hebrew city, distributed his *Prospectus* in Jaffa, in all of five copies. It said:

> We must urgently acquire a considerable chunk of land, on which we shall build our houses. Its place must be near Jaffa, and it will form the first Hebrew city, its inhabitants will be Hebrews a hundred percent; Hebrew will be spoken in this city, purity and cleanliness will be kept, and we shall not go in the ways of the goyim. [. . .] In that city we shall arrange the streets with paved roads and sidewalks and electrical light. In every house we shall bring in water *from the sources of redemption* that will flow to us in pipes, as in every modern European city, and even sewers [in Hebrew: *kanalizatsiya*] will be arranged for the health of the city and its inhabitants. [. . .] And in time this will become the New York of Eretz-Israel. (Shkhori 1990:33–34)

Cleanliness is a central motif in the documents and memoirs of the founders of Tel Aviv (see how many times the word is repeated in Shkhori 1990:31–54), and the planned city is explicitly opposed to the crowded quarter of *Neve Tsedek* that looked "like a Jewish Diaspora *shtetl*" (1990:31). David Smilanski tells of the historical assembly in Jaffa toward building the new settlement, in the summer of 1906: though the participants spoke other languages among themselves, the assembly was conducted in Hebrew, and it was decided that, in the new city, all the protocols, accounting, correspondence, and office work would be conducted in Hebrew only (1990:25). Thus the relations between a frame language and an embedded language were doubly reversed: In Diaspora, Hebrew had been embedded within the frame of Yiddish speech and now it became the frame, with Yiddish (especially at home) still embedded in it; and in Jaffa, Hebrew was an embedded language within a frame of several other languages; but in Tel Aviv it became the official frame language of the city. The establishment of the first purely Jewish city in the world (after two thousand years) created a territorial base for Hebrew as the frame language of society, later duplicated in the kibbutzim.

In 1912, the new Hebrew Language Committee demanded that the national bank and other institutions insist on speaking only Hebrew with their customers (Eisenstadt 1967:73); and in 1913, Yehoash reports that the official language in the Anglo-Palestine Bank was indeed Hebrew: a special announcement was posted, requesting the public to speak Hebrew, the forms to be filled out were in Hebrew, and so on, and one of the important officials was the former teacher

---

61. Compare such American expressions as HIAS, *Hebrew Immigrant Aid Society*, and even "Hebrew National" salami.

Yehuda Grazovski (later: Gur), who was working on his new Hebrew dictionary (Yehoash 1917,1:171). In Tel Aviv, according to Yehoash, "Yiddish here is as impure as pork. To speak Yiddish in the street, a person must have tremendous courage" (1:158). His heart was moved by the "Marranos" who, to make a living, had to accept the "faith" of Tel Aviv (i.e., Hebrew), but after a young man in a *Maspeira* (barber shop) had finished all the words he knew in Hebrew and discovered that Yehoash would not betray him, he revealed to him the awful secret in warm "*mame-loshn*" (1:162).

Thus, the enlightenment saying, "Be a man in the street and a Jew in your home," was inverted into: "Speak Hebrew in the street and your own language at home." Hebrew triumphed in the framework of life. The reversal took place within four years of the city's existence!

In the Hebrew city, there was also a second wave of dissociation: the children who grew up in Hebrew in the school. The Hertseliya Gymnasium, one of the earliest buildings in the new city, had an important function: this was not a rural school only for the lower grades; it promoted instruction of genuine culture and language on the highest level, all in Hebrew. Yehoash (1872–1927), a Yiddish American poet who had no stake in Hebrew propaganda, tells of a group of Gymnasium students playing soccer in Tel Aviv in 1913:

> There were the usual screams and tussles, but not even in the exciting moments of the game did a non-Hebrew word come out of their mouths. For me, that was the best proof that the language had penetrated to their souls and was an organic part of their personality. A great victory for the pioneers of the revival of the language. (Yehoash 1917, 1:160)

The Hebrew they spoke united the children of the Hebrew city. That is, here too, *a horizontal age stratum* embraced the new language as its own, creating *a second wave of severance*, and distinguishing them from their Diaspora-born parents. Characteristically, in countries of immigration, the first-generation immigrants work hard attempting to assimilate but are still perceived by their children as immigrants, ignorant of the new conventions and speaking a broken language with a foreign intonation. The children then try to dissociate themselves from their parents—in fact, in order to fulfill their own parents' dream of belonging to the new language and culture (see, for example, Henry Roth's *Call It Sleep*). In this case, the language and its ideology were imposed on them by the idealist school, including the revulsion for the Diaspora as portrayed in Hebrew literature.

Indeed, the separation of age cohorts was the prominent sign of the emerging *Yishuv*: a child-oriented society if there ever was one. In Diaspora, the celebrated warmth of the Jewish family, expressing the drive to preserve the ever-threatened nation, was intended as a continuation of the chain of generations rather than as a break in it. Now, the children were one or two rather than twelve to a family, and the devotion to children was transformed into an apotheosis of the new "healthy" and "strong" race of the future. It was a society without parents, and, for the children growing up, without grandparents; the former admiration for grandfather as the source of wisdom was turned upside down, and the orientation of life was toward the utopian future, to be implemented by the next generation. Hebrew newspapers and weeklies used to carry special columns of language teaching (mainly arguing about the meanings of words and fighting against "distortions" of the spoken language) as well as columns quoting the wisdom and language innovations of "our sweet *sabras* [native-born children]."

The whole society was based on ideology, hence the authority of the ideologically sanctioned institutions: the school, the youth movements, the kibbutz, the underground army. The awareness of the ideological supremacy of the school and its Hebrew knowledge; the centrality of the youth movement; the intensive group activity of one age cohort (in a warm country, with small apartments, where life is centered outdoors); and later, the *Palmakh* (voluntary military units) located in the kibbutzim—all of it separated the young age group from their parents, strengthened Hebrew as the language of the young generation, and created a new life-style and a new culture.

Various statistics show a much higher percentage of Hebrew speakers among the Israeli-born or the young as compared with the adult population, and this is true, with fluctuations, from 1914 to this day. In part, this reflects an identity statement: certainly, Hebrew schoolchildren could speak Hebrew, but even if they did not do so well enough, or all the time, they could not afford to say so. But beyond that, children really created their own social cells and separated from their immigrant parents' world by a magic circle of Hebrew speech.

During the time of the Second Aliya, however, most education in the cities outside of Tel Aviv was still in foreign languages—until the big strike of teachers and students, the "war of languages" of 1913, gave a serious blow to German education. Even in the "Hebrew-speaking" communities, evidence about the extent of actual Hebrew speech varies greatly, depending on the ideology of the witness. Brener, the idolized literary authority of the Second Aliya, who settled in Palestine in 1909, mocks the level of spoken Hebrew in that period. For example, in *From Here and From There* (1910) the character Diasporin says:

> The Jews speak *jargon* [= Yiddish] here... Maybe in the editorial staff of *The Plow* they speak Hebrew, maybe the teachers with one another, but all the Jewish inhabitants of the place—the "aristocrats" speak Russian and the masses speak *jargon*... (Brener 1978a)

And even in *Bereavement and Failure* (1920), we read:

> So, Shneurson was captivated lately by a Sephardi woman... The Sephardi woman, like all her friends... of course, knows Ashkenazi jargon [= Yiddish] very well—no less than Shneurson himself (the fools abroad imagine that Hebrew is dominant... That's a story too!) [. . .] [Yet] the two of them pretend that only the Hebrew language is what brings them together. (Brener 1978b:1636)

Or elsewhere:

> After them, a refined young couple comes and sits down, a Hebrew-speaking couple.
> He is about nineteen, she is about sixteen—students in a national school. And
> amazingly, the content of their Hebrew talk this time is not about the pressing need
> for Hebrew speech, as usual, and not even about the emptiness and lack of meaning
> in life, but about another subject—about art itself! (Brener 1978b:1666–1667)

Despite the satire, however, an important principle was achieved: Hebrew speech
was the ideal horizon, Hebrew chatting was already possible, and in social life it
was considered *bon ton*.

In sum, what was established just before World War I was not a complete Hebrew-
speaking society but two bases: 1) Several *social cells*—primarily groups of workers and groups of children and youth—whose lives were conducted in Hebrew;
2) Several *public frameworks* that conducted their affairs in Hebrew. Within about
seven years, from the decision of *Ha-Poel Ha-Tsayir* to accept Hebrew as the
national language—to the control of the schools (i.e., between 1906 and 1913),
Hebrew in Eretz-Israel turned into the frame language of the Hebrew city, of the
Labor organizations, and of the "Hebrew" schools, and the base language of elite
social cells.

   During World War I, the Turks expelled most foreign citizens from Eretz-
Israel, including the Jews of Tel Aviv, and the Jewish population shriveled (from
85,000 to 56,000, which included the Orthodox "old *Yishuv*") and constituted
only 10% of the population of Palestine. When the *Yishuv* recovered, in the wake
of the Balfour Declaration and the British conquest of Palestine, and when waves
of immigrants arrived after the pogroms in Russia in 1919, that is, in the Third
Aliya that Brener dreamed of, a Hebrew Secular Polysystem was established on
the basis of the myth and ethos of the founding nucleus, the Second Aliya.

In 1918 the British army conquered all of Palestine and in 1922, the League of
Nations officially established the British Mandate over Palestine, with the condition that the Mandatory power be responsible for the implementation of the
Balfour Declaration; in paragraph 23, Hebrew was proclaimed one of the three
official languages of Palestine. Thus, what had been a language of several small,
isolated groups of teachers, workers, students, and the pioneers of the First Jewish
City became the *frame language* of the whole country. It was precisely because
the avant-garde of the Second Aliya consisted of only small numbers of "stubborn
people" compressed in ideologically controlled social cells that Hebrew could be
implemented almost in laboratory conditions. When some of them returned from
exile, they imposed their myth about the revolutionary conquest of work and
conquest of the language on society as a whole. The leadership of the *Yishuv* at
the beginning of the British Mandate came from this small group (including the
labor leaders Berl Katznelson, Yitzhak Tabenkin, David Ben-Gurion, Yitzhak Ben-

Tsvi), perhaps because they had the moral authority of having attempted self-realization and because they could speak Hebrew.

Berl Katznelson insisted that candidates for the Assembly of Representatives in 1919 could only be Hebrew-speakers, even though this decision affected some of his own comrades-in-arms, the soldiers of the Jewish Legion in World War I (many of them, from Britain and the United States); and that was barely nine years after he himself struggled to speak the language! His argument came from a pan-historical destiny: "In the life of the Hebrew worker in Eretz-Israel the question of languages does not exist. Hebrew history gave our people the land of Israel and the Hebrew language [only] one time. And the complete revival of Israel lies in the reinstatement of our people in its land and in its language, and in the renewal of a full, organic life." (See Berl Katznelson 1919b, "On the Question of Languages," translated in this volume.) Thus, Berl and the other Hebrew speakers of the Second Aliya dominated the institutions of the *Yishuv* when a new flood of immigrants arrived after the pogroms in Ukraine in 1919, the so-called Third Aliya, filled with socialist ideology, revolutionary impetus, and national pride. They also were socialists and could adapt to the revolutionary spirit and discourse of the Second Aliya, and enhance it.

If the Second Aliya created separate Hebrew social cells, a Hebrew city, and several institutional frameworks, it was only during the British Mandate that the Hebrew network spread over all of Palestine. Mandatory Palestine was what some sociologists call a *consociational State*, and the Hebrew society had its own separate network of political and educational institutions, officially conducted in Hebrew. Secular and religious political parties became legal and formed statewide networks. Since Turkish and French disappeared, Hebrew education took over and formed a statewide network, including a central Education Department, textbooks, and Teacher Seminars (as a matter of fact, there were several, separate educational organizations, affiliated with various political parties). The network of information and literature was covered by the modern Hebrew newspapers. Eventually, several underground military organizations that developed a system of wide-reaching mobilization emerged. But, except for the elected bodies, all these were voluntary frameworks.

A coherent and unified Hebrew Secular Polysystem, covering all aspects of social life, was launched by the labor movement—and to a large extent that accounts for the decisive power it attained in the *Yishuv*. Shortly after demobilization from the Jewish Legion in World War I, in 1919, Berl Katznelson wrote a proposal for the unity of the workers' movement. The proposal clearly appealed to a nation on the move, a nation of immigrants. In the spirit of the Second and Third Aliyot—and just a year after the Bolshevik Revolution in Russia, which impressed all of them—he opens with the statement: "The workers' movement in Eretz-Israel is a branch of the Socialist workers' movement in the world, striving to free man completely from the oppression of the existing system which imposes private capital on the life of the nation, on its economic and cultural creation, on the relations between people and States" (1919a:129). But, at the same time, it is a branch of the Zionist movement and its goal is: "The revival of the Israeli nation returning in masses to its land, striking root in its soil, creating its settlement and its work, and becoming a free nation, governing its own country, speaking its Hebrew language, arranging its life in its own domain, and creating and developing its material and spiritual treasures." In view of those twin goals, the united workers' movement would establish stations for the absorption of immigrants, a labor exchange, health services, a network for the distribution of products, a central cooperative of workers' kitchens, a workers' bank, a center for cultural action ("for spreading the language; and human, social, and professional education"), a free press, and a publishing house ("for the education and cultural enlightenment of the worker"). Though some socialist parties in Europe had similar ambitions, here it is a program for the invention of a centralized State rather than a labor party.

Berl Katznelson and the leaders of the *Histadrut* ("Hebrew Labor Federation in Eretz-Israel," founded in 1920) implemented this vision when they established under its wings not only a federation of professional labor unions and a network of collective settlements but also: a construction company, *Solel u-Boneh* (Pave-and-Build); a concern for the production of building materials, *Even ve-Sid* (stone-and-plaster); an industrial concern, *Ḥevrat ovdim* (Workers' Company); a distribution network, *Ha-Mashbir La-Tsarkan* (Provider for the Consumer); a mutual-aid health organization, *Kupat Ḥolim* (Sick Bank); workers' kitchens, *mis'adot poalim* (Workers' Restaurants); a publishing house, *Am Oved* (Working Nation); and a network of schools, *Zerem Ovdim* (Workers' Trend) (typically, those were two-word names like those of the old Religious Polysystem, e.g., the hospital society *Mishmeret Kholim* [Sick Guard], the burial society *Khevre Kadishe* [Holy Society], or the aid society *Gemiles Khesed* [Alm of Grace]). The major mouthpiece and informational base of this cluster was the newspaper *Davar*, founded in 1925 and edited by Berl Katznelson, which promoted Hebrew as the prevailing language in the society and allocated a place of honor for belles-lettres, as did newspapers in the Diaspora. (Its one-word name—like the one-word names of Diaspora Hebrew newspapers, *Ha-Melitz, Ha-Magid, Ha-Shaḥar, Ha-Shiloaḥ*, or the Eretz-Israeli *Ha-Aretz*—was a plurisignifying term, meaning: "[concrete] thing," "Word," "[prophetic] sermon," "message," all in one, and thus epitomizing the return to Biblical connotations.) And soon enough, a whole network of journals covered the institutional network: a women-worker's weekly, a teachers' journal, a kibbutz kindergarten-teachers' journal, health publications, and so on.

The sweeping creation, almost overnight, of a secular polysystem with Hebrew as its frame language was so impressive that in 1922, the British Colonial Secretary, Winston Churchill, wrote:

> During the last three or four generations the Jews have recreated in Palestine a community, now numbering 80,000, of whom about one-fourth are farmers or

workers upon the land. This community has its own political organs; an elected assembly for the direction of its domestic concerns; elected councils in the towns; and an organization for the control of its schools. It has its elected chief rabbinate and rabbinical Council for the direction of its religious affairs. Its business is conducted in Hebrew as a vernacular language, and a Hebrew press serves its needs. It has its distinctive intellectual life and displays considerable economic activity. This community, then, with its town and country population, its political, religious, and social organizations, its own language, its own customs, its own life, has in fact "national" characteristics. ("The Churchill White Paper," Laqueur 1969:47; also quoted by Ornan 1976)

Horowitz and Lissak wrote perceptively about the immigrants from Oriental countries that came to Israel in the 1950s:

The exposure of the immigrants from Islamic countries to the combined influence of the *industrial revolution*, the *secular revolution*, and the *national revolution*—occurred only upon their arrival in Israel. Here they had to integrate into a society whose institutions were formed by elite groups whose universe of values was crystallized under the influence of those three revolutions, and they strove, accordingly, to create in Eretz-Israel a nation-State, modern in its cultural character and economic development. (Horowitz and Lissak 1990:18; my emphasis—B.H.)

True. Yet almost the same can be said about those very "elite groups," the Ashkenazi founders of the *Yishuv*, when they first arrived in the country. Almost all of them were born in small towns, with no electricity or running water and little tolerance for secular behavior. They did not see there any industrial, secular, or national revolutions. Most of them broke out of the "medieval" confines of the *shtetl* for a few years before they emigrated, but they derived the *secular* and *national revolutions* not from real life (in tsarist Russia?) but from books, ideologies, and arguments; it was no political reality they could have experienced, but the freedom of their own, voluntary, multiparty, Jewish Secular Polysystem in the making—conducted in Yiddish—where they could experiment with the new sensibilities, disregarding the totalitarian tsarist regime. After a few years of going through this revolution in their youth, a few of them went to Palestine and tried to implant those sensibilities in the new country by means of the new language. Certainly, very few of them had any experience with the *industrial revolution* until they accomplished it themselves in Palestine. Thus, modernization, embracing the secular, national, and industrial revolutions, and promoting avant-garde literature, was part and parcel of their Zionist realization and helped to expand the domains of the new language. The difference was that they underwent this triple revolution in their own lives, whereas the immigrants of the 1950s had to adapt to a ready-made situation.

The kibbutz movement too was not just a return to Jewish peasants or farmers; it strove to combine agriculture, industry, culture, and defense, that is, to create in its small settlements a new, utopian class that would merge the classes of peasants, workers, soldiers, and intelligentsia. Every kibbutz movement established a publishing house, educational institutions, journals, and museums; and today, almost every kibbutz has a factory besides its fields, and often a museum or another cultural institution.

The kibbutzim, formed after World War I, were the quintessential form of the new society. Like Tel Aviv, those were purely Jewish settlements and, like the workers' collectives, they constituted new cells of young people conducting an intensive social life. Their social framework was Hebrew: the weekly assembly, education, cultural activity. For them, Hebrew was not simply a new language to supplant their first language while talking about customary matters; Hebrew carried a whole new universe of discourse and a new semiotics, reflecting domains of life entirely new both to them and to the Hebrew language. The terms for nature and agriculture—the entire context of their existence—were unknown to them in any previous language; in those domains, Hebrew was their first language. Hence, the "conquest of the language" was intertwined with the "conquest of work," and with a new understanding of nature, love, the independence of women, armed self-defense, and a democratic or communist-democratic society. They learned all those new worlds of life along with the Hebrew words denoting them, which they uncovered or invented as they went along.

Unlike the workers' groups of the Second Aliya, the kibbutz was not an itinerant collective of mostly male laborers, but a village on its own land; it had to become a normal settlement to last for generations, and children now occupied an important place. The children were separated from their parents and received a "collective education," intended to breed the New Hebrew, of sound mind and body, a person of the commune, endowed with collective consciousness. The parents' generation had already cut themselves off sharply from the Diaspora world of their parents. Now a second wave of dissociation was implemented, taking the main tasks of education out of the hands of parents, who might still retain some "Diaspora mentality" and "bourgeois" or "individualistic" habits. Collective and separate education included the exclusivity of the Hebrew language, which was separated from the mutterings in Yiddish or Russian in the parents' tent. The kibbutzim constituted only a small minority of the *Yishuv*, but, outside of Tel Aviv, those were the only purely Jewish territories; this is where the lofty myth of the new Eretz-Israel was implanted, and this was the educational goal of most Zionist youth movements in Diaspora (even if many of their members eventually ended up in the city). Hundreds of thousands of young people went through the kibbutz, its Hebrew society, and its Hebrew educational system. In the 1930s, children brought from Germany were also educated in a separate Hebrew framework of *Aliyat Ha-No'ar* (Youth Aliya), located mainly in the kibbutzim.

Thus, *several stages of severance from the chain of generations and several waves of horizontal social cohorts* in this young, antitribal society, combined with an orientation toward the future instead of the past, under conditions of a voluntary society governed by an ideology, compressed on a small island isolated from the Jewish world of that time, and preserving dominance over newspapers and schools—created the frame of a Hebrew society.

The general outline of the evolution can be summed up thus: in the First Aliya, a few individuals emerged who could speak Hebrew but did not use it regularly. Several teachers with no formal education devoted themselves to learning how to teach the language, and their pupils carried the torch, mostly as individuals. The Second Aliya demonstrated the possibility of setting up *enclosed Hebrew social cells* in opposition to their non-Hebrew-speaking Jewish environment, and *a public framework of life* in Hebrew. In the Third Aliya, however, a *Secular Hebrew Polysystem* was constructed and imposed on the new Jews of the whole country, politically sanctioned by the Mandatory government. The written frameworks, the meetings and assemblies, the technical literature, and so on—everything was, at least nominally, conducted in Hebrew. The entire "organized *Yishuv*" operated like this.

At the same time, there is a great deal of evidence (mostly overlooked by the ideological studies of the history of Zionism) that, within this framework, the embattled Yiddish and other native languages continued their daily existence, though they were incessantly attacked, especially by the fanatic "Brigade of the Defenders of the Language." On the third anniversary of the Brigade in Jerusalem, in 1928, Menakhem Usishkin, a prominent Zionist leader, said:

> The Hebrew language was turned into "the solemn language" or "the beloved language": official assemblies and Zionist conferences open in Hebrew; the official Zionist leaders, among them some who don't know Hebrew even after thirty years of membership in the Zionist organization, express sympathy for the language, and then the assembly or conference continues not in Hebrew. [. . .] Even today, "Hebrews" are treated as "Natives" in the full sense of this term [i.e., in the British colonial, derogatory sense—B.H.]. (Usishkin 1928:3)

The dangerous enemies Usishkin observed were "jargon" (i.e., Yiddish) and English, "the language of making a living" (*sfat ha-parnasa*). Of course, Usishkin was a fanatic; even in Odessa he threw the greatest Hebrew writer Mendele out of the *Bney Moshe* lodge for writing Yiddish. But, ultimately, the precarious balance in the "war of languages" was won for Hebrew in Eretz-Israel. Although, at home, many Jews still held on to other languages, the growth of a new generation, whose language was presented as the social ideal and who refused to learn the language of their parents, brought Hebrew speech into their homes as well. Whether or not they knew Hebrew well, they spoke it under the pressure of society and of their own children. As soon as Hebrew was established as the base language of society and the exclusive language of education, the matter was simply turned over to the young generation that grew up in the Hebrew schools.

The continuing waves of immigration did not upset the balance, first because many pioneers coming from Europe acquired the language in the new Hebrew schools and Zionist youth movements that emerged there; second, because of the powerful pressure the established ideological society exerted on all immigrant waves; and above all, because it is relatively simple to adapt to a language of an existing society, as in all countries of immigration.

The youngsters who carried out the revolution were a generation unto themselves. As a small, select kernel of stubborn, inspired, self-made men and women, they knew their own importance, unique in history. They shook off the established leadership of their own parties in Diaspora and, with time, took over the world Zionist organizations. Neither would they easily transfer the reins of revolution to the next generation. The power in Eretz-Israel, the leadership of all parties and institutions, was in the hands of those "converts to Hebrew," like Berl Katznelson and David Ben-Gurion; Israeli-born and Hebrew-educated young people had no access to power. It is only the generation that emerged as young officers in the War of Independence, that provided a second echelon of a new leadership (Yigal Alon, Yitzhak Rabin, Moshe Dayan). To this day, most ministers in the Israeli governments are not Israeli-born. That may not be a language problem per se, but it certainly reflects something about the semiotics of culture.

TWENTY-SEVEN

Ashkenazi or Sephardi Dialect?

The rejection of the Diaspora and the "*shtetl*" world of their parents made the Ashkenazi revivers of the language choose what they thought was the "Sephardi" dialect for the new, spoken Hebrew. That was such a radical social and ideological decision that it needs further clarification.

In English and other languages, speech patterns have changed in the course of history, and only much later did the spelling stabilize; in Hebrew, the opposite was true: the sanctified spelling of the Bible was preserved in its minutest details throughout the ages, but different dialects, developed by Jews in distant lands and under very different foreign influences, gave rise to several different pronunciations of the same spellings.

Ashkenazi Hebrew pronunciation was formed in Central and Eastern Europe some time after the thirteenth century, then branched out into several dialects and survived in Orthodox communities until the present. This was the Hebrew language that had brought the Zionist immigrants to Eretz-Israel. Once here, they threw out even the Hebrew of their childhood, repressed whatever their memories could express in it, and chose a fundamentally different, foreign accent. Ben-Yehuda and the first Hebrew speakers in Jerusalem had compelling social reasons: the established Jewish community in Jerusalem was Sephardi, it carried the respect of the glorious Spanish Jewry, and the title "Pure Sephardi" (*Sfaradi tahor*) had an aristocratic ring to it. A similar connotation carried over to the language, as is indicated by the name of the society, *safa brura*, meaning "clear," "precise," or select language. Hebrew was not used in the daily affairs of the Sephardi community, except for precise reading of holy texts, hence the vowels were not changed and the words not contracted, as in the living language, Yiddish. Thus the Sephardi pronunciation sounded more prestigious than that of the Ashkenazi Orthodox Jews of the "Old *Yishuv*" in Jerusalem (who excommunicated Ben-Yehuda twice). It was also part of his romantic attraction for things Oriental.

There were also "scientific" justifications for the choice of the Sephardi pronunciation. For example, the blurring of the distinction between the Biblical vowels *patah* and *kamatz* (and reading both as **a**) can be found in the Septuagint (the Greek translation of the Bible) and hence in European transcriptions of Biblical names (e.g., *David* rather than the Ashkenazi *Dovid*). The Biblical distinction between *milra* and *mil'eyl* (the place of stress on the ultimate and the penultimate syllable, respectively) was known to the Hebrew grammarians of the Vilna Enlightenment, Ben-Ze'ev and Adam Ha-Cohen Levinson (following the tradition of Hebrew and Christian medieval grammarians). This distinction favored the ultimate stress on most words, as performed in the "Sephardi" accent of the Near East. More important, it is indicated in the accent marks of the Bible, and a fundamentalist return had to consider it. But Biblical fundamentalism could also have claimed that the precise distinction of *vowels* in the Bible was better preserved by Ashkenazi and not by Sephardi Hebrew and that it was the Ashkenazim and the Yemenites who maintained the distinction between *patah* (**a**) and *kamats* (**o**) and between the hard *tav* (**t**) and the soft *tav* (**s**).[62]

Yehoash, who was impressed by the natural language of the young people who learned their Hebrew in the new, "national" schools, describes the effort and artificiality of the speech of the adults, even those who knew Hebrew well:

> As for the language itself, that's half the grief. But the Sephardi accent... A pious Jew told me with a sigh that he tried over and over again to pray in the *Sephardi accent* but his tongue stuck to the roof of his mouth and he didn't understand the "meaning of the words"... Since then, he decided that, in the street, he would do as they did in the street but, in the synagogue, give him the old accent of Shnipishok! [A Jewish suburb of Vilna] (Yehoash 1917, 1:161)

When the immigrants of the Second Aliya arrived in Eretz-Israel, the so-called "Sephardi" pronunciation was already a *fait accompli*; the rural school in the agricultural settlements introduced the study of Hebrew and instruction of other disciplines in Hebrew, and the authority of the sages of Jerusalem was decisive for the few Hebrew teachers. But this was a grammar school that did not teach literature and did not even suspect that a great Hebrew poetry in the Ashkenazi dialect had emerged in Europe at that same time and had, indeed, influenced a new wave of Zionist immigrants.

Parents vehemently opposed the Sephardi dialect, strange to their ears, their prayers, and their understanding of Hebrew, but the few nationalist Hebrew teachers felt superior and imposed their will in the schools. The Teachers' Assembly in 1903, organized and influenced by Menakhem Usishkin (an activist characterized by his virulent hatred of Yiddish), who arrived specially from Odessa, decided on the Sephardi pronunciation for the new language. The teachers' orga-

---

62. Indeed, the Nobel Prize–winning Hebrew novelist Agnon, who never fully learned to speak in the Sephardi accent, regretted that the Yemenite pronunciation was not accepted; he apparently did not dare to mention the Ashkenazi.

nization was the major vehicle for teaching the young generation Hebrew and played a decisive role in implementing the accent. But they compromised too: the handwriting they selected was Ashkenazi!—Unlike speech that had to be invented, handwriting was inherited for generations, and that was, apparently, too hard to change, even for devoted teachers.

Thus the last gasp of the First Aliya determined the language of the Second. It was a fluke of history, the last collective effort of those few who, in principle, spoke the language and hardly knew the new Hebrew poetry that flourished in Diaspora, the teachers (and even that effort was organized from the outside). Indeed, the Second Aliya starts officially in December 1903, with the arrival of the refugees from the Homel Self-Defense. But it began in earnest only after the failure of the Russian Revolution and the mass emigration of Jews from Russia, in 1906, and was enhanced around 1910, when some of the intelligentsia of the Second Aliya arrived. The ideological, labor wing of the Second Aliya did not think about educating children until after World War I—and then it would be too late to change the language. And the immigrants to the cities surrendered their understanding to that of the established new school.[63]

But, outside of this historical accident, there were strong social and ideological motivations in favor of the "Sephardi" dialect. For one, accepting the "Sephardi" dialect was eventually important for the melting pot of Jewish tribes in Israel; it was designed to bring the Sephardi Jews closer to the new Ashkenazi establishment, and the other tribes would follow suit. The Jerusalem propagators of the language, Ben-Yehuda and David Yelin (who intermarried with a Sephardi family), had the socialization with Sephardim in mind; and they did influence the teachers and the normative Language Committee. But this argument was irrelevant at the time of the formation of a Hebrew-speaking society in the lowland of Palestine. The labor movement and the settlers of Tel Aviv were absorbed in their own Russian-derived, intensively pursued, and "superior" world of ideas; they did not even see the Yemenites with their distinct accent and paid little attention to the Galitsyaner S. Y. Agnon (until their own Brener discovered him).

Not less important: accepting the "Sephardi" accent helped overcome the boundaries between the various Ashkenazi subdialects, which provided a linguistic garb to the animosities, mutual contempt, and even hatred between Jewish ethnic groups that had lived for centuries in different territories: the *Litvaks, Poylishe, Galitsyaner, Romanians, Russians,* and *Yekes* (German Jews). Shlomo Tsemakh describes his first attempts to speak Hebrew:

---

63. As a matter of fact, we don't know much about the actual pronunciation of Hebrew by people who learned their first Hebrew in the Ashkenazi accent. Agnon, who arrived with the Second Aliya, preserved Ashkenazi features in his speech to his last day; and so did many members of his generation. In the old kibbutzim, you could still hear Ashkenazi traces in a general "Sephardi" stress-pattern: **oMARtsi** rather than the contemporary Israeli **aMARti**.

All the time, my words were accompanied by mighty waves of laughter rolling out of all mouths. My Hebrew language, this broken language of a Jew from Poland, which makes every U into I, every O into U, every long E into AY, and every long O becomes a prolonged OOY—this distorted language was certainly quite ridiculous. (Tsemakh 1965:80)

In Tsemakh's Polish dialect, the pronunciation was **BUrikh Atu** rather than the Lithuanian **BOrukh Ato**; instead of **eyn** they say **Ayen**, instead of **MElekh** they say **MAYlekh**, and so on. Also characteristic was the complaint about the diphthongs frequent in the Ashkenazi dialect, reminiscent of the sighing "oy" of the Diaspora Jew.

Tsemakh's inferiority complex for his Polish dialect—which in Diaspora was expressed in reverence toward the "pure" and "rational" Litvak Yiddish or Hebrew—was now transferred to the new "Litvaks," to the "pure" Sephardic pronunciation of the language (which he admired even in the speeches of the Ashkenazi teacher Yudelevitsh, delivered "in a beautiful Sephardi accent"). The new dialect would erase all tribal differences between East European Jews.

But the issue goes deeper than that: the basis for this inferiority complex lies, paradoxically, in the very fact that, in Ashkenaz, Hebrew was a semiliving language. Indeed, there were three modes of using Ashkenazi Hebrew (in all its dialects): Ideal, Spoken, and Fluent Ashkenazi.[64] a) *Ideal Ashkenazi* was reserved for reading the Torah in the synagogue; it consisted in pronouncing precisely every single sign of the canonical vocalization, with a fixed vowel assigned to each diacritic sign. b) *Spoken Ashkenazi* was the Hebrew that merged in Yiddish and hence was used as part of a living language; here, all final syllables lost their specific vowels (for some neutral **e**) and compounds were contracted into shorter words. Thus, the night-prayer was called *krishme* rather than the Ideal Ashkenazi *kriyas shma* ("calling the *shema*"); *balebos* rather than *ba'al ha-bayis* (homeowner; boss); and the feminine *baleboste* rather than *ba'alas ha-bayis*. Those who looked at the written words felt that the original sounds were distorted, "swallowed," abused. This, however, is a natural process in all living languages: French has, similarly, lost the last syllables in its verb declensions (still preserved in spelling); English can be seen as having "perverted" the German disyllabic **Na-me** into a monosyllabic **name** (pronounced **neym**), or **lachen** into **laugh** (**laf**). c) *Fluent Ashkenazi* was the way authentic Hebrew texts were pronounced in study and argument, mostly under the influence of Spoken Ashkenazi—and this was the dominant way of pronouncing and hearing Hebrew. And on top of this, the Yiddish dialect distinctions were superimposed on all three ways of pronunciation.

From the position of a fundamentalist return to the written, pure and precise,

---

64. I described the three modes in *The Meaning of Yiddish* (1990a:55–57) under the labels "Ideal," "Merged," and "Practical Ashkenazi Hebrew."

Biblical language, this seemed a perversion, reflecting the perverse, sloppy, irrational behavior of Diaspora Jews. Even worse, the spelling of Hebrew in Rabbinic and Hasidic writings was influenced by this semispoken language and often disregarded Hebrew grammar.[65] Also, the gender of Hebrew words was often changed, under the influence of the spoken language, where Hebrew was part of Yiddish. The *Haskala* writers viciously parodied this style (notably, in Yosef Perl's anti-Hasidic satire, *Megale Tmirin*) and saw in it the deterioration of the Holy Tongue rather than the evolution of a living language and its dialects. The Zionist movement inherited this revulsion toward Rabbinic and Hasidic Hebrew, especially in its wish to skip two thousand years of history and return to the wholesome Bible.

The stereotype, first formulated most harshly by Moses Mendelssohn, that Yiddish was a perverted language (as compared to literary northern German), reflecting the perversion of the soul of the Diaspora Jew, was as relevant for Ashkenazi Hebrew (as compared to the written Bible). The revulsion from this dialect, therefore, is a recoil from Diaspora existence, from the Yiddish language—the mother tongue, intimate and hated at the same time, from their parents' home in the *shtetl*, corroded by idleness and Jewish trading, and from the world of prayer, steeped in the scholastic and irrelevant study of Talmud, and the irrational and primitive behavior of the Hasidim. The decision in favor of the Sephardi dialect was part of the ideological package the individual forced on his life. It seemed that the Sephardi dialect would free them from all those ugly sounds and dialectal discrepancies. Since its language was not spoken, it mirrored precisely the written words, clearly pronouncing especially the last syllable, now stressed, which was so contorted in Ashkenazi. In short, it was easier to learn a new language, beautiful and dignified, than to correct their own contructed, "cockney" Hebrew. But that move was aided by various ideologies.

Like other proponents of Hebrew, Eliezer Ben-Yehuda, born in a small town in Lithuania, first abandoned Yiddish for Russian culture and even Russian nationalism and Slavophile ideology (influenced by the wave of Russian patriotism during the Russian war against Turkey in 1877–78, defending the Slavs in Bulgaria). Then he went to Paris, where he met a Russian named Tshashnikov, who encouraged him in the idea of Jewish national revival:

> I happened upon a "Goyish head," a man with a simple mind, a natural man, who saw things in the world as they were and not through broken and perverted light beams, the way things looked to the crooked brains in the over-clever head of the Diaspora Jew. (Ben-Yehuda 1986:66)

---

65. For example, the suffixes pronounced in Israeli Hebrew as **at, ut, ot** (feminine genitive, collective noun, feminine plural, respectively) and in Ideal Ashkenazi as **as, us, oys**, were all conflated into the same **-es**. In spelling, they were often confused and interchangeable.

Under the influence of this idealized Russian, Ben-Yehuda shifted his nationalist fervor from Russian to Hebrew. He had no respect for the Hebrew of the Ashkenazi religious world but, on the contrary, was impressed by anyone who spoke with a hint of a Sephardi accent: the writer Yeḥiel-Mikhel Pines, who came from Jerusalem to Paris; Getzl Zelikovitsh (later a Yiddish poet and professor of Semitics in Philadelphia), who brought it from his travels in the East; the Jews whom Ben-Yehuda encountered during his own sojourn in Algiers; and, later, the people of the Sephardic cultural milieu which he knew during his long years in Jerusalem. In his memoirs, he describes his shock when he and his wife first came to Jerusalem and were invited to the home of the editor of a Hebrew newspaper, *Havatselet*: they spoke Yiddish there and Ben-Yehuda's wife was asked to cover her head with a kerchief—and there she was, a "young woman who just came *from Europe* where she was exposed to a *free life* and had very nice brown hair" (Ben-Yehuda 1986:90; emphases mine—B.H.). The opposition is: European culture and individual dignity versus the "Diaspora" (i.e., Ashkenazi) restricted Jewish world. Ben-Yehuda also aspires to edit a "Hebrew political national [i.e., secular] newspaper, in the European meaning of those words" (90). But he finds the ideal of beauty in the Eastern world. Even on the ship to Eretz-Israel, he is impressed by the Arab passengers: "Tall, strong men [. . .] I sensed that they felt themselves citizens of that land," while "I come to that land as a stranger, a foreigner" (84). The admiration for the East also included Sephardi Jews:

> Most of the people of the old *Yishuv* [i.e., the Orthodox Ashkenazim] were not natural human beings, leading natural lives, making a living like everybody else. Only the Sephardi community [. . .] was more or less a natural community, for most of them were simple people, uneducated, supporting themselves with crafts and simple work. (95)

And he goes on:

> Why should I deny it? It is a better, much nicer impression that was made on me by the Sephardim. Most of them were dignified, handsome, all were splendid in their Oriental clothing, their manner respectable, their behavior pleasant, almost all of them spoke Hebrew with the owner of *Havatselet*, and their language was fluent, natural, rich in words, rich in fixed idioms of speech, and the dialect was so original, *so sweet and Oriental!* (97; my emphasis—B.H.)

Clearly, the language was part of a total package in which the Ashkenazim were on the negative pole, as he said explicitly:

> The Ashkenazi visitors of all classes all had a Diaspora countenance. Only the older ones [. . .] were already a bit "assimilated" into the Sephardim and looked a bit like them. [. . .] And the Diaspora stamp was a bit wiped off their faces too. (97)

In another place, he gets excited:

> How much the Sephardi Jews love cleanliness and how strict they are about it even in the secret places, the most private rooms. [. . .] And all household and cooking utensils were truly sparkling with cleanliness. (106)

Ben-Yehuda is aware of his one-sided value judgment: "I mentioned this detail here incidentally *because it is one of the reasons that influenced me later in my relationship toward Sephardim and Ashkenazim*" (107; my emphasis—B.H.).

Although Ben-Yehuda knows "that, scientifically, there is no true or false pronunciation" (205), he assumes that "the dialect used among western [i.e., European] Jews is from a late period, from the time of the spoilage and distortion of the language" (212), and he fights for "the Oriental dialect": "It is the dialect of the Hebrew language that is alive in Eretz-Israel, and everyone who heard it spoken by the new generation is stunned by its beauty" (212). But the admiration combines beauty and strength:

> [because we lost the Oriental ring of the letters *tet, ayin, kuf,*] we deprive our language of its force and power by the contempt we have for the emphatic consonants, and because of that, the whole language is soft, weak, without the special strength the emphatic consonant gives to the word. (203)

Despite the acceptance of the Sephardi accent in the schools, Ben-Yehuda understands its superficial nature and the prevailing general tone of the Ashkenazi heritage; he fears that we may be too late: there are already thousands of children speaking Hebrew, and their language is "so un-Oriental, so lacking in the ring and force of an Oriental Semitic language!" (204). Indeed, when the new Language Committee begins to work again in 1911 and sees its main task as coining new words, they decide to appoint among its members persons "whose knowledge of both languages, Hebrew and Arabic, is beyond any doubt." In the *Foundations* of the new Language Committee, written by Ben-Yehuda, presented by David Yelin, and accepted by the Committee (published in 1912), the first paragraph defines "The Function of the Committee" in two points:

1) to prepare the Hebrew language for use as a spoken language in all matters of life [. . .]
2) to preserve the Oriental quality of the language [. . .] (Academy 1970:31)

The conclusion is: to demand the study of pronunciation in special classes and by a teacher of the Arabic [sic![66]] language. In 1915, the Hebrew Language Committee in Jerusalem decided

> to compel all schools in Eretz-Israel to appoint a special teacher for pronunciation and to select for this position in particular one of the sages of Aleppo [that is, not a trained teacher, nor a member of the Ashkenazi community to which the children in the new settlements belonged, but a Syrian Jew whose native language is Arabic!—B.H.]. (207)

---

66. Reuven Sivan, the editor of this text, assumes that there must be a mistake here and that he meant to say "Hebrew," but there is no evidence for this conjecture, and why would one have to stress that the Hebrew teacher must be the one to teach Hebrew pronunciation?

(The "Sephardi" dialect that was chosen was essentially the dialect of the Jews of Syria; Aleppo, or Haleb, in Northern Syria had an influential Jewish community.) Ben-Yehuda, who was opposed to absorbing words into the new Hebrew from any non-Semitic languages, thought it advisable *to use all the roots of Arabic to enrich the Hebrew language.* Since Ben-Yehuda and David Yelin had influence on the few Hebrew teachers, the Sephardi accent was, basically, accepted, but the Oriental nature of pronunciation he dreamed of was contrary to the whole mentality and intonations of the new immigrants, and never took root.

On the contrary, the ultranationalist and gifted poet and writer Ze'ev (Vladimir) Jabotinsky, in his book *Hebrew Pronunciation* (still trying to mold the pronunciation of the new language in 1930!), opposed the Arabic pronunciation and claimed that our ancestors did not speak with an "Arabic accent" either. Canaan, he argued, was teeming with races, including the "remnants of the nations of Europe and Anatolia," that is, *Aryans* (sic!), all of whom were swallowed up within Judea and Israel:

> Thus the Hebrew was formed as a Mediterranean man, in whose blood and soul several aspirations and several flavors of the nations of the North and of the West were blended. [. . .] To set the rules for the pronunciation of the renewed Hebrew, if we must seek points of support in other languages, let us look for them not in Arabic but in Western languages, especially in those which were born or developed on the shores of the Mediterranean. I am sure, for example, that the general impression of the sound, the "prosody" of ancient Hebrew was much more similar to that of Greece and Rome than to Arabic. (Jabotinsky 1930:6–8)

And he adds:

> I admit openly and confess that the guiding "taste" for the outline proposed in this manual is a European taste and not an "Oriental" one. In my proposals, the reader will find a clear tendency to get rid of all those sounds which have no basis in the phonetics of Western languages—*to bring our pronunciation as close as possible to the concept of the beauty of sound prevalent in Europe*: that concept of beauty, that musical yardstick according to which, for example, the Italian language is considered "beautiful" and the Chinese language is not. I chose this yardstick, first of all, because *we are Europeans and our musical taste is European*, the taste of Rubinstein and Mendelssohn and Bizet. But also from the objective side of the problem I am sure, for reasons I explained above, that the pronunciation proposed in this book is truly closer to the "correct" pronunciation, to the ancient sound of our language as spoken by our ancient forefathers than is the pronunciation that imitates the Arabic gutturals; let alone the slovenly pronunciation, lacking any line or rule or taste, with which we jargoned [i.e., Yiddishized] our speech and defiled *our language, one of the most splendid and noble languages in the world,* to the point of a noise without variation or character. (9; my emphasis—B.H.)

Thus, Jabotinsky too preached the renewal of pronunciation as part of the ideological and emotional package; but, according to him, "beauty" is exemplified not by Arabic but by Italian, and Yiddish (which he himself used in political speeches and articles) is even uglier than Arabic. He even ingeniously finds a similarity in the ideal language English: "A *furtive patah*, for example,[67] is a characteristic quality of English pronunciation: *pair, deer, door, poor*, pronounced **peyah, deyah, doah, poah** [sic!]" (7).

Although, in his opinion too, it is impossible to guess the sounds of the Hebrew pronunciation in the time of our forefathers, Jabotinsky has no doubt that

> one thing is clear—their pronunciation was marked by an outstanding precision. They did not speak hastily, they did not swallow syllables, did not confuse vowels—in short, they did not know the sloppy way of speaking that is heard now in our streets. (3)

The hatred for Yiddish stands out:

> First of all, we have to avoid the Yiddish **ch**, which is like the hoarse cough of someone with a throat disease. Even the German **ch** in the word *doch* is too guttural. *We should learn from those Jews of Russia who speak without a Yiddish accent* the proper pronunciation of the Russian letter *X*. (My emphasis—B.H.)

Thus the Russian writer Jabotinsky, himself a native of the Yiddish-speaking city Odessa, barely one generation out of the "ghetto." Like the teachers of modern Yiddish secular schools in the cities of Diaspora, he too regarded the singsong of the provincial Jew as something melodramatic and harmful. And what venom permeates his words, ostensibly written as a scientific, medical recipe:

> Do not sing while you speak. This ugliness is infinitely worse than every other defect I have mentioned and, regrettably, it is taking root in our life. Both the school and the stage are guilty: the first, out of sloppiness, the latter, out of an intention to "revive" for us the ghetto and its whining. *The tune of the ghetto* is ugly not only because of its weeping tone which stirs unpleasant memories in us: it is also *ugly objectively, ugly in the scientific sense*—ugly as all superfluous or exaggerated efforts. [. . .] That sick frenzy, which we also suffer from in our social life, is also the result of the Diaspora—an abundance of forces with no field and no outlet for the repressed storm except to explode in a bowl of soup—the "singsong" of ghetto speech is nothing but an echo of this national disease. The exercise that helps against the disease is very simple: exercising monotony—"monotony" in the scientific sense of the word, that is, lack of all vacillation in intonation. (37–38; my emphasis—B.H.)

In the debate over the dialect among the teachers in Rishon Le-Tsiyon in 1892, someone brought up the advantage of hearing Hebrew from parents and in the synagogue, in the Ashkenazi dialect, and the danger that if the school introduces the Sephardi dialect, the student's "mind will be confused." Y. Grazovski (Gur) responded:

---

67. As in the Hebrew letters *ayn* and *het* at the end of a word, which acquire an additional *a* vowel after a previous vowel: *reah, koah, luah*, etc.

It is better for the children not to understand the mistakes of their fathers, who read without preserving the vocalization and not correctly. Let the child talk in a correct Sephardi accent, let him get used to that, and there is no damage if he does not understand his father's dialect. (Karmi 1986:80; my emphasis—B.H.)

Thus, the second dissociation from the past was supported by education. Indeed, the religious "old *Yishuv*" and the parents of schoolchildren in the settlements fought against spoken Hebrew, the national school, and the Sephardi accent, all of which seemed to undermine the religious tradition. Mrs. Pukhatshevski from Rishon Le-Tsiyon told proudly of a demonstration in Jerusalem organized by two wagonfuls of settlers from Rishon, headed by the teacher David Yudelevitsh, and speaking Hebrew aloud in the street; the Jews in Jerusalem said: "Look, *goyim* speak Hebrew!" (by *goyim* they meant secular heretics). She tells the story as evidence of the miracle of living Hebrew speech but does not recognize the religious scorn for the national movement.

But, out of great concern for the correct pronunciation of the future farmers, the connection was also broken with the new Hebrew poetry, whose flourishing was no less miraculous than the revival of the spoken language, even though it happened in Europe.

Secular Hebrew poetry grew in the soil of Hebrew study in the religious society, against which all Hebrew poets rebelled in their youth. At the base of his poetic language, a poet will use his most intimate vocabulary as he heard and absorbed it in childhood, with all emotions and connotations attached to it and in the multidirectional context of texts and images it evokes. This is especially true for a language remembered from childhood and youth, when they were immersed in it for long days, year after year, and not heard in the adult milieu. Hence, in spite of the knowledge of grammar that claimed a different, "correct" (as Bialik later admitted) pronunciation, Hebrew poetry accepted the intimate, Ashkenazi pronunciation of their childhood and created many variations of musical meters and sound patterns in it, both in original poetry and in translations. With the change of pronunciation, all this poetry of the Renaissance Period, in fact, has been lost as rhythmic texts. From the point of view of Hebrew poetry, this was the second language revolution, a tragic one. If Bialik's poetry is taught today in Israeli schools, it is not taught as poetry that activates the reader's sense of rhythm, but rather as a bundle of well-known ideas, a reconstructed biography, or a texture of devices and figures.

Many poets were opposed to the "Sephardi" shift and felt that the musicality of the Ashkenazi pronunciation, with its many vowels and diphthongs and its flexible and balanced stress position, was lost in Israeli Hebrew. But Hebrew poetry was not in Eretz-Israel when the decision was made (by such estranged and pro-Oriental zealots as Ben-Yehuda or coarse agitators as Usishkin). Bialik was the idolized "National Poet" and had an immense influence on his readers around the world; Hebrew literature in Europe educated the generations of immigrants, but did not understand or believe in the importance of the dialect revolution that occurred in the "primitive" *Yishuv*. Most of them did not believe in the language revival altogether, in its feasibility, or in the cultural level of the Palestine Jewish peasants.

With the exception of Brener, most important Hebrew writers settled in Eretz-Israel only after the Bolshevik government banned Hebrew in Russia in 1921, and many went first to Western Europe and came back even later. Thus a new alienation between literature and living speech was artificially created—and this was the very literature that developed the language to an extent that it could be activated in speech! The poet and critic Ya'akov Fikhman, for example, tried to oppose the shift to the Sephardi accent in poetry up until the mid-1930s; the master lyricist Ya'akov Shteynberg wrote poetry in Ashkenazi Hebrew to his dying day (1947); Tshernikhovski compromised, wrote declarative poems and ballads in Sephardi Hebrew and went on writing many of his important works in Ashkenazi Hebrew; even Shlonski and Uri-Tsvi Grinberg, the avant-garde poets of the pioneers, persisted in writing in the Ashkenazi accent in Eretz-Israel until 1928—an accent their readers did not speak. The poetess Rachel, however, who did not know Hebrew from religious education, wrote in the simple, new Hebrew spoken around her, combined with words from the Bible she read in the "Sephardi" accent. And there were a few other poets like that. One of them, Tsvi Shats, who founded a Zionist commune with Trumpeldor back in Russia and was later killed by Arabs along with Y. H. Brener in Jaffa in May 1921, wrote an essay entitled "The Exile of our Classical Poetry," in which he posed the problem sharply:

> The main reason why [Hebrew] poetry cannot be absorbed among us is its foreign accent. With all its beauty and depth, it will not make our heart beat *because it is not molded from the coarse clods of our life or from the harsh or joyous tones of our life, which vibrate on our lips every day* [. . .] *Its value is like that of poetry written in a foreign language.* (Shats 1919:24; my emphasis—B.H.; see his essay in this volume)

But he admires the poets of the Revival Period and concludes: "*May we wish that Shneur, Tshernikhovski, and Bialik be translated into our pronunciation!*"—a wish unfulfilled to this day (my emphasis—B.H.).

This is the perspective: our language is pioneering, coarse, strong, masculine—like the "masculine" rhyme imposed by the Sephardi accent as opposed to the soft, "feminine" rhyme dominant in Ashkenazi poetry (as in Italian). There is no better example of that than the harsh, emphatic stress on the ends of words which Ben-Gurion emphasized with great energy as if he had to overcome an opposing tendency.[68]

The "Sephardi" accent quickly spread all over the Diaspora, especially in Zionist-influenced Hebrew schools. It represented the challenge of secular nationalism

---

68. In Ben-Gurion's pronunciation, paradoxically, even though a strong stress falls on the last syllable, the last vowel seems to be contracted, even swallowed, as in the Yiddish of his native central Poland: **poaLM vekhayaLM, beyaMM truFM Ele** (but there the last syllable is not stressed!).

to the religious tradition. Those were schools that had to break away from the religious world steeped in Ashkenazi reading of the Holy Tongue. But the Ashkenazi accent fights for its position to this day and is clearly the only legitimate accent in the eyes of many Orthodox Jews in Diaspora, as can be seen from the English transliterations of Hebrew words in newspaper advertisements by Orthodox groups, including the Lubavitsher Rebbe in the *New York Times*, or from his long lectures, delivered in Yiddish with some 80% Hebrew words pronounced in his ultra-Lithuanian Ashkenazi dialect. A typical case was in interwar Vilna, "Jerusalem of Lithuania," where a compromise among the secular Hebraists was made: elementary school in Ashkenazi (called, accordingly, **beySEYfer aMOmi**) and Gymnasium in "Sephardi" (hence called **tarBUT**—and not **TARbes**).

But here comes the surprise: *the Hebrew finally accepted as the basic language in Eretz-Israel is not Sephardi Hebrew at all, but rather the lowest common denominator between the two main dialects, Sephardi and Ashkenazi.*

The group that established Hebrew speech in social cells were young Ashkenazi Jews from Eastern Europe, from a Yiddish background, who went through processes of restraint (Jabotinsky's plea for "monotone") and aestheticization. This group accepted the Sephardi accent in principle, without having much contact with Hebrew-speaking Sephardim, but filtered it through its previous linguistic habits. Indeed, it was a harsh passage, as to a completely new language, when a person who read or wrote Hebrew had to give up **KEYses** or **KOYsoys** ("glasses" or "goblets") and say **koSOT**; the stress is reversed, the vowels reduced and changed, and the soft **s** at the end turns in Israeli Hebrew into a hard **t**. The harshness of the language was felt in the strongly accented endings of most words, mostly on closed syllables.

Indeed, the entire system of sounds shifted, yet ultimately, both **s** and **t**—that is, familiar sounds—remained in the language (with many more **t**'s than before). As the linguist Haim Blanc showed, *in Israeli Hebrew, not a single sound was added which was not in Yiddish*, except one—the glottal stop—which is not a consonant requiring pronunciation but a zero sound, a pause before a vowel: the Israeli speaker distinguishes between **lir'OT** ("to see") and **liROT** ("to shoot"), **mar'A** ("mirror") and **maRA** ("gall bladder"), **TSA'ar** ("grief") and **TSAR** ("tsar"), **me'IL** ("coat") and **MIL** ("mile"). The Ashkenazi dialect made no distinctions here and pronounced both words in each pair as its second member in our list (many Ashkenazi Jews, including Prime Minister Shamir, cannot pronounce the zero consonant and still use the short form in both cases). As Haim Blanc demonstrated in the 1960s, high-school graduates of Oriental origin speak like Ashkenazi high-school graduates, disregarding the Arabic gutturals and other consonantal distinctions. In recent years, perhaps a stratum of Oriental Jews who pronounce the guttural **ḥet** and even **ayin** has been added; as for all other consonants, the Ashkenazi filter succeeded among all educated people.

With the vowels, however, it was the "Sephardi" filter that succeeded in Israeli

Hebrew. All Biblical vocalizations are pronounced with only five basic vowels—**a, e, i, o, u**—instead of the eight vowels and diphthongs in Ashkenazi, the ten vowel-signs in the canonical Bible (or the seventeen differently pronounced vowels in the Random House English Dictionary).[69] Ashkenazi speakers accepted this minimal, "Sephardi" norm, partly out of hatred for the dipthongs **ay, oy, ey,** which symbolized Diaspora whining (**oy vey, ay-ay-ay, oy-oy-oy**), partly to create a more dry, matter-of-fact, rational, and "monotonous" intonation, and especially because they accepted the authority of the Sephardic "pure" language without a second thought. As a result of this extreme reduction, in Israeli Hebrew about half of the vowels in an average text are **a**; for example, what is pronounced **khaZOke (a-O-e)** in Ashkenazi becomes **khazaKA (a-a-A)** in Sephardi Hebrew. Simplicity has been achieved, but what is lost is the rich variety, that "culture of language" which accustoms the speaker to subtleties of nuance and serves as a base for poetic musicality. Even worse, the majority of the nation, including many of its poets, does not know how to write correctly the vocalization marks, indispensable in Bible and in poetry, because the vowel distinctions, preserved in Ashkenazi Hebrew, have been erased from Israeli speech. (Most publishers employ a specialist "vocalizer" (*nakdan*) who can place the vowels in poetic texts or in children's books.)

Thus, *Israeli Hebrew combines the range of Ashkenazi consonants and Sephardi vowels—the minimal range in each case.*

A similar process took place with stress. The so-called "Sephardi" stress is totally artificial and was never used in this form in a living, spoken language. In terms of rhythmic balance in long words, the predominant Biblical stress on the end of the word was possible when, in the middle of the word, there was a rhythmic variation of another kind, namely of long and short syllables. Indeed, that variation between long and short—rather than the end-stress—became the basis of the meters of Hebrew poetry in medieval Spain. The great linguist Roman Jakobson defined a general rule for all languages: when the distinction in length of vowels in a language disappears, the stress shifts from the margins toward the middle of the word. But in Hebrew pronunciation, the distinction between short and long vowels disappeared in all dialects, under the influence of other languages, at a time when the language was not spoken and natural processes could not take place. In Ashkenazi Hebrew, perhaps because of its strong integration in the spoken Yiddish, such a shift of stress to the penultimate syllable did occur. But in the artificial, "Sephardi" (actually, Syrian) reading of Hebrew, the rigorous stress on the ultimate syllable was preserved—which is not characteristic at all of the living language Ladino or in Sephardic ballads. As a result, a "Sephardi" stress often comes at the end of a long word of three or even five syllables,

---

69. Naturally, when two vowel signs, or a vowel followed by the consonant **y**, come together, a diphthong is created, but for every single sign there is only a single vowel; and the combined diphthongs are a small minority in the language.

with no rhythmic balance in the middle, and must be strongly emphasized in pronunciation, to carry the whole word.

The living Israeli language accepted that artificial norm for traditional word patterns but balanced it by profusely extending the groups of words with penultimate stress: proper names, emotional and slang expressions, and foreign loanwords. Most proper names are simply pronounced with penultimate stress, even if the nominal pattern is end-stressed: **DAvid, SAra, meNAkhem, MEir**, even **Itamar**—though by the Bible they should be stressed on the final syllable. In the use of non-Hebrew words, Israeli Hebrew adopted the Yiddish model, which absorbs most of the international words with a penultimate stress and in the feminine gender: **gymNASya, traGEDya, koMEDya, filharMOnit, simFONya** (though the major foreign language influencing Hebrew today, English, often stresses the third-to-last syllable: **TRAgedy, COmedy, SYMphony**). That same model which originated in Eastern Europe is also applied to words borrowed directly from Western languages: **teleVIzya, kaSEta, eksistentsiaLIsm** (though in French, the accent is on the last syllable: **existentiaLISME**, and in English on the fourth from the end: **exisTENtialism**); and such adjectives as: **baNAli, reAli, elemTAri, popuLAri** (all different from their English counterpart: **BAnal, POpular, eleMENtary**). However, in foreign words that get in Yiddish (as in German) the stress on the ultimate syllable, the stress shifted in Hebrew to the third from the end, as in Russian: **poLItika, FIzika, MUzika, uniVERsita**, a stress position otherwise almost unknown in Hebrew.

This pattern may have come from the language habits of the East European immigrants. But then this became the productive mode of accepting foreign words in Hebrew. Since most of these penultimately stressed words end in **a** and are therefore automatically feminine, the proportion of feminine nouns in the language—otherwise a minority of nouns—is considerably enlarged. Furthermore, such nouns are coordinated with their adjectives and verbs, which all become feminine and penultimately stressed too. Poetry and songs also soften the language and tend to rhyme with alternating masculine and feminine rhymes; hence, the large number of nouns in the feminine gender in poetry and song, which enable a penultimate stress: **oMEret–khoZEret, oHEvet–nilHEVet, simloTEya–hishtaGEya**, and so on. Feminine patterns are also popular in neologisms, such as **taYEset, raKEvet, matKOnet, mishMEret** (squadron, train, recipe, shift). And, in addition, an emotive emphasis may draw the stress of a word toward its beginning. Thus the impression of the language as a whole is tipped against the Sephardi final stress.

This is not just a phonetic issue, it gives a specific character to Israeli speech and its speakers. And beyond that, *this is the basic mode of the whole revival in Eretz-Israel*: an ideological decision and a drastic imposition of a new model of behavior, radically different from the Diaspora past, is accompanied by *a subtext of old behavior*, which reemerges with time: the Jew comes out from under the Hebrew.

TWENTY-EIGHT

Remarks on the Nature of Israeli Hebrew

An analysis of Israeli Hebrew in a broad cultural perspective—including the language of literature, journalism, and science—still awaits detailed research and comprehensive models. I will sketch here a few general ideas, as hypotheses for further discussion.

Opposition to the Diaspora was initially expressed, as in other countries of immigration, in changing last names (see Toury 1990) and preferring new first names. The names of central Biblical figures, popular in Yiddish, seemed too Jewish and fell into disfavor (though some still gave such names after their grandfathers); those include the names of the fathers of the nation and its prophets: Moshe, Avraham, Sara, Dvora, Rivka, Yitshak, Yirmiyahu, Yeshayahu, Yehezkiel, also the non-Biblical Hayim. Instead, some preferred "meaningful" names (*Zohar, Rina, Tikva, Geula,* i.e., "Light," "Joy," "Hope," "Redemption") or names from nature (*Ilan, Ayala, Rakefet, Narkis*—"Tree," "Deer," "Cyclamen," "Narcissus") or "Biblical" names that are not typically Jewish, that is, of unfavorable Biblical characters that were not widespread in European Jewry (*Boaz, Ehud, Yoav*). A well-known Israeli writer, born Monyek Thilimzoger (literally, "Psalm Reciter"), arrived in Israel at age 15 without his parents from the impending Holocaust in Poland; his name was changed in the youth colony Ben-Shemen to *Moshe Shaoni* (from "watch" or "clock"; apparently, *thilim,* "psalms," seemed too religious, and *zoger,* Germanized to *zager,* was misunderstood as *zayger,* "watch"); but becoming a real Israeli, he disliked "Moshe" and realizing the artificial nature of his new last name, changed his name again to *Dan Ben-Amotz* (for a long time, he did not reveal in his biographies that he was not a native-born Sabra, until he told the story himself, in his fifties).

Hebrew words identified with Yiddish words were also rejected. The Israeli says *Yareakh* (moon) and not *levana,* as in Yiddish; *tsibur* (the public), not *olam; me'unyan* (interested), not *ba'alan; rotse* (want), not *hafets; yimama* (a 24-hour day), not *me'et-le'et; ta'anug* (pleasure), not *mekhaye; mikhya* (sustenance), not

167

khiyuna; adam (man), not *yehudi; isha* (woman), not *yehudiya; menahel* or *akhrayi* (person in charge), not *ba'al-ha-bayit* (boss; though this too is used in slang); *more* (teacher), not *melamed; totsa'a* (result), not *po'el-yotsey;* le-hashpiya (to influence), not *lif'ol; bekhayay* (my word!), not *bene'emanut; sofer* (writer), not *ba'al-mekhaber; petsa* (wound), not *maka; shoded* (robber), not *gazlan; khabibi* (term of endearment), not *rotseakh; rekhilut* (gossip), not *leshon-ha-ra; ivrit* (Hebrew), not *leshon-kodesh; goy* (Gentile), not *arel; beit-kvarot* (cemetery), not *beit-olam.*

Most of the Hebrew expressions in Yiddish came from post-Biblical strata of Hebrew and were rejected in Eretz-Israel either because of the tendency to get away from both the world of religion and that of Yiddish or because of a more precise differentiation between synonyms (for example, *olam* in contemporary Hebrew means "world" and cannot also denote "the public"). A contemporary Israeli reader is not likely to understand precisely the language of Brener or Agnon—the preceding generation of Hebrew literature—especially when a Yiddish phrase or idiom stands behind the Hebrew sentence.[70]

The fate of Aramaic is a separate case. In the Religious Polysystem and in the world of Yiddish, Aramaic was part of the "Holy Tongue." In the Traditional Library, there were pure Aramaic texts (the *Kaddish*, parts of *Gemara, Akdamuth Milin, Had Gadia,* and the classical book of the Kabbala, the *Zohar*). Yet the active "Holy Tongue," the language of writing, was primarily Hebrew: the syntax was Hebrew, and the framework of discourse was Hebrew. Aramaic was not fused into the Holy Tongue but was *embedded* in it: Aramaic texts embedded in the Hebrew Library, and Aramaic phrases embedded in a Hebrew text.[71] With the revival of Hebrew literature in Diaspora, Aramaic received a special position and an important stylistic function; in Yehuda Leyb Gordon and Mendele Moykher Sforim, it signaled living speech, that is, Yiddish. Berditshevski, in an affectionate essay, wrote: "We do not have one literary language but two, [. . .] two nations bickering in your belly, [. . .] Hebrew and Aramaic. [. . .] the Hebrew language loves the sublime. [. . .] And the Aramaic language [. . .] is a language of the sharp proverb and morality, [. . .] the language of the humility in your heart, the language of religion, the language of the *Jews*" (Berditshevski 1987:101). In his stories, Brener embedded many Aramaic phrases, sometimes coined by himself, intermingled with International, non-Hebrew words.

But the Hebrew purists also fought against Aramaic. Klauzner claimed that *casus belli* is permissible in Hebrew but not *sadna d'area* ("human nature is the same everywhere"). Uri-Tsvi Grinberg, of the other camp, called his journal *Sadna D'Area* (published in 1925 in Eretz-Israel). Those who came from the yeshiva or from Yiddish loved Aramaic. But victory in the struggle went to the purist Klauzner: some Aramaic spellings were Hebraized and only a few overtly Aramaic

---

70. See examples in my Hebrew essay, Harshav 1990b.

71. Of course, the ancient influence of Aramaic on Hebrew itself is a different matter. "Hebrew" includes here whatever was absorbed by it in the texts of the Library: Greek, Arabic, Latin, Aramaic.

expressions remained in the Israeli literary language, seasoning it like Latin expressions in English, such as *sui generis* or *casus belli*, which have not been fused into the language but signal the technical use of a learned language. It seems that the Hebrew speaker wants one, recognizable Hebrew language, and if some foreign language is quoted in it, it had better be a language he knows. The religious connection between the two is meaningless to him today.

The new Hebrew language had to define its boundaries against both Yiddish and the Holy Tongue, though it drew on the resources of both. Thus, expressions from the world of religion and Talmud and translations of Yiddish proverbs and idioms were often rejected when recognized. Nevertheless, after all the purges of the purists, Yiddish ways of expression have penetrated Israeli idiomatic speech and Israeli slang (Yiddish itself derived many of those from Talmudic as well as European sources). Vast layers of Yiddish subtext underlay the ostensibly archaic, "Holy-Tongue" Hebrew of Agnon. It is interesting that also distinctly Biblical elements were exposed as naive and outmoded. Thus the three basic European modes of time, reflected in three tenses of the verb, were accepted; and the Biblical reversal of future into past, abolished. Despite the veneration of the Bible and its endless study in schools and adult circles (including Ben-Gurion's Bible Circle), the language of the Bible is markedly not Israeli Hebrew—and is kept apart. Though many know large portions of the Bible by heart (having studied it for ten or twelve years), the use of a Biblical phrase in Israeli Hebrew has the function of a quotation from another language. Thus, the return to the Land of the Bible and to the Language of the Bible involved a national and social ideology formulated in the language of European thought, and included a rejection of the innocent world of Mapu's "Love of Zion."

In sum, every stratum of language that is too reminiscent of one of the religious texts—Mishna, Talmud, Torah, or Prophets—is rejected in the Israeli base language and may be used in literature as a stylistic device (as we said earlier, the vocabulary of all those texts is an open store for modern Hebrew).

The result of these tendencies is that, from the perspective of the Hebrew sources, the Israeli language is a fusion language. It uses a certain range of language options from the past, on condition that the words or idioms are context-free, do not demand expertise in their sources, and do not mark the text as a mosaic of styles. From the point of view of the language user, a radical reversal occurred: in the past, there was a library of texts, from which the individual could draw words and phrases; now, there is a fused "repertory" of the living language, an active vocabulary and word-combinations employed in the base language or in specific idiolects and genres of discourse, irrespective of their origins. This "living" vocabulary may be used by anyone, irrespective of whether or not he is a "native" speaker.

In morphology and basic syntax, most of the forms were determined unequivocally, and most do prefer Biblical to Mishnaic forms. The real revolution took place in semantics and macrosyntax. The structure of the complex sentence and the paragraph follow the constraints and licenses developed in the logical writing, political commentary, and belles-lettres of Europe and America (although not all the long-winding, complicated periodic sentences of German or Russian were absorbed into Hebrew). The revival of the Hebrew language began from this world and attempted to match it with Hebrew expressions, rather than the opposite. It is not a case of speakers who grew up in Hebrew and had to expand their horizons but of people who learned Hebrew in the religious library of their childhood, then discovered the modern world and were absorbed by its ideologies, which had an overwhelming explanatory power—provided to them in Yiddish and other languages—and from here they went back to find Hebrew words for the new needs. Hence, it was relatively easy for Israel to become a modern nation. Instead of a base of Biblical Hebrew or Rabbinic Hebrew, which would have slowly grown and absorbed concepts from outside, *a European base was formed within modern Hebrew which observed selected Hebrew rules of morphology and absorbed concepts and expressions from all directions: from the international vocabulary and from the Hebrew library as well.*

Most of the words in an Israeli Hebrew text—a journalistic, scientific, or literary text—are new words, in form or meaning. It is precisely the indefatigable effort of the purists to substitute "Hebrew" or Hebrew-shaped words for foreign words that has filled the Israeli language with an international world of concepts, disguised in Semitic garb. *The law of style* encourages the "seasoning" of texts with words and expressions deviant from the medium, including words from foreign languages, original innovations, and non-Israeli collocations from Hebrew sources. This law also includes the rules of "good taste," which does not allow such "seasoning" to go beyond a certain limit, so as not to damage its status of an *embedded minority.* Hence, it is precisely the processes of change of non-Hebrew words into Hebrew or Hebrew-looking roots that made room for the introduction of new foreign words and translations of new concepts. As a result, Hebrew is a Semitic language only in the genetic and etymological sense, concerning only basic vocabulary and morphology. From every other perspective, it is an ally of the modern European languages.

Here, for example, is the opening of an editorial in the Israeli newspaper, *Ha-Aretz* of Friday, October 27, 1989:

The Missile Race

One of the television networks in the United States, NBC, has broadcast information stating that a missile built jointly by Israelis and South Africans was launched on the fifth of July from a certain place in South Africa, to a distance of fifteen hundred kilometers toward a group of islands in the direction of Antarctica.

Our broadcast network reported that the Prime Minister "denied reports" on the aforementioned subject, while the Minister of Defense confined himself to stating the standard version that Israel will not be the first to introduce nuclear weapons into the area. The Minister of Trade and Industry could say that the cabinet discussed nuclear weapons and came to a decision on the subject under discussion.

יום ו', כ"ח בתשרי התש"נ
27 באוקטובר 1989

מערכת, הנהלה, מודעות, הפצה ומנויים: תל אביב, רחוב זלמן שוקן 21, טל': 5121212
ת"ד 233 תל אביב 61001; פקס: 810012 (מערכת), 815857 (הנהלה), 815859 (מודעות)
ירושלים: רחוב החבצלת 2, טל' 6־224245־02, ת"ד 273 י-ם 91002; פקס' 224249־02
חיפה: רחוב נורדאו 20, טל' 8־6611166־04, ת"ד 5259 חיפה 31052; פקס' 670715־04

המו"ל: הוצאת עתון הארץ בע"מ, רח' זלמן שוקן 21, תל־אביב
העורך: גרשום שוקן   עורך המשנה: חנוך מרמרי

אין המערכת אחראית לתוכן המודעות ואינה מחזירה כתבי־יד
HA'ARETZ Daily Newspaper, P.O.B 233 Tel Aviv 61001 Israel
21 Salman Schocken St., Tel (03)5121212, Fax 810012

מירוץ הטילים

אחת מרשתות הטלוויזיה בארצות הברית, "אן־בי־סי", פירסמה
ידיעה לפיה טיל שנבנה במשותף על ידי ישראלים ודרום־אפריקאים,
שוגר בחמישה ליולי ממקום מסוים בדרום־אפריקה למרחק של אלף
וחמש מאות קילומטרים בכיוון קבוצת איים השוכנים בדרך
לאנטרקטיקה.

רשות השידור שלנו מסרה כי ראש הממשלה "הכחיש דיווחים" על
הנושא הנ"ל, בעוד ששר הביטחון הגביל את עצמו להשמעת הגרסה
השגרתית כי ישראל לא תהיה הראשונה שתכניס נשק גרעיני לאזור.
שר התעשייה והמסחר ידע לספר כי הקבינט דן בחימוש גרעיני וקיבל
החלטות בנידון.

Clearly, the Hebrew text can say the same thing and in the same way as the
English text (and vice versa). The excerpt includes:

1. International words: *kilometer, television, Antarctica, July, cabinet, Africa,
   NBC*.
2. New Hebrew words for international terms: *race, [television] networks, missile, launched, report, nuclear weapons, Minister of Trade and Industry, area*
   (in the sense of geographical area), *the United States*.
3. Phrases that represent Euro-American concepts: *"has broadcast information
   stating that," "a certain place," "standard version," "denied reports," "nuclear
   weapons" "fifth of July," "Israel will not be the first," "confined himself to stating
   the standard version."*

In this editorial, there are almost no older Hebrew words with their old meanings.

4. The microsyntax, concerning contiguous words, or immediate constituents,
   is essentially Hebrew: the coordination of verb and noun; the use of the

definite article, prepositions, and connectives; the genitive phrases. Yet, the macrosyntax is European: the sentence in the first paragraph accumulates five stages of states of affairs, which could not be done in the syntax of traditional texts.

Despite all that, as a result of the renewal of the language, the roots of most of the words are Hebrew or quasi-Hebrew. Thus, new concepts and the European macrosyntax were absorbed as part of the base language of Israeli Hebrew, which is open to absorbing new material just as the entire culture of Israel is open to the changing world.

This was the real achievement of the revival of the language: the creation of a language to absorb the culture and civilization of the Western World on the basis of the forms of words in traditional Hebrew. It was accomplished by Hebrew literature, Hebrew journalism, the secular Hebrew high school, and the Hebrew labor movement.

TWENTY-NINE

Principles of the Revolution:
A Retrospective Summary

Now we may disentangle the twin strains, the social and the linguistic, and observe that the revival of the Hebrew language was accomplished in two different large moves, one linguistic and one social:

1. *The revival of the language itself*, that is, the transformation of a language of a library of religious texts into a comprehensive, modern language.
2. *The transformation of a nuclear society to a new base language, Hebrew.*

These two moves were interdependent but not overlapping. They are, indeed, two diachronic processes, or *intertwined systems*, hence both repeatedly mirroring each other and asymmetrical.

1. *The first move, the revival of the Hebrew language*, was a long-range process, beginning in the middle of the nineteenth century (with earlier antecedents) and continuing uninterrupted to this very day. It was a cumulative, evolutionary process, with three distinct stages:

    a. The revival of "Hebrew literature" in the broad sense, that is, the extension of a religious language into the secular, representational, and aesthetic domains—which took place in Europe, especially from the end of the nineteenth century.

    b. The transformation of Hebrew from an embedded language into the base language of a minority society, which has to cover all areas of life and imagination encountered by that society, including daily affairs, social-political relations, and the imaginative world of their reading habits—this took place in Eretz-Israel just before and after World War I.

    c. The transformation of Hebrew into the language of a State, responsible for the linguistic base of all the institutions and systems of a modern State—this took place with the establishment of the State of Israel.

2. *The second move, the transformation of Hebrew into the base language of a society*, began as the result of a unique historical junction of three social-

cultural polysystems that intersected in the consciousness of the members of one generation:
  –the Jewish Religious Polysystem;
  –the Secular Hebrew Polysystem evolving in Diaspora;
  –the emergence of new social cells in the "social desert" of Eretz-Israel.

This was a revolutionary event, concentrated in a short time, with three stages:

a. In the period 1881–1904, the method of teaching "Hebrew in Hebrew" was introduced; teachers and students could speak Hebrew on occasion; but perhaps only a few individuals actually turned it into their base language.
b. In the period 1906–1913, two forms emerged: i) *social cells* whose group life aspired to be conducted in Hebrew (groups of laborers and schoolchildren); ii) *institutional frameworks* formally conducted in Hebrew (the first Hebrew city and Hebrew schools).
c. At the beginning of the British Mandate (1918), Hebrew leaped from those spotty small cells into a *network of institutions encompassing all of Palestine*; this occurred as the result of the political and educational autonomy granted the *Yishuv*, the recognition of Hebrew as an official language in Palestine,[72] the freedom of movement between all parts of the country, the mass immigration of the Third Aliya, and the establishment of the Labor Federation, Histadrut, as a full, nationwide, secular polysystem.

It must be noted that there was no complete overlap between the two moves, the linguistic and the social, as is natural with twin systems. Not everything achieved in the first move, in written Hebrew, was absorbed as an active asset into the life of the Hebrew society. And vice versa, the extent of the openness of the Hebrew base in society (e.g., the Yiddish idioms and jokes of Eshkol and Sapir, or the English phrases embedded in the conversation of educated Israelis today) did not pass into written Hebrew (outside of reported speech in realistic fiction or reportage in popular newspapers).

Thus, a full-fledged Secular Hebrew Polysystem was created which transformed Hebrew into the base language of the entire "Hebrew" *Yishuv* (however, most of the adult population still spoke Yiddish and other languages at home). But before 1948 that was not yet the base language of the entire "Jewish" population in Eretz-Israel since the orthodox "old *Yishuv*" still conducted its study of Hebrew texts and all of its life in Yiddish. Nor was it the language of the Zionist establishment in the rest of the world, where Hebrew still served as "a ceremonial language"

---

72. For the first time in history did Hebrew appear on official stamps, though in the lowest place of the trilingual stamp and with the name in Hebrew: *Palestina* (A"Y). The British government would not allow the full Hebrew name of the country; the compromise A"Y was an acronym for *Eretz-Israel* and was read by Jews as the Yiddish interjection for trouble: *ay-ay-ay*.

(in Usishkin's 1928 description), used to open meetings, while the language of the Zionist Congress up to the time of the Holocaust was the so-called "Congress Deutsch," that is, Germanized Yiddish. Even the new secular Hebrew schools in Diaspora that introduced "Sephardi" Hebrew were embedded within another base language of society in which the children spoke at home and in the outside world (or two languages: e.g., Yiddish at home, Russian or Polish in frames of the State).

Ultimately, a new Hebrew language arose which is the *base language* of the society, the individual, and the text:

The base language of a society means that social and cultural frameworks are conducted primarily in that language but that other languages may be embedded in it (like conferences in English at the Hebrew University).

The base language of an individual is not necessarily his mother tongue: Berl Katznelson, David Ben-Gurion, Natan Zach, Yehuda Amichai, Dan Ben-Amotz, Lea Goldberg, Dan Pagis, Shimon Peres, and many others, whose basic language of thought and expression is Hebrew, were not born into that language. Nor is it necessarily the only intellectual language of an individual: many Israelis read literature and scientific and technical texts in non-Hebrew languages, but the base language of their lives and consciousness is still Hebrew.

Nevertheless, one distinguishing characteristic of the base language of a normal culture is that there is a generation that was born into that language in which they achieved their early socialization and which is their exclusive or primary language. Since the revival of Hebrew achieved that goal, the status of the language in Israeli society is secure.

The base language of the text means a language in which the framework of the text is presented and in which most of its sentences are formulated, even though, on this basis, there can be various kinds of embedded material. Such a structure enables the dynamic development of the Hebrew language because the ever-growing base absorbs new materials—both from the world at large and from Hebrew sources as well—and assimilates them into tomorrow's Hebrew base.

These three—the base language of the society, the individual, and the text—are interdependent: without many individuals whose base language is Hebrew, no language of a Hebrew society could function; and vice versa, without a living society in Hebrew, a Hebrew-speaking individual is nothing but a curiosity or a Don Quixote (or a "Ben-Yehuda"). Also, without the continuous development of a rich language of texts, there is not a full life either for the individual or for the society in our complex world (unless they preserve their language as a "tribal tongue" as many African nations do, and require another language, e.g., English, for cultural life); and vice versa, without a society living in this language, the world of texts has no foundation, as Hebrew and Yiddish literature in Diaspora died out.

The connection between the three intertwined systems is circular. Hence the difficulty of the revival of the language was inherent in the need to break into the circle and establish its three interdependent areas almost at the same time. Hebrew literature had prepared the first move (in the expansion of the written language); Zionism opened a territory for a society formed in the new language; and the ideological emphasis in the life of the individual turned his third language into his base language: the combination of these factors enabled the revolution in all three dimensions. As soon as such a three-dimensional and circularly interdependent network was established in principle—even though the language was at first poor—it could be filled with ever more material in all three dimensions. The integration of these three enabled the uninterrupted absorption of groups of population and of world concepts, assimilating them into a living Hebrew culture.

THIRTY

Remarks Toward a Theory of Social Revolution

An explanation of the revival of the Hebrew language allows us to draw some fundamental conclusions about the processes of change initiated in society:

1. The transformation of an idea into the reality of social life is like the transition from a line to a three-dimensional sphere. An idea is a logical, linear content, formulated in language. Its realization, however, fills the multidimensional texture of the entire society. In such a transition, we can distinguish four stages: *formulation, rhetoric, realization, acceptance* (which also act in combination and not necessarily in this order). In the formulation of the idea, various arguments and schools of thought take part, resulting in a gradual clarification and development of the idea. Rhetoric is the ensemble of arguments, models, propaganda, and emotional influences on the public. Personal realization, like that of Eliezer Ben-Yehuda, is a change in the life of the individual for the sake of implementing the idea. But it is only the social acceptance of the idea and of its realization that can guarantee its embodiment in a society.

   Because the life of a society is multidimensional, the realization of an idea cannot be put into effect without a cluster of additional ideas that aspire to encompass many aspects of life. The revival of the Hebrew language was not identical with Zionism—there were Hebrew writers who were not Zionists and Zionists who did not live in Hebrew—and yet only in the cluster of Zionist realization could the language also be revived. Yet such "Zionist" clusters were very different with different persons, generations, and ideologies.

2. Revolutionary innovation does not appear *ex nihilo*. On all levels, it is founded on a two-stage *reversal of relations*: a) the development of a new element embedded within the old society; b) the reversal of the *embedded*

into the new *framework* or the new *base*. The Hebrew language that was rejuvenated in writing but still embedded in the cultural life of the society in Diaspora turned into the base language of the new society. In the life of the individual, knowledge of Hebrew, embedded in his intellectual world as a third language, turned into the base language of his life. In the schools in Eretz-Israel around the turn of the century, Hebrew, just one of the languages studied (along with French, Arabic, and Turkish), turned into the framework language of education and ultimately into its base language.

Examples of such a process can be found in all of modern culture. For example, free verse emerged in France as one option, embedded in the poetics of Symbolist poetry; later, the relation was reversed and free verse became the base of Modernist poetry in Europe and around the world.

3. In terms of the social carrier of the revolution, we can distinguish two steps:
   a. The creation of a small nucleus that implements the new concept in a clear form. The nucleus is voluntary and activates self-control. It has two advantages: on the one hand, it constitutes a society in miniature and, on the other, it is small enough to realize the idea in its perfect and controlled form. Such nuclei were the groups of laborers, the Gymnasya Hertseliya, and even the entire city of Tel Aviv.
   b. A historical change or shock from the outside which enables such a peripheral nucleus to move to the center of culture. Thus, for example, Expressionism was created in Germany or Futurism in Russia among small groups of radical artists and poets before World War I and moved to the center of the cultural stage after the shock of the war. The BILU group (only thirteen of whom arrived in Palestine) was organized in Russia before the pogroms of 1881, but only in their wake did it become central to creating the First Zionist Aliya, followed by a larger immigrant wave. The workers' movement of the Second Aliya included just several hundred people, but only after World War I was their ethos taken up by thousands and placed in the center of society.

In the Hebrew labor movement and in the youth movements established by it, there was an awareness of being an avant-garde, the "vanguard preceding an army." In this, there were two intellectual influences: 1) the idea of the holy Jewish community of Safed in the time of Lurianic Kabbala in the sixteenth century believing that a small community of saintly people can bring about a cosmic upheaval. This idea, though watered down, influenced Hasidism in Eastern Europe. The Hebrew labor movement imbibed the atmosphere of Hasidism, in the notions of a voluntary sect and of collective excitement and dancing, and in the role of the "Rebbe" in it (Katznelson, Tabenkin, Ya'ari). 2) Lenin's idea of the small and disciplined nucleus as the seed of the future revolution, an idea based on a profound distrust of the masses and democracy.[73] The notion is that a small, dedicated minority willing to sacrifice must retreat from the majority of the nation to create a new image of life which is the only solution for the entire nation (and which the nation will ultimately accept). Not just in politics but in culture too this elitist notion may be extremely influential—for example, the role of Ezra Pound and T. S. Eliot, who retreated to England and changed the notion of poetry in America. For twenty-five years, Eliezer Ben-Yehuda had little following, but the kernel, the principle of reviving Hebrew, was there; then the revolutionary situation, which swept up Jewish youth after the Revolution of 1905, instantly ignited the fires of Hebrew in Eretz-Israel and in Diaspora. Now a new kernel was established, the Hebrew-speaking cells of the Second Aliya—to be picked up by an even bigger revolutionary wave after the Balfour Declaration, the Russian Revolutions of 1917, and the pogroms of 1919, in the Third Aliya.

4. A key characteristic of the creation of such nuclei is a severance from the chain of the past: a biological, geographical, cultural, and/or ideological severance. A small group of Russian revolutionaries in Switzerland or Jews in Palestine, for example, distant from the masses of their people; the establishment of a Hebrew "national" (i.e., secular) school on the background of a religious society that did not have schools in the modern sense at all and especially not in Hebrew; or the creation of collective cells of young laborers without the generations of fathers and grandfathers.

Hebrew literature in Eretz-Israel also crystallized in two such severing waves: 1) The literary avant-garde of the 1920s (Shlonski, Uri-Tsvi Grinberg, Almi, Talpir, Shteynman) suited the avant-garde self-perception of the pioneer *Yishuv* and was embraced by it; it did not grow out of the Hebrew literature that preceded it ("the generation of Bialik") but started all over again under the influence of the avant-garde of Russian and German literature. 2) The *Palmakh*, select paramilitary units, made up of youngsters who were born or grew up in Eretz-Israel, and trained in kibbutzim in the 1940s, was a society separated from its parents in the city (who themselves were the masters of the first separation). They created a "native" Israeli life-style and literature, which did not know about Jewish life in Diaspora one generation earlier (their parents hardly told them of their own childhood). Their "Bible" was *Panfilov's Men* (the Hebrew translation of Alexandr Bek's Russian novel *The Volokolamsk Road*, describing the heroism of the defenders of Moscow in 1941); that is, they were influenced by Russian heroic Socialist

---

73. For Lenin's influence on Borochov, see Jonathan Frankel, *Prophecy and Politics* (1981). There was a cognate imagery too: Lenin's Bolshevik newspaper was called the *Spark* and carried the slogan *From the spark, a fire will be ignited*; Bialik's famous poem, "I Didn't Get the Light for Free," talked of the lonely spark in his poetry that will ignite a fire in the people; and Ḥana Senesh's widely sung poem said, *Happy the match that ignited a fire.*

Realism rather than by the earlier Hebrew avant-garde of Shteynman or Berdit-shevski. These were new beginnings, from ground zero, introduced into the continuous history of Hebrew literature only in retrospect.

Indeed, the history of Western culture—particularly in the revolutionary and radical period of the last hundred and twenty years—proceeds in fits and starts, and it is only later that old elements are absorbed again, consciously or in the subtext, and the new is "domesticated" into the old history.

5. The new development is neither linear nor continuous. It takes place on several parallel lines, which begin at different times and in various areas of life, under the influence of a single idea; some of those lines fail and some are renewed and succeed. Such lines of change may include individuals, schools, ideologies, newspaper, and organizations. Ben-Yehuda was the first visible propagandist who launched the idea of the revival of Hebrew and started the momentum of creating new words in all areas of life. He had almost no social influence. But two lines of development inspired by him—the innovation of words and the Hebrew Language Commit-tee—continue to operate to this day, although not in the center but at the periphery of the life of the language.

Schools in the agricultural settlements realized the idea of teaching "He-brew in Hebrew," but this line also died out and did not lead to the creation of a society living in Hebrew. It was only the new line, the social cells of the Second Aliya, that actualized Hebrew speech in a social framework. The urban *Gimnasya* and the education in the schools of the labor move-ment were, again, genuine new beginnings and not continuations of educa-tion in the agricultural settlements (just as kibbutz agriculture was not a continuation of the private agricultural settlements but rather emerged in opposition to them). Only in a continuous historical tale can we narrate all these lines as following one another.

But we must not forget the Diaspora. Parallel to the "Precise Language" Society of Ben-Yehuda and his friends in Jerusalem, similar societies arose and Hebrew education emerged throughout the Diaspora: their number was small in terms of the Diaspora but was quite large when compared with all the Hebrew speakers in Eretz-Israel. After World War I, in the wake of the Balfour Declaration on the one hand and the rights granted at Versailles to minorities in Europe on the other—and under the inspiration of the myth of the revival of the Hebrew lan-guage in Eretz-Israel—a network of Hebrew schools, gymnasia, teachers' colleges, and Zionist youth movements arose in Diaspora. From all these parallel lines, there was a constant stream of people to Eretz-Israel, which reinforced the Hebrew project. This multilinear effort not only revived the language but also spread it throughout the society, supported by the political establishment of the voluntary *Yishuv* and later of the obligatory Hebrew State.

PART III: SOURCES ON THE HEBREW LANGUAGE REVIVAL

Translated from Hebrew by Barbara Harshav

Rachel Katznelson

1885–1975. Born in Bobruysk, Byelorussia. Studied in Berlin and at the Bestu-
zhev Institute for Women in St. Petersburg. Immigrated to Israel in 1912. Taught
Hebrew and history at the farm for young women in Kineret. In 1920 married
Zalman Rubashov-Shazar, later President of Israel. 1928–1961, editor of *Dvar
Ha-Poelet* ("The Word of the Working Woman"). Literary critic and writer.

LANGUAGE INSOMNIA[74]

I

In the Kineret commune,[75] there were discussions of the crisis in Socialism.
From these discussions, I clarified for myself the concepts of *Movement* and *Revolutionary Literature*. I realized the revolutionary nature of Hebrew literature as opposed to Yiddish, and thoughts arose in my mind about our betrayal of Yiddish
and about the difference between those two languages.

At the beginning of the Jewish labor movement in the Pale of Settlement in
Russia, Jewish youth began to return from Russian to Yiddish. This started with
a free choice, as later on we chose Hebrew. We have not yet assessed that period
in our lives. We were a small group of people who absolutely had to speak
Yiddish. That language took the place of our homeland in Diaspora. With every
word we uttered in it we were reminded and confident that we had a homeland:
the street, the workers. The mystery of Judaism dwelled only in the small and
poor houses. It was strange to think that those who live in abundance were also
Jews. It seemed that the secret and the beauty of the race was hidden only in the
children of the poor street, in their faces. On spring evenings, we would go listen
to the rousing commotion of the workers, as you go to listen to the commotion
of the forest, because there was life there. The first word we read in Yiddish, or
which was read to us, revealed that street to us, and whoever lived there discovered himself in it. We also found our writers: Morris Rosenfeld, Peretz; and our

---

74. The title, *nedudey lashon*, is untranslatable. Literally, it means "language wandering," meaning
"shifting from language to language"; but it is also an allusion to *nedudey sheyna*, "sleep wandering,"
i.e., insomnia. [All notes in the translations are the translator's, unless indicated otherwise.]

75. The Hebrew term *kvutsa* preceded the use of *kibbutz* for a communal settlement living according to the same principles but in a smaller, familylike society of several dozen members.

contemporaries, companions of our spiritual development: Z. Y. Anochi, Rachel Feygenberg. Later, we understood the simplicity of Avrom Reyzen. And above all, and later than all others, we gradually realized the riddle of Sholem Aleichem.

We gratefully accepted every word that was written or said in Yiddish and that had a spark of feeling, youth, and art. It was a greeting for us from "our land." We did not "lack words" even though the language was poor. It was perhaps the only period in our lives when there was truth in our speech: the language was poor, many of us knew one or perhaps two other, richer languages; but without seeking it, we found in Yiddish an expression for the totality of our inner lives. Then, we felt proud and happy to hear in speech the music of every word, to know that only you and your people understood its tone and value and that, for everything that stirs in you, "somebody" has prepared an expression and it is latent in your soul and responds to you whenever you call it. How much we suffered then from the artificial Yiddish of others! And it was incomprehensible how the false tone could not be distinguished when there were so many teachers of good taste in language. Many of us also knew the Hebrew language. The awakening to Hebrew came with the awakening to Yiddish. There were quite a few of us whose knowledge of Hebrew was, until then, unusable. In Hebrew there was a national treasure—that was obvious both to those who knew a little and to those who only wanted to know. That was during the period of Bialik, in the years of his poems "The City of Slaughter" and "The Pond."[76] Even those who did not read Hebrew knew about Tshernikhovski, Fayerberg, Brener, and Shofman. They were translated and talked about. It never occurred to us to speak Hebrew. Would we abandon what was natural and choose what was artificial?

And these were the strong connections we betrayed when we came to Eretz-Israel. For here, we no longer feel like children of Yiddish and are no longer impressed by its beauty and intimacy. And even while speaking Yiddish and hearing its confident tones with pleasure, our pleasure is that of a person speaking a language whose secrets he knows but to which he has no connection or attachment. We are masters of that language, but it no longer masters us.

We had to betray Yiddish even though we paid for this as for any betrayal. And do we need to justify ourselves and explain how we could so quickly abandon what had become the substance of our lives? The fact that the Hebrew language was the language of our forefathers could not return us to it. Such facts could never compel people to desert their living language. Even the fact that there are Jews who never knew Yiddish, or that the language is gradually being forgotten, could not be decisive. After all, many of our people do not know Hebrew either. And Yiddish is forgotten on the one hand and, on the other, is learned and loved. And, above all—we are members of our generation, and the major thing for us

76. Bialik's poem "The City of Slaughter" described the horrors of the pogrom in Kishinev in 1903 and scolded the Jews for not resisting their enemies. It influenced a wave of self-defense groups in Russia. "The Pond" is a romantic celebration of nature and individualism.

is recognition of the truth and peace of mind. And if we are only a few (for, in our relation to Yiddish, we were then a smaller minority than in our speaking Hebrew now)—there is no need to worry. We have seen how a minority becomes a majority. The wealth of the Hebrew language certainly did not make our betrayal of Yiddish easier, for the poverty of the pauper is befitting to him. And what happened in Eretz-Israel to the wealth of the Hebrew language, how did we use it? Wasn't our Hebrew bereft of the movement of life and, for the little bit of picturesqueness of our speech, do we not use foreign expressions, influenced by the wisdom of a foreign spirit, not a Hebrew one? Do we not see fine Hebrew speech as a wonderment?

True, even now, after two thousand years, Eretz-Israel resonates with the Hebrew language, and the Bible comes to life when we read it here, but the distance between our spiritual life and the spiritual life invested in Hebrew by previous generations is immense. Nevertheless, there is an essential complementarity, which is lacking between us and Yiddish. We understood this even before we came here, we were amazed by it but we had to see it.

The essential thing was that, even though Yiddish is a living language, the language of the people and of democracy, there is a trend of thought, which for us was revolutionary, that expresses itself in Hebrew; whereas Yiddish literature is ruled by narrow-mindedness, mostly inert and reactionary in our eyes and, at best—only a weak echo of what was revealed in Hebrew. And we, in our situation and in the situation of our people, yearned for revolutionary thought.

II

"Revolutionary" usually means what stimulates war against the environment, against others. We mean that blessed revolutionary thought which stimulates an *internal* war, inside yourself, which can then lead to a clash with the environment. Revolutionary thought opens our eyes to see reality and saves us from delusions and conventions, from seeing something where there is nothing and from overlooking the substance. And because revolutionary activity demands our constant renewal and vivid observation (if not, it is not worthy of the name), hence its source is in the personality. Personality is the source of an incessant "revelation," and we are rescued from routine only if everything is built on the person, his defeats and his triumphs, his degradation and his purity.

The expression of revolutionary thought is simple, like the style of scientific formulas. Such is the expression of ethical imperatives, emerging from the most original thought that is most opposed to all the ways of our life. "Justify the righteous and condemn the wicked"—that is obvious. The "obvious" must exist.

The value of revolutionary thought is not in its innovation. The same phenomena are repeated throughout human history. "Love thy neighbor as thyself" was pronounced a long time ago, but the influence of that command depended on the situation in which it was declared, on the moods of the environment, on the form and the connection that were understood only by the people of the time, and on the authority they believed in. The Bible could be a source of revolution in Germany only in Luther's time and by him, and in the modern period of our nation—only in the nineteenth century. And how can something that reveals the errors of his life to one person not mean anything to someone else? Why will one man get a revolutionary impulse from a tune and another man—from some occurrence in the street? And why do the results of a sudden revolutionary illumination seem so illogical to us? Who can say what connection there is between the revolutionary decisions of a person—to answer "yes" to a close friend, to change the content of his life—and the moments that illuminated reality for him and gave him the courage to decide? Oh, how much we need the intensive spiritual life, restlessness and constant return to nature, the whole movement of revolutionary activity that is the soul of life for us! And how inert and misleading is what is sometimes called "revolutionary"!

The revolution, the revolt of our generation against itself—we found it in Hebrew literature. And that seemed strange. According to our hopes for Yiddish, according to our relation to Hebrew, Brener should have written his stories of the life of the masses in Yiddish; and Sholem Asch's idyllic novel *A Shtetl* should have been written in the classical language, Hebrew. But it was not like that. And it was also amazing that the writers who were youths from one street, sometimes friends, and mostly knew both languages—split: into Hebrew and Yiddish writers. Why was one talent drawn to one language and another to the other? Why did the war of languages occur? If it had a lot of blindness, gratuitous hatred, and ephemeral influence—it also had profound reasons.

III

Every language is a treasury of national energy. The chronicles of the nation, not just the annals recorded for memory but the feelings, the desires, and the life events of every individual—all those live and exist forever in the language. Hence, every language has its own atmosphere, and a person cannot learn a new language that doesn't influence his spirit. The person who knows his nation well, its history and its language—will discern the ring of each of its phrases as opposed to a parallel phrase in another language, and from what historical event, from what leader, or from what quality of the national soul it got this special tone. Those expressions created or used in moments of profound shock, of religious revelations, of national danger, at the appearance of a chastising prophet or a beloved hero, are etched forever in the national memory. And even if, at first, they are heard only by individuals—from those individuals, the same tones will be heard by everyone.

Not only the exceptional days in the life of the nation, also everyday life—especially that—their reverberations go in the language forever; and in these terms, the creation of the language doesn't cease as long as people live and think and speak in it. The more our internal lives revealed in language are important, the more we add to this invisible national treasure and create for ourselves, and for those who come after us, a purer atmosphere of life. Every word we invested with feeling and thought had an effect on somebody, and he can't utter it without feeling what we ourselves felt in it. And, vice versa, the conventional thought of individuals makes words cheap and hollow and thus decreases the value of national thought.

Every language has its own magic circle, and he who enters it surrenders to the influence that breathes on him from every word. Anyone who has learned a few languages knows that every time he changes his language, he changes himself as well. We've often heard the line: "When you speak this language your voice is different from your voice when you speak another language." The natives of the Pale of Settlement in Russia, even those who didn't have any opportunity to get close to Russians, received something of the qualities of the Russian soul from the influence of the Russian language and literature. For language is not a collection of expressions but the ephemeral past leaving its soul in the language.

"In times of doubt, in times of hard thoughts about the fate of my homeland—you are my support, only you, our great and mighty, true and free, language, for such a language could not have been given to a people that wasn't great" (Turgenev, "The Russian Language").

A language gives, but it also imposes duties, and the richer the ancestral legacy, the harder it is to live. It is difficult for nations with a great past. But our nation did not deny its past, it continued it. The national strength latent in the Hebrew language lived even in Diaspora. The religion preserved it. And because of that latent force, Tshernikhovski wrote Hebrew after two thousand years of exile. Religious life, which filled the Jewish heart with a new and living content, which penetrated all its aspirations, all the events of its life, restored to Hebrew its intimacy, which the second language had diminished, the language of mother, the family, and everyday life. And vice versa, religious thought—whether it was poetry, philosophy, or science, it was always religious—that sublime spiritual enterprise, was nourished by the treasury of energy of the Hebrew language, and itself enriched that treasury with expressions, intentions, and nuances, in which the lives of generations were preserved.

Now, for hundreds of years, our nation has spoken Yiddish; we could almost say: our nation. And that language is also a treasury of national energy. We lived in it. And what was invested in its sounds—motherhood, childhood, the history of our nation in Diaspora, the life of the national soul—is precious and genuine and belongs to us. And the writers of our period, the period when the fate of the languages was decided, found these two worlds. And if a person, a writer chooses this language rather than the other—he does so because he feels close to it. This is the genealogy of the internal life enclosed in the two languages, the continuation of the tradition. We continue the tradition of the language we live in even if we don't intend to and maybe even against our will.

The intellectual and spiritual content of the language indicates the height of all expressions possible in it. Even the person who lives a more complex life than is latent in his language is limited to some extent by the line it drew for him, and an expression can also descend only to the limit allowed by the language.

IV

When we wanted to name the special line of the original Yiddish literature, we sometimes said: "This literature is more national than Hebrew." We said that because we felt a warmth in it that was lacking in Hebrew. There they loved us as we were—us, our street, and our little town. This is one of the essences of Yiddish.

The softness and the quiet in Sholem Asch's *Shtetl* and Peretz's *Folklike Stories*; the weakness of popular thought and the strength of popular truth in Avrom Reyzen, the dear poet—in their day, all those were revelations for us. The impression that *Folklike Stories* made on us was just as strong as the impression of Bialik's poem "The City of Slaughter." In our hearts, we called those tales "self-sacrifice." That was poetry of self-sacrifice and admiration for our nation in Diaspora, for only in Diaspora could such wonders take place.

There was something maternal in Yiddish literature. The writers who wrote in that language could not see or penetrate artistically into the internal life of our exhilarated comrades—just as a mother cannot see in her son's soul all his internal struggles, all his sins; for, after all, he is her son and she is only a mother.

So, after the failure of the Russian Revolution of 1905, when the situation of our nation was extremely tense, there was something tranquilizing in the best writing in Yiddish, a lack of wings—and it became too narrow for us to breathe in its air. Once upon a time, the small town was for us too what it had been for Asch: an unusual world, dependent on itself and nourished by its own beauty, but that was not what we needed then, on the verge of the Second Aliya. For if we had had only the possibility of seeing and thinking revealed in Yiddish, we could not have thought our nation was still one of the great nations.

There is bitterness in our judgment of Yiddish, the bitterness after a disappointed young love: with all the pain, there lingers the awareness that the soul's freshness, revealed only once in a lifetime, was spent in vain. And the awareness that Yiddish bound us again to the life of the Jews and added loyalty to the nation is no consolation.

Why is it that, although there were real and sincere talents in Yiddish—it wasn't Yiddish but Hebrew literature that restored our self-respect? Why did Bialik, Fayerberg, and Gnesin have a fascinating and compelling force when there wasn't even a trace of it in Yiddish? It did not depend on talent but on the *free Man* with which Hebrew literature and its language captivated us. We yearned for Man, and for us—Bialik's poem "A Twig Has Fallen," and Tshernikhovski's preface to his translation of "Hiawatha," and Fayerberg's questions, and women's nature in Gnesin—for us, all those became the music of *Man*. And, where there is Man—there is the nation. And on the other side, there was in Yiddish all the charm of literature that lacks clear thought—humility, a folk tone, softness, and subtle eroticism that particularly filled the whole Polish branch of that literature. To be sure, the eroticism that penetrated the Hasidic stories or the nature of *A Shtetl*, and was perhaps the source of the magic of Peretz's *Folklike Stories*—it too reveals to a person the secrets of life and helps him shape his worldview. But there are periods in the life of a person and of a nation when nothing is more dangerous for them than the idyllic. Such was the period that was supposed to answer the question of languages. If Brener had written in Yiddish, that alone would have changed the answer. Not because of the force of his talent but because it could have been a symptom. But since the talents were so clearly separated, since the vehicle of original revolutionary thought was the "dead" language and not the living one—that was the verdict.

For there was a discrepancy between the difficult situation of the nation and the assessment of the situation in Yiddish literature and political commentary. Only the current that was an echo of the Hebrew, that was a kind of Yiddish translation from Hebrew, behaved differently.

On the one hand, sometimes the reforms Yiddish writers wanted to put into our lives were surprising for their lack of tact and reminiscent of a man who interferes in the intimate affairs of a stranger; and, on the other hand, there was in Yiddish thought a cowardice and lack of criticism concerning everything national, and an inability to take a single free step for fear that the tattered clothes would be torn. Yiddish was conservative and did not see beyond today. Do I need to mention the important newspaper *Fraynd*, the "Bund," Zhitlovski? Only Hebrew literature—in the part of it that is important to us—lacked the "censorship" that had depressed us in the radical currents of Yiddish. Here, people allowed themselves to think about the Hebrew nation out of freedom, as Aḥad Ha-Am, Berditshevski, and Bialik thought. Freedom of thought and expression came not because they were aware that they were writing for a few readers, that the street would not read them. The awareness that they were writing for a few did indeed influence the Hebrew writers very much, for good and for bad; but the freedom of thought and the ability and courage in Hebrew literature emerged out of an internal need and an internal permission. This is the tradition of the Hebrew language, the continuation of the revolutionary thought of the Bible. One generation gave its voice to another.

By coming to Eretz-Israel, we wanted to liberate ourselves from nationalism as an *idée fixe*. In Diaspora, nationalism hindered us in living. Our thought and feeling always focused on one thing, and there was no freedom to devote ourselves to other aspirations. Any devotion to general human issues always caused, or seemed to cause, getting close to an alien world. It was impossible to be a socialist, a Tolstoyan, an artist, a public leader, a scientist, without fearing assimilation. Personal freedom—and alienation; activity in general society—and alienation. There were very few exceptions. And in Eretz-Israel we liberated ourselves from that. Here we are Jews anyway, and that was essential to us. And the Hebrew language is the same refuge for us. The Hebrew writer will always be more of a citizen of the world than the Yiddish writer. The Hebrew writer will always have more confidence and his sense of authenticity will be fuller, for he has the unmediated awareness that, through the Hebrew language, he connects and continues to spin the thread of eternity in some hidden ways.

V

The revolutionary force of contemporary Hebrew thought consists in its ability to affirm and negate. About two years after the publication of Peretz's *Folklike Stories*, Brener's book *From Here and From There* appeared. Did Brener know that this book would be a greater source of confidence and strength and hope for us than *Folklike Stories*? But we felt that if it was still allowed not to pity us, it was a sign that we were alive. And the hope that he drew for us—in the characters of the old man and the grandson—was our only hope, but a true hope. And this book came at a time when national political commentary—in Yiddish and in Russian and partly in Hebrew—was dominated by such courtesy, advocacy, and caution toward our nation that it sometimes seemed that we had already died, that nothing was left and that this was a kind of burial service. But it was not only from Brener that we drew affirmation, the knowledge of the good we had to go to; it was also from A. D. Gordon, who did not need Brener's negation to reach the affirmative.

And a light we didn't find in others we found in Fayerberg, who was more than a guide for us, even though we didn't understand him properly then. For if Bialik had written for only three years like Fayerberg[77]—would we know much about him? But it was impossible not to sense that in this stammering—Fayerberg's words, burning with the fire of feeling and concentrated thought, are stammering only in contrast with what he might have said—in this stammering of one who was almost a lad, there is something without parallel in the new Hebrew literature. These stories have a natural attraction, and the basis of this attraction is that Fayerberg was even more independent than other great writers of his generation. There were connections between him and Hebrew history which others lacked. If only he had had time to write the novel *From the Life of the Besht*,[78] which he thought of writing! For he was the real heir of the Besht and his Hasidism, and he could have given us a new revelation of the new Hebrew history and of ourselves.

Indeed, there are still untrodden paths in the chronicles of our nation and there are internal aspects Fayerberg envisioned, and that source of knowing our nation remains closed to us. The first time I thought of Fayerberg like that was in Eretz-Israel when I read the chapters on Hebrew uniqueness and the redemption chapters of the Prophets. It was impossible to live in the world of thought of

---

77. M. Z. Fayerberg (1874–1899), influential Hebrew writer, died at the age of 25.
78. *Besht*—Israel Baal Shem Tov (c. 1700–1760), founder of modern Hasidism.

Jeremiah, Isaiah, and Ezekiel and not sense that there is a depth in the being of our nation which even the best of us have not reached. Isaiah's "Thou hast chosen us" was different from what was scorned in our literature. And then we felt there were outside influences that prevented us from seeing the essence, that we lacked the self-knowledge and the full life within the Hebrew circle which Fayerberg had.

Hence, too, the painful and difficult alienation we felt toward the literature of our time. The writer must reveal to the readers what has been revealed to him, and, to a certain circle of readers, everything must be revealed—and there is such a relation of good Hebrew readers toward other literatures. The good reader evaluates writers by what he gets from them, and where there is esteem, there is also genuine respect and love. This does not depend only on knowing the language, for the amazing thing is that we sometimes read a European language with the help of a dictionary and there is no limit to our complete and genuine enjoyment.

But we don't have such an attitude toward our own literature, either in Hebrew or in Yiddish. There is no confidence in our evaluation, as if one more part of the life of our nation was revealed to those individual writers, but the work of those writers was *not* revealed to us. People with discernment in European literature grope in Hebrew literature. Sometimes, we love the Hebrew poet who grants us something, but we won't know for sure how to answer who he is, if he really does have great talent or if he does grant us something because we came to him empty-handed and he touched the romantic chord in our hearts, in our love for our nation. And as the enigma of our nation is closed to us, so is our literature, and there is no genuine evaluation and there is no faith in the writers.

When we read a Hebrew work, we always want to compare it with the works of foreign nations, but it is impossible to compare. And we don't know who is Peretz or what attitude we should have for him. The same is true of our relation to Sholem Aleichem. It seems that, according to the worldview of European literature, he has weaknesses that are forbidden even in a minor writer: some descriptions of nature—"the moon shines, the trees sprout," a desire to amuse, a stereotyped structure of his works, and a few other "sins." But why is he so beloved, why can you read him endlessly and, most important—why do both good Jews and assimilated Jews read him, and converts, grownups and children, the whole nation? And it seems that only a few know that Sholem Aleichem—is a marvel, a phenomenon, something other nations apparently don't have, and the marvel is that Sholem Aleichem isn't just a writer, isn't just himself, but is—our nation. Thus, we should not attribute Sholem Aleichem either to the Yiddish trend or to the Hebrew trend of our literature, just as we should not attribute the nation as a whole to either trend. And just as the internal life of our nation is full of substance and is genuine, so is Sholem Aleichem genuine and profound and full of wisdom.

But where is the criticism that will draw from him, where are the persons who will teach him?

There is something that stands like a demon between us and our individual writers, as there is, so it sometimes seems to us, something dividing them from the historical soul of our nation. This is the curse of a person's not understanding his own spirit. A curse that weighs on our nation—we see it only in the assimilationists and their negation, but it lies on all of us. Does all this emanate from the influence of education in a foreign cultural environment, which creates for us a split heart, or are the reasons more profound?

There are very few to whom the past and the present will be revealed in both their creative achievements and their weaknesses. For there is no limit to weaknesses. And if we approach as strangers—what won't look weak among us? And what did we create after the Bible that we can trust? And there are some who don't even trust the Bible. And one person to whom both good and bad, weakness and heroism, the uplifting and the degrading were revealed—was Fayerberg. He had an unmediated relation both to the Talmud and Rabbinic literature on the one hand, and to our generation on the other; and many secrets were buried with him when he died; for a man with such a sense of history is like a prophet among us.

VI

A few years ago, there was a lot of talk in Russia and America about the need to translate the Bible into Yiddish. Those who were opposed to it harbored a vague and illogical feeling: Can the Hebrew Bible be translated into all languages and not Yiddish, the language of the Jews, so that those Jews who know only Yiddish won't know the Bible? Anyway, there are Yiddish translations of the Bible from hundreds of years ago! Indeed, is there any relation between the Yiddish of *Tsene-Verene*[79] with its own demands of itself (such as they are) and its literary requirement, on the one hand, and a translation of the Bible into the Yiddish of our time and its goals? At any rate, the translations were published by Yehoash in America and, as soon as we opened them, we knew why we were opposed. The possibilities of translation and its success are based on the law of "I am a human being and nothing human is alien to me." You can translate the Bible into the languages of all cultured peoples, because no cultured people is alien to what we experienced during the Biblical period, and synonyms were created in all languages for common concepts. Hence, the Bible could be one of the bases of the classical literature of another people. But how can the Bible be translated into Yiddish? How can it be translated—for us? Did we also create idioms in Yiddish for the spiritual life of the Bible? Who created, when and why and in what moment did we need such a thing? You can translate the Bible into German or English,

79. The popular Yiddish retelling of the Bible for women.

because there is an equality between those languages and the language of the Bible, an equality that does not exist between that language and Yiddish; because no two languages have such different programs as those two, because we divided the contents of our lives between them. And every important translation from one of the languages into another (even if the spiritual content of the literary work can be translated—Mendele, Sholem Aleichem) would always demand a great effort. Only Mendele could translate himself, and only Berkovitz could translate Sholem Aleichem.

The open war against Hebrew is not its main impediment but the war that is fought, with an invisible weapon, by Yiddish, by foreign languages, and by all the conditions of our lives, although we must not forget that Yiddish and Hebrew also aid each other. But those who fight against Hebrew so as "not to endow it in the schools with a value that does not fit its value in life," and sometimes even those who defend it, do not know who are the decisive participants in the war. Those are not the main speakers in assemblies. Outside the debating rooms, in all the space of our world, Hebrew fights the war herself; and how powerful are her weapons: every Hebrew word in which we still hear its genuine content; and with it are fighting for Hebrew among us: Moses and Jeremiah, the prayerbook and the Haggadah, Rabbi Jehudah Ha-Levi and Rabbi Nachman Krochmal.

The Hebrew language is striving to be a spoken language, and it cannot exist without that aspiration even if our Hebrew speaking sometimes offends the language sensibility living within us.

In our day, when the book has become common property, no literature can exist for just a few. Nor does Hebrew literature have the features of aristocratic literature. It lives in everyone and hence wants to find a way to everyone. And it is also out of the question to agree that most of the nation will hear about the most precious and original intellectual activity of the nation either from its friends or from its enemies. And, although Hebrew is not yet everyone's reading language, it is already the spoken language. The creation of the spoken language began in Hebrew at the same time that the danger to its existence appeared, when we reached the possibility that a Hebrew person who can read will read a foreign book and not a Hebrew one. This is the war of survival of the Hebrew language. The transition of Hebrew from a reading language to a spoken language was done in literature. It was the Hebrew writer who listened to our life and found its echo in Hebrew, for only in Hebrew could it be found. The language created by Mendele and Bialik will save us from the dominion of foreign languages, and the New Hebrew Man will speak the language of Brener and Gnesin.

Just as music requires a fitting resonance to be understood, so a great work of literature requires comprehending readers and many readers.

And when an important thing is created among us and is read by a handful of people—is it not offensive that a wonderful thing vanished like music getting lost in a low room? It is also hard to arrive at a correct evaluation of the writer if only a few understand him. True, an evaluation is made by individuals, but these individuals evaluate empowered by the nation. For ephemeral mortals are forgotten by a nation's verdict, but great writers live forever. Hebrew literature does not have a *nation of readers*, and this also deprives individuals of the power to evaluate. The Hebrew nation and literature have no hope of rising as long as Hebrew is not a spoken language, for a literature not only requires many readers but also many who live a common, organic life with it. And vice versa, the language of speech and thought of the nation must draw from the source of its national literature. Who can imagine that Tolstoy could write what he did without hearing spoken Russian around him? Who can imagine that the Russian people could understand Tolstoy's works without speaking his language? Because they do not imbibe organically from the nation, our genuine poets stop writing and turn to whatever they turn to also for lack of real evaluation; for only the living language gives the many, and not just the exceptional individuals, a musical ear and the knowledge of the value of every word, and without these, no evaluation is possible. For a certain time after Pushkin, there were a few poets who wrote poems no less beautiful than his; but the Russian who *speaks* the language his nation inherited from Pushkin could discern that there was no novelty or truth in those imitations.

A large number of readers and speakers is not enough for a language. Every minority that does not live in the national language and speak it detracts from and reduces its image. Only the whole nation has the power to restore its force to the language. And the future of the Hebrew language is still dormant in the future of the nation.

(1918)

Yitzhak Tabenkin

1887–1971. Born in Bobruysk, Byelorussia. Came to Israel in 1912. Spiritual leader of the largest kibbutz movement, *Ha-Kibbutz Ha-Meuḥad*, and the *Aḥdut Ha-Avoda* (left Zionist-Socialist) party.

THE ROOTS

We must not assume that members of the Second Aliya shared a single world of thought. On the contrary, the roots of their thinking were different and distant from one another; but all of them emerged from one soil, and the reality of their lives was the same. The forces operating in that period influenced everybody because its manifestations affected every single individual, even though the responses to them may have been completely different. However, we are not concerned here with their responses but rather with the fact that they were all immersed in the same horizon of life, in a single *landscape*. The landscape includes all circumstances surrounding a person—the social identity, the economic factors, the political atmosphere, the ideological and cultural-psychological influences, quite variegated and distant from one another—all those together combine to form the complete landscape of the generation.

In my mind's eye, I see familiar figures of that period, members of various Socialist and Zionist small circles of young people. All of them belonged to the same landscape of life in Russia during the first revolution [1905]; all of them were born to the same factors and events. Some belonged to a stratum in which revolution per se was something foreign, that saw revolution as a form of slavery in freedom, of toil in alien fields; others lived on the horizon of this revolution, the horizon of life of the Russian worker and his revolutionary movement. One, native of a Jewish *shtetl*, son of the town *rav*, raised on folk beliefs and alien to the Bund with all his heart, seeing it as the home of ignoramuses, was puzzled by and estranged from the "guys" of the *shtetl* who wore red shirts and followed the call of the revolution. And on the other side, there were people who participated in the revolutionary movements, in the Self-Defense, in the Russian Revolution itself, who welcomed the revolution enthusiastically.

But we are not concerned here with the nature of their responses. The main point is that both of these types lived in the same period, breathed the same air, were immersed in the social-public milieu of that Diaspora Jewry which motivated them to immigrate to Eretz-Israel. Both of them lived in the landscape of that generation.

What was that generation? What did that period mean to the cultural-spiritual world of the Second Aliya? A time of revolution and the formation of a fighting working class, decisive changes in the life of the Hebrew individual, a period of the rise of man as an active individual altering life. The passivity of the days of Mendele Moykher Sforim no longer characterizes this period. Tevye the Milkman's seven daughters—each of them had a different mate: one goes to Eretz-Israel, one is a Bundist, one a craftsman immigrating to America, and some go and return, but they all move in the same circle of life. David Pinski's well-known play, *The Family Tsvi*, is reflected in every home: one son strives for a territory, the other for assimilation; one has a positive relation to Eretz-Israel, another—to an assimilated life in a foreign land. *Something has moved in the life of the Jews.* Everyone participates in the revolution—positively or negatively, with it or against it, brings Jews to Eretz-Israel or to a "territory."

This is one of those periods in history designated as turning points, a *special* period in the life of the people—not just in the social perspective but also in all the transformations in the spiritual and cultural domain. And in that period, the years when the Second Aliya type was created were a *time of renaissance*. What an *outburst of forces*! An abundance revealed in many aspects of human expression: in literature, painting, music, and poetry. Close up, you can also see in it signs of decay, and a deeper and sharper feeling of general and Jewish decline. But from a distance, this is a renaissance period, perhaps not less valuable than the golden age in the Hebrew spiritual and creative life in Spain. Here are the roots of the new Hebrew and Yiddish literatures.

Indeed, for the last hundred and fifty or two hundred years, there has been a Yiddish literature, and modern Hebrew literature began some sixty or seventy years ago. But the period we are talking about was immensely enriched in expression—in fiction, poetry, and essays. Here was the beginning of secular literature, the best reading book for the Jewish individual, a book expressing his needs and questions. Hebrew literature is no longer a matter of "Questions and Answers" [i.e., religious Responsa] and yet more commentaries on the Bible, but a rich world of thought about the destiny of the people in relation to the destiny of the world, and the destiny of the individual vis-à-vis the destiny of the universe and the destiny of society. *For the first time*, Hebrew thought raised the question of the existence of the nation and its destiny, and the very asking of that question was revolutionary vis-à-vis previous centuries. All the foundations of life and existence were reexamined, all the values of life and relations of life—the relation to man and to nature, to religion and to labor, the relation to child and family, to Eretz-Israel and the "Gentiles"—everything is raised as problems to be discussed. *For the first time*, an attempt was made to understand Hebrew history, to recognize that there is a Jewish national poetry and folk poetry, and Jewish music. Painters and sculptors whose art is drawn from Jewish life emerge, and an original style is created for the response of a Jewish man in the world of art.

In our lives, the discussion never stopped: what was the nature of that period? Was it a period of rise in creative life—a rise in economic, political, and cultural forces, or a period of decline, exhaustion of all forces? No doubt both. Economic reality in that period knew both rise and fall. The collapse of social positions, the destruction of the ghetto and the crumbling of an age-old mode of existence, pogroms, and tempestuous and shaken lives—in the wake of all that came fundamental changes in the life of the Jews: an economic rise, changes in the economic structure, the transition to new professions and countries; the emergence of new centers in the life of the nation, internal immigration from villages to small towns to big cities and to distant lands, to new countries and continents; social differentiation, the emergence of new classes among the the Jews. Only people with a *homeland* find a solution in immigration: the nation occupies a new land by settlement. But immigration within Exile, from one Exile to another, without a port and without a homeland, turns into a constant reality of contradictions, turns from a solution to a *destiny*. This immigration makes the Jewish man a nomad; the whole generation is thrown into a nomadic existence that fills the whole space of its life: they breathe in it and are nourished by it.

And out of all that—emerged a striving to give a new shape to the life of the Jews; the destruction of petrified forms and threadbare thoughts with sharp and brutal criticism in order to pave the way for a new world of concepts and values. None of those efforts finds an anvil in the rootless Jewish existence. Whether it is a war of enlightenment—Hebrew, Jewish, or assimilationist, fighting for a bourgeois shape—or whether it is a Socialist war for the creation of a working class with a proletarian shape and a new culture and independent values—either of those winds up badly in the Diaspora existence that pulls the ground out from under their feet and cancels every attempt at original creation. But those manifestations of destruction were also the foundation for a rich and multifaceted spiritual fermentation. Spiritual life was suddenly filled with a war of opinions, a tempest of searching that also received artistic and critical expression—there was a plethora of definitions, for there was social differentiation and there were influences of various factors and various cultures. The national and social questions appear as tangible factors in the life of the Jews.

This is the greatest period of fermentation, *there never was one like it and never could have been* in the life of Diaspora as long as the Jews were confined to the ghetto. Indeed, great minds, giant figures rose out of the ghetto, but they were bound by that fixed frame of religious life, set for generations. In this period, everything *deviated* from the fixed route of generations, all life was called in question, and suppressed forces suddenly burst out of it, storming toward a different life, toward wide-open spaces. Every Diaspora awakens hopes and destroys hopes, every Diaspora has its own specific manifestations, every place has its own attempt to get out of the ghetto into the wide-open spaces, to get out of those specific streets to the field, the forest, the "general" human street—to get out of the economic and geographic ghetto, to get out of the spiritual ghetto to the wide-open spaces of thought and free life of man and the generation, self-renewing and independent.

II

For many years this period will seem to us a period inundated with great and unusual forces. We shall see its figures—Aḥad Ha-Am, Bialik, Berditshevski, Peretz—as incomparable giants. For a long time, we shall be nourished on that rich treasure revealed then in all branches of artistic creativity. In that period, the Yiddish artistic theater also emerged, influenced by Y. L. Peretz, Herman, and others; the first buds of the Hebrew theater sprouted (Y. Katznelson, N. D. Tsemakh, M. Gnesin), which later led to the founding of *Habima* in Moscow and Eretz-Israel; serious treatment of Jewish folklore and folk songs began (Marek, Ansky); daily newspapers in Hebrew and Yiddish started appearing. This feeling of renaissance was also shared by some of Western Jewry, especially in Germany, which had contacts with the Hebrew spiritual treasures. In Germany Hasidic stories as well as selections from lyrical poetry and the treasures of Jewish legends appeared as expressions of a specific philosophical thought. The Berlin *Jüdischer Verlag*, influenced by Bertold Faivel and especially Martin Buber, gave its readers respect for the values of Jewish culture and revealed Hasidism, Rabbi Naḥman of Bratslav, and so on, to German Jewry. And there was a Jewish party (*Vozrozhdenie*—"Revival") whose worldview was based on the rise in the nation's forces: here Hebrew and Yiddish literature were created, a Jewish working class appeared, political organizations, public and democratic movements and secular community councils were all formed; they will achieve Jewish autonomy and that autonomy will lead to the unification of all *Sejms*[80] ("Parliaments") and finally, both as a result and as the apogee of the Jewish renaissance, also a territory and Jewish independence. Thus it was a conception that fed on the feeling of elevation in the life of the people. Members of that movement, of the same circles, Labor Zionists by their various labels—*Worker Zionists, Poaley Tsiyon*, and so on—assembled in those days and created a radically inverse theory. Their theory drew on the recognition of the destiny of the generation and annihilation in Diaspora; they saw the economic degeneration, the destruction of classes without a formation of a new class. The recognition of the weaknesses of the Jewish proletariat led to different theories: to the negation of its very existence, to the evaluation of it as a lumpen proletariat, for it found a foothold only in backward professions. They saw Hebrew and Yiddish culture increasingly uprooted, and the fear of degeneration led them to look for a territorial solution.

---

80. The *Sejmists*—a Jewish workers' party (in 1905–6) that affirmed Diaspora and saw the goal as Jewish autonomy governed by Jewish *Sejms* (in Polish: "Parliaments").

All of them then seemed to be gospel, with no contradictions between them, although theoretically the contradiction was paramount. For in all that process of fermentation, there was at the same time an expression of rising forces and a sharp expression of the dead end of the Diaspora. The literature that expressed the period was not only born of fermentation but was also a constructive and consolidating factor, encouraging and exuberant. This abundance of spiritual fermentation found its expression in both languages—Hebrew and Yiddish—which turned in that period from the "Holy Tongue" and "jargon," respectively, into languages of the people, national and popular, languages of the spiritual life of the individual personality. The quarrel between the languages itself both expressed and influenced the new attitude toward language, to its positive and spiritual value. From a narrow, utilitarian attitude—as in the language of "Responsa," "Targum," the language of "give and take" among our coreligionists—it turned into an attitude toward language as a means of national existence, a consolidating cultural value. Language, per se, assumed an importance in man's consciousness—precisely because of that competition for "the national linguistic priority," both languages had an impact on the individual. The whole generation was influenced by both and by the quarrel between the two. In this struggle of the people for its language and the language for the people lies the root of that fanaticism of the self-realizing vanguard, of the *Ha-Meorer* group around Y. H. Brener; of the worker in Diaspora in his attitude toward Yiddish and of the worker who laid the groundwork for the revival of Hebrew in Eretz-Israel. The writers—though they were not the ones who shaped the parties—did influence the minds and spirit of masses of people, and insofar as they faithfully expressed life, they also shaped it.

We cannot speak of the spiritual world of the Second Aliya without mentioning the special influence of the Bible, which had been a living and influential factor in previous immigrations to Eretz-Israel as well. The Bible influenced all generations, not just in its religious value and content; on the contrary—religion was nourished by it, but the influence of the Bible was greater than that of religion. The Bible is a spiritual reflection of the life of agriculture and war, the image of a conquering nation, a working nation, a nation of "this world." The land, its conquest and life in it, the emergence of a Hebrew personality, the unification of the tribes, the primeval attitude toward the universe, nature, love and death, wisdom of life, its poetry and grief, social and national wars—all that is reflected in the Bible with the genius and educational value of artistic simplicity. The Bible molded the spiritual world of the Jewish child. For thousands of years, Jews have taught with the Biblical figures of the Hebrew myth. Every other religion takes pains to turn their personalities, heroes, and spiritual giants into naive, untainted saints. Every personality is abstract, either all good or all bad. But the heroes of the Bible are men of flesh and blood, they rise and fall, have plenty of sins, weakness and valor, like all mortals. With this realism and its involvement, this book educated and influenced no less, and perhaps more, than with its religious feeling.

Eretz-Israel lives in the memory of the Jews as a homeland, and this memory was contained in the Bible. In all the generations, no other Bible was created, for the Jewish nation did not have another land. Only in this land did we live our independent lives and our culture drew its strength from it, and in no other land did we know such upright bearing.

The influence of the Bible on the Second Aliya served as a tangible link to the whole country, reviving the threads that connect the immigrant to *every spot* in the land, through associations evoked from childhood (Jerusalem, Judea, Shomron, the Galilee, the Jordan, mountains and valleys). The Bible served as a kind of birth certificate, helped to break the barrier between man and the land, and nourished "a sense of homeland." This "ours" raised forces in man which helped him to strike roots and hold on to this land whose climate, nature, and landscapes are so different from the land of his childhood. All this was expressed in the close and courageous contact with this book and in the phenomenon so unusual in a working-class milieu—that the Bible was in almost every worker's room.

In those days of fermentation and questioning, when life was so problematic and the existence of the Hebrew individual and the Hebrew nation were in question, the great strength of our literature surfaced, accompanying and enriching all of life. Insofar as the political and economic consolidation in the life of the Jews was weak, the consolidating value of the cultural and spiritual life grew strong.

For the masses of rootless people, lacking ground and a homeland, lacking consolidating values of life, the artistic and literary expression of their desires and suffering served as a great and involving unifying force. Bialik was not read just by Zionists. A Bundist who knew Hebrew would secretly read Bialik's new poem. All of us, members of different and rival parties, read this Hebrew poem; many knew it by heart; for all of us, its appearance was an event. And every genuine Hebrew reader also read a Yiddish work by Peretz, Sholem Aleichem, or Nomberg, and the pleasure of literary expression was shared by all this complex and factionalized intelligentsia. All were "for" or "against," but none was outside. Some were "for" Bialik, some were "for" Peretz, but both of those writers expressed the fermentation of the period; for in both of them, the weary Jewish soul with its tragic contradictions found a voice. All came from the same world, whose foundations were doomed to destruction, and they sought the truth of the fermentation and the destruction, strove for a new image of life and a revamping of all values; because, in the destruction and fermentation of the life of the Jews, many creative forces were crying for a way out. Masses of young people were uprooted from their world, were torn out of their past, began looking for a new grasp on life, but there was no basis for their seeking and they remained with no homeland and no outlet; Hebrew and Yiddish literature—were both born of that destiny, both are results of that helplessness and that tragic dead end of Diaspora, both raise the same problems to the extent of their expressive abilities.

Hebrew and Yiddish literature were a highly valuable influence in the life of the Second Aliya; they put their stamp on the individual, on the formation of the human type; and there is no better tool to educate the immigrants today than the art of those years. Therefore, we call for a return from time to time to the assets of that period and its creations: to Mendele, Berditshevski, Peretz, Brener—to all those whose art became a revolutionary force in life and expressed the problematics as an experience of life.

Both literatures influenced the generation. Indeed, every literature has its own special traits as every writer has his own individual image, but the generation has one countenance and there is one image for the period as a whole. In their beginnings, both literatures were highly unified. There was also the personal unity, for the same people created in both languages: Mendele, Sholem Aleichem, Berditshevski, Peretz, Bialik, and Nomberg.

The unity of all Jewish generations, the link with the beginnings of national existence and with all the generations of Diaspora found its stronger expression in Hebrew, in its creative literature; and, on the contrary, Yiddish expressed more the positive aspects of Diaspora. That doesn't mean that Yiddish literature out of its very essence had to affirm Diaspora, its life forms and values; and that, out of some other linguistic essence, Hebrew literature had to express the unity of the generations and of destiny, the sense of history. But it is true that the historical link in the life of the nation, its historical destiny, its national separateness, were factors in the life of Hebrew and its preservation in all generations and Diasporas; while the stable, existing, continuous Diaspora was the source and guarantee for the possibility of the existence of Yiddish in the future. These facts caused various tendentious attitudes in Hebrew and Yiddish literature. The nation, the House of Israel, the link and the opposition to the culture of generations, the stability or shakiness of Jewish existence—those are central topics in Hebrew literature and the air it breathes. Moreover, the Hebrew writer turned toward himself and not toward the outside, not toward the Gentile and not toward the Jew outside his culture, hence—less self-justifying, less apologetics. In *Haskala* literature, in general essays, and in Socialist and Zionist literature in Hebrew, the writer was freer toward himself, more virile, educed less pity for the life of Jews and Judaism. The Yiddish writer expressed a softer, more compassionate attitude toward life; hence also the wish to teach and console, to cover up, justify and defend.

More than Hebrew, Yiddish literature expressed questions of class relations, social issues, contradictions among the people; Peretz, Reyzen, Lyesin, Pinski served and accompanied the formation of a Jewish fighting working class. The stories of Peretz, "Bontshe Shvayg," "Shtrayml," and so on, even served as propaganda in the formation of the Bund, as educational material in all Jewish Socialist movements and parties; the attitude toward the Russian Revolution was nourished by them. But the revolutionary attitude to the life of the Jews, to the Jewish man, to all foundations of his life and customs—found its expression primarily in Hebrew literature.

The idealization of Diaspora reality, romanticism, the defense of Hasidism, of the idyllic aspect of the *shtetl*, of the "virtues" of the Jewish man—all those prevailed in Yiddish literature; while the same reality found its revolutionary-relentless criticism in Hebrew. Hasidism at that time did not serve Berditshevski as a romantic ornament or sentimental emotion, but was an auxiliary weapon in his spiritual war inside Judaism. For Brener, the reality of the *shtetl* did not need a revolution, because it was overturned in its very being. Exposure of the revolutionary truth of the naked Jewish reality, Brener's strong, open-eyed, critical, and analytical attitude—that is what Hebrew literature taught us. And it was this literature of that period, along with the ancient Bible, that educated the individual for his immigration to Eretz-Israel.

The spiritual influence of that generation was not confined to the boundaries of Hebrew and Yiddish literature. World literature, especially the literature of Eastern and Central Europe (Russia, Germany, Poland), influenced that whole period through various channels, either directly or through Jewish literature. Either by the circumstances of their lives or in their wanderings as well as through their movements, masses of Jews were thrown into spheres of foreign influences. Contact with the surrounding world in that period was not merely an economic contact; masses of Jews left their domain, traveled to centers of learning and culture, and penetrated the liberation movements of those countries. The whole atmosphere of the first Russian revolution (1905–1907) and the literature accompanying it engraved their features on the image of that generation.

We must not identify the transformations in the life of the Jewish people only with events in Russia. The year 1904–5, the date of the first Russian revolution, is a turning point not just for Russia but also for most of the countries where Jews lived—Russia, Poland, Galicia, Romania, and Bessarabia. Those are years of revolutionary movement in Austria too: the struggle for general voting rights and for a democratic parliament, and the years of debate over the general strike and the role of the professional and political movement in German Socialism—Rosa Luxemburg, Kautski, Bernstein. Indeed, in Russia it was an immense explosion, for many revolutionary forces had accumulated there which had been oppressed for a long time, but those revolutionary phenomena were not unique to Russia; in those days they grew on the soil of European life in general, especially in Eastern and Central Europe. All the sources of cultural and spiritual influence on the Jewish individual—were themselves ablaze with revolution. And this atmosphere encompassed masses in all those countries, large movements and various parties. No doubt our literature absorbed a great deal from the world expressed in European literature. Tolstoy and Dostoevsky, Gorky and Ibsen, Hamsun and Żeromski, Wyspianski and Hauptmann—their works served as a source for the whole generation of the Second Aliya.

When we examine the period and its influence, we see it as a period of stormy changes, events and upheavals in the life of the nation and the individual. In a very short time, people were hurled from one extreme to another. It was a *period of conflagration*, a whole generation went up in flames. Values were burned, worlds and ideas were burned—people were constantly on fire. No doubt this literature expresses a great deal of the positive and constructive, building values and forging man's soul; but all of it was stamped by the conflagration. All Hebrew and Yiddish literature then passed through this crucible.

This fire of spiritual worlds, of values, which accompanied the destruction of the foundations of economic life and Jewish life-style—became a typical phenomenon. In a brief time—ten or fifteen years—many writers and thinkers in our literature and our lives moved from being rebels, igniting and dousing lights, to being penitents. And this phenomenon of burning worlds prevails in the education of the whole generation. Lilienblum, Aḥad Ha-Am, Peretz, Berditshevski—all share this trait in their spiritual life and influence. Lilienblum, this sedate, rational man, was hardly the type of person to light fires. His main virtue was measuring everything profoundly; in his perception, he was hardly an idealist revolutionary, realism was his natural mode; but reality itself was overturned, in the best sense of this word—and he of all people took a *revolutionary* path. That is how his religious world burned down and he arrived at reform in religion and enlightenment. But that world too was completely burned. And this destruction, this criticism of the *Haskala*, ended in a return to the nation, its culture and tradition. His path to Zion, to "The Lovers of Zion," is the path of a penitent. And this problematic of the generation and the warpath in it are often connected with that phenomenon that every value we raised, every idea we ignited suffered from a lack of inflammable material in our Diaspora reality, in the limited possibilities of realization in our Jewish lives. In the Pale of Settlement of Russia, Poland, Lithuania, Galicia, all the ideals burned down very fast, and in many people that fire was accompanied by hesitation and reevaluation as well as by manifestations of penitence.

In our literature, many carry *Sins of Youth*[81] of heresy, revolt, Socialism—and many are penitents. And when we want to pass on the spiritual world of that generation to the generations of new immigrants, we do not face one world, but a world and its opposite. For example, Aḥad Ha-Am—how should we see him as a whole, how convey him? *Which* Aḥad Ha-Am? The fighter against assimilation, against spiritual and religious slavery, against the bureaucracy and patronage [of the officials in Eretz-Israel during the First Aliya], against the sense of inferiority toward rich Western Europe; or Aḥad Ha-Am, fearful lest the foundations will be undermined, who returned to the "bottom line," to fear of the Hebrew worker, of freedom of thought in our lives, who participated in ostracizing Brener, etc.,

---

81. The title of M. L. Lilienblum's autobiographical book, showing his revolt against religion.

etc.? And the works of Peretz? *Which* Peretz? That Peretz who heralds the beginning of a Jewish workers' movement, of the rebel among the people, who puts the individual against the conservative *rav*, or that Peretz who later beautifies that world and feels the need to find a way for apology for the *rebbe*, for Hasidism, to find a symbolic form for our hesitation? And many more.

True, many had their "sins of youth" and burning of worlds and many went through the "road of penitence." During that period, many things were ignited and there were many fires, and in all of them "penitence" appears as an accompaniment. But penitence does not embody the full truth of the value you return to. Let us not learn faith from the "penitent"! And let us not learn the faith in revolution from the "penitent" to revolution! But the values—they were important, they influenced. And the influence of literature was primarily by *paving the road for the Jewish revolution*. It was not literature alone that did it, but as far as literature paved the road to revolution, it also built the possibilities for our immigration [of the Second Aliya] and our creation in Eretz-Israel.

(1937)

Berl Katznelson

1887–1944. Born in Bobruysk, Byelorussia. Immigrated to Eretz-Israel in 1908. In 1911, elected secretary of the Council of Judean Farm Workers. Was a volunteer in the Jewish Legion in World War I. Was among the founders of the Histadrut and editor of its newspaper *Davar* from its inception in 1925. Chief ideologue of the Israeli labor movement.

ON THE QUESTION OF LANGUAGES[82]

We may assume that the executive committee of *Aḥdut Ha-Avoda* did what was necessary to explain our position to our allied organizations abroad, the exact situation of the question of language in Eretz-Israel, the essence of the decision of the Constituent Assembly, as well as the loss and disrespect revealed in the debate on the decision of the Constituent Assembly in the American Jewish press. That debate had only one purpose: under cover of "democracy," to sully Hebrew and the Hebrews in the eyes of their readers.

But, by presenting the decision of the Leeds Conference literally, the *Kuntres* found it necessary to accompany it with a few words addressed to its authors. A few, clear and sharp words:

In the world of the Hebrew worker in Eretz-Israel, the question of languages does not exist. Hebrew history gave our nation Eretz-Israel and the Hebrew language only one time. And the complete revival of the Jewish people lies in the regeneration of the life of the nation in its land and in its language, and in the renewal of a full, organic life. For us, there is only one practical question of language: how to hasten the complete revival of the language among the entire nation, how to make the treasures of Hebrew culture the property not only of exceptional individuals but of the entire nation, how to bring the masses of the nation as an active force into the making of the new Hebrew culture, how to implement this matter most decisively and effectively.

The decision of the Constituent Assembly requiring that those *elected* to the Assembly of Representatives know Hebrew was accepted not by pressure of out-

---

82. Original title: "Statement of the *Kuntres* (On the Question of Languages)"; *Kuntres* was the journal of one wing of the labor movement, *Aḥdut Ha-Avoda* ("Unity of Labor").

siders but by general agreement. We workers of Eretz-Israel *participated in it and supported it.* This decision is not intended to deny the rights of anyone. The Assembly that made the election law did not deny any right of *the voters.* It was this assembly that gave voting rights to members of the Hebrew brigades from England, America, Argentina, and Canada, without asking whether they knew Hebrew. This decision which was accepted expresses our firm conviction—and we are sure that *this is* the conviction of the Hebrew people—that the Hebrew legislative body in Eretz-Israel has only one language: Hebrew. And this, our innermost conviction, will not be changed by all the powers of East and West. In fact, the accepted decision fits a minimal education requirement. It is not a requirement for "learning" and examinations but for an ability to speak the language. And a candidate, who has been in Israel no less than a year (before that, according to the law, he has no right to be elected) and has not learned the language of the people, that is, doesn't know the issues of the country, doesn't read what is written in books and newspapers, and won't understand what is said at meetings, including the Constituent Assembly itself—why should he be elected and what will his function be? Only one function remains for him—to obstruct Hebrew and to demand another language. Perhaps there is someone abroad who wants the Assembly of Representatives to be occupied with such issues. Here there isn't.

So this is the awful decision, the "decree" salted and peppered with some vain rumors,[83] which infuriated the Jewish press in America, caused grief for several innocent people, raised the scream: Hebrews upon you, Israel! And provided Jews with contempt and scorn for the language, the land and its workers, things reminiscent of the period of Territorialism, may it rest in peace.

And to our comrades abroad, let it be said: Stop the vestiges of national opportunism. The Socialist Zionist movement is a revolutionary movement in the highest sense. It triumphed over the concepts prevalent among the Jews, concepts of accommodation and socialization to the equal rights and the annulment of the Pale [of Settlement, in Russia]; it stood against the plague of rational and logical Territorialism. Should it give in to linguistic Ugandism? In the great Hebrew revolution, the revival of the Hebrew language takes its place. And, my brothers, please do not waste forces so necessary for the work of redemption in a war against us, *the vanguard that has advanced before you.* If this is not clearly understood by you in Diaspora, we promise you that, when you come to Eretz-Israel—you will listen and understand. Will you throw stones into that spring of blessing and redemption whose waters you will soon come to drink? The transition of the

---

83. Like the lie that went around the world that soldiers aren't accepted for regular agricultural labor in Mikveh Israel unless they know Hebrew and that the gates are locked for the rest of them. In fact no knowledge is examined and no one was rejected in Mikveh because he didn't know Hebrew; on the contrary, scores who don't know Hebrew come there, and leave after two months speaking Hebrew. [Author's footnote]

worker who comes to Eretz-Israel to our language is natural, the fruit of internal necessity—why burden it by compounding false concepts in Diaspora? It is natural for you there to do your educational work in whatever language the people understand. But the Jewish worker must be educated right away to recognize that here, the language of the nation, the only language, is revived. And this recognition will also make his own transition easy for him. You have accepted the decision about *He-ḥalutz* and about the preparation of pioneers by working the land and learning Hebrew. This is the way!

(1919)

Yosef Klauzner

1874–1958. Born in Olkienik, near Vilna. Studied at the University of Heidelberg, where he received his doctorate. Succeeded Aḥad Ha-Am as editor of *Ha-Shiloaḥ* in 1903. Immigrated to Palestine in 1917. In 1925, appointed Professor of Hebrew Literature at the Hebrew University.

ANCIENT HEBREW AND MODERN HEBREW[84]

I would like to take the liberty of beginning my lecture with a sad event in my life.

Last year my mother died. I sat *Shiva* and began reading the Book of Job, as is customary. But right after the "opening" of the book (chapters 1–2), I came upon a difficulty: instead of *reading* the book of Job, I had to *study* it; for most of its verses are written in an ancient language and require interpretation. And where you need an interpretation—you cannot savor what you read. The words of consolation lost their flavor and I didn't enjoy the lofty argumentation. And I am ashamed to say: I took the French translation of Job by Louis Segond and began to read it chapter after chapter. Naturally, much of the sublimity of the wonderful Hebrew rhetoric and of the unique expressions of this divine book was lost in the foreign translation; but, on the other hand, as compensation I didn't need any interpretations, the *language* was simple and intelligible, so that I could direct my thinking to the *idea*, admire the lofty arguments, and find solace in my grief.

And that is I who have been steeped in Hebrew literature all my life. For over sixty years, from my early childhood, I have not only written but spoken Hebrew.

Yes, I write and speak Hebrew. But the Hebrew of the Book of Job is not my Hebrew, namely, the modern Hebrew in which I write and speak.

This event broadened and deepened in me the idea I had several dozen years ago: There is ancient Hebrew and there is modern Hebrew, which are certainly very close to each other and linked organically to each other, but, after all, *are*

---

84. Excerpts from Lecture at the Fifth National Conference of the "Brigade of the Defenders of the Language," Tel Aviv, Passover, 1929. We excerpted here the discussion of ideas and have deleted the specifically linguistic parts that require a knowledge of Hebrew.

not the same thing. For not only do we not speak and write in the language of Isaiah and Job, but neither in the language of *Mishnah* and *Midrash*. [. . .]

Here is an example of a vital change. The Bible says: "Jacob shall not now be ashamed, neither shall his face now wax pale" (Isaiah 29:22); and the Talmud says: "He who *whitewashes* his friend's face in public" (*Avot* 83:51); but in our day, we don't think that the face of an ashamed person "gets pale" or "white," but "*turns red*" from shame. Should we now use the language of the Bible or the Talmud against our own *senses*? [. . .]

Furthermore, we must open our eyes and see the truth: whoever is not a "scholar" and has not devoted at least ten of his best years to studying all the periods of our literature now no longer understands even Mendele, Bialik, or Tshernikhovski. Soon they too will require an interpretation for their language as we need it for Job, the *Mishnah*, the *Midrash*, and the medieval research books. We already include considerable masses who can speak Hebrew but cannot read it. That is, they can read a newspaper, can read things written in a language close to spoken Hebrew, but cannot read texts whose language is Biblical or that alludes to typical Talmudic or Tibbonite[85] expressions. You may call this ignorance, you may get excited and angry at this sad phenomenon which the alumni of *heder, yeshiva,* or *shul* cannot come to terms with; but that won't change the fact.

And the modern *school* is not to blame: modern *life* is to be blamed. In *heder,* they used to study seventeen hours a day for twelve months of the year (except for short breaks)—and only one discipline: the Torah and Rashi and Talmud. Nevertheless, only 20 percent of those who finished *heder* were capable of studying by themselves; 80 percent remained ignorant and hardly knew a verse of "Torah with Rashi." In the new school, they study nine months of the year, and parents demand that they study history, geography, mathematics, English, and Arabic (or, in the Diaspora, two other foreign languages). How can you expect even the best students to know of our ancient literature what a *ḥeder* graduate knew? But on the other hand, there is not one graduate of our new Hebrew school in Eretz-Israel who could not master the Hebrew language, write a Hebrew letter, or read a Hebrew book; but this Hebrew book must be written in modern Hebrew, not in a mixture of ancient, medieval, and modern Hebrew.

What do our writers today do?—Ostensibly they write modern Hebrew; but, in fact, it is a "language medley." They mix Biblical Hebrew with Mishnaic Hebrew with Tibbonite Hebrew and think this is modern Hebrew *par excellence* because it is "synthetic Hebrew"—and nowadays "synthesis" is very popular: it serves instead of "compromise" which people are a bit ashamed of... And now the grammarians come and provide a grammar of the Hebrew language "in all its styles"—and think they have thus enriched and perfected the Hebrew language.

---

85. The Tibbon family in the twelfth and thirteenth centuries translated many research and philosophical works from Arabic into Hebrew and created the style of Hebrew medieval philosophy.

Those "synthesizers" don't understand that their deeds are like yoking an elephant and a mastodon together.

For if there is development in the world, it is an evolution. An old layer is covered by a newer layer that is the same old layer with some additions and innovations. Of course the new is embodied in the old; but since the birth of the new, we no longer need the old unless we are interested in the evolution of the new; while in vital usage, the new pushed out the old and took its place. This is how evolution works, and this is the nature of things all over the world. The elephant derived from the mastodon, and scholars of antiquities are happy to prove that the mastodon preceded the elephant and that, if not for the mastodon, there would be no elephant in the world; but for various natural reasons—because the elephant was more fit for the new conditions—the elephant triumphed over the mastodon. And now whoever wants to revive the mastodon and use it instead of an elephant or whoever wants to yoke a mastodon and an elephant together would be a grotesque romantic and a hopeless Don Quixote.

Words and forms of a language change and evolve like animals. They too undergo a struggle of survival. A form that fits better for clear expression, a word that is easier and clearer, will always win over forms and words that are less fitting for the given expression or are less easy and lucid. Once upon a time, Martin Luther translated the word *alma* in Isaiah—which religious Christians see as an allusion to the Holy Virgin: "Behold, a virgin shall conceive, and bear a son" (Isaiah 7:14)—with the German word *Dirne* (which is still remembered in the popular emotive word *Dirnchen*); but today, the word *Dirne* is a derogatory word for a whore and no German writer would use it to refer to the Holy Virgin or even to a plain, modest virgin. [. . .]

This is not the case in modern Hebrew literature, which is a pantheon of words, forms, and expressions from all periods, living peacefully next to one another. [. . .] For our language today is really not a language at all but a Biblical patch on top of a Mishnaic patch with a Tibbonite patch on top of it. And he who masters all those "languages" and can juggle them and combine them in various strange blends is a "language virtuoso." This is the above-mentioned "language synthesis" our writers boast they have used to enrich the revived Hebrew. But in fact it is nothing but "language syncretism": as our forefathers in the time of Ahab and Jezebel worshiped both Ba'al and Jehovah with no distinction, so we mix various language periods together—and that's our new Hebrew. This is a kind of linguistic ragout or vinaigrette, but not a real language. In a real language, there are earlier and later phenomena—and the earlier are always supplanted by the later: for this is the way of natural evolution. [. . .] And our modern language must be preferred over all the others, for it is new: it is the last of our four linguistic layers. And as in geological strata, plants and animals of earlier strata were supplanted by those of the most recent stratum, so in language strata—the *newest and latest* stratum precedes all the rest.

It may be argued that the Hebrew language was not spoken until these very days. Therefore, it cannot have a natural evolution. It was only a literary language, and hence cannot rely on anything but literary examples. It was alive only in the Biblical and Mishnaic times. Later, when it lived only in writing and not in speech, it became very distorted, and we have no criteria to judge what is right and what is wrong except for the ancient examples from the time of the Temple. Otherwise—our language will become barbaric and grow wild.

There is a *lot* of truth in this argument but not *all* the truth. Even a language that lives in writing undergoes an evolution. If we agreed to that decision about the Hebrew language, we would have to admit to the Yiddishists that we came today to revive a corpse—which we absolutely must not do. The Hebrew language, which was alive in writing, also evolved in writing, even if not in an entirely normal way. And the vitality of the "dead language" was so great that it even influenced the "living languages" spoken among the Jews. [. . .] The literary Hebrew language did not cease weaving the thread of its life (or half-life) even for one generation in the whole fifteen hundred years of its existence. But we consider only the language of the Bible and to some extent the language of *Mishnah* and *Midrash*; and only just now have some begun to pay attention to the style of the Tibbonites. No one paid any attention to the modern language, to the conscious and subconscious changes made in it during the hundred and fifty years of intensive and uninterrupted development. Let us admit that, to this very day, not just for our grammarians but even for all the Hebrew teachers and for most writers writing Hebrew today, the Hebrew language is only the Biblical, vocalized Hebrew. For them, all the rest is simply a deviation, a "medley-language," considered distorted and barbaric.

We must put an end to this. How long will we waver: if we have a living and spoken language—it is the language of now, *with* its natural (not accidental) changes which our conservatives call "barbarisms"; and if the Hebrew language is only an imitation of the language of Job and Rabbi Yehuda Ha-Nasi, then writing and speaking it is nothing but magic tricks, a talented attempt to imitate the ancients, but not natural writing or real speech. There is no "synthesis" in it at all, but this is really the "mixed language," and not the one with a few barbarisms: this ostensibly "synthetic" language is a mixture of Bible, *Mishnah*, and Tibbonite and has no trace of a unified language or language evolution. [. . .]

We must emphasize that we are not the only ones in this hesitation between an ancient and a modern language. There is another ancient nation that is proud of the splendor of its forefathers which, like the Jews, enriched the whole world with their culture; and their children have now declined, for they too were deprived of a government and a state for several hundred years and returned to life only a hundred and thirty years ago. I am referring to the *new Greeks*. [. . .]

The strength of the Hebrew language vis-à-vis the Ashkenazi and Sephardi jargons lies in her uninterrupted evolution for thousands of years. Our Hebrew script is twenty-five hundred years old (approximately from the time of Ezra). And if we cut off that thread of development, we weaken ourselves. *Mendele*

Moykher Sforim said in a speech at a celebration of his eightieth birthday in Odessa: "The force of forty thousand horsepower will not vanquish the force of four thousand years of the uninterrupted existence of the Hebrew language." We must not, therefore, make a breach in this ancient force. And yet modern Hebrew is the latest summary of this evolution uninterrupted for thousands of years: it absorbs and swallows, takes in and integrates the selection of all language periods, and grasps the latest and most developed in them. Hence, the demand to write and speak modern Hebrew does not mean ripping the historical thread but rather its continuation, without lagging or retreating. It means spinning the historical thread with no interruption; hence, this spinning involves opposing a return to a language period that is past and gone.

It may be argued that there are not sufficiently important changes between one language period and another language period in Hebrew and that it is therefore premature to distinguish ancient Hebrew and modern Hebrew. In my opinion, this is wrong. A Christian theologian who knows the Bible well does not understand the language of the *Mishnah* and the *Midrash*, which means there is a big difference between them. And a Jewish scholar in Western Europe, who is an expert in *Mishnah, Midrash*, and medieval literature, can barely read modern Hebrew literature and will always prefer reading a scientific book in another language to reading an equally important scientific book in modern Hebrew. Which means that even between the language of *Mishna* and *Midrash* and the language of the Tibbonites, on the one hand, and modern Hebrew, on the other hand, the difference is not that small.

Of course, the language of the *Mishna* must be at the base of modern Hebrew, for it is the later layer of the two language strata that emerged when Hebrew was still a spoken language in Eretz-Israel. The language of the Tibbonites, the language of the later rabbis, and the modern language up to Ben-Yehuda were formed at a time when Hebrew was no longer spoken on a regular basis. Nevertheless, we must not freeze at the *Mishna* language either. Many reasons have caused the changes in Hebrew in the last hundred and fifty years—and we must take account of those changes. [. . .]

Did you ever see a forest in early spring?—The first soft, young sprouts are burgeoning; yet heaps of dry, withered leaves are scattered on the forest ground and won't let the soft sprouts emerge into the air. The same is true of modern Hebrew. There are new, soft sprouts—and even if there are few of them, they are signs of a new development; but our pedantic and rigorous conservatism won't let them grow—and they dry up before they grow strong. [. . .] An important grammarian found mistakes in the poems of *Bialik* and in the stories of *Frishman!*—We must approve such literary forms and stop thinking of them as "mistakes": they are mistakes when you write ancient Hebrew, but are not mistakes at all when you write modern Hebrew. They must stop scaring us constantly that we are writing with mistakes because in phrase X in *Mishna* Y and in *Midrash* Z, the phrase is different. For if we are consistent in this matter, we may conclude that modern Hebrew has no right to exist at all, as the scholar Nöldeke always argued: it takes Biblical words out of their context and their literal meaning in the Bible. To which we answer: the meanings of ancient words evolve and change willy-nilly. [. . .]

Of course we must be aware of barbarisms. Simple people in Eretz-Israel say: "*Ha-yeled ose li mavet*" [literally, "The child makes me death"] (from Ashkenazi-Jewish—i.e, Yiddish: *Er makht mir dem toyt*) or "*na'asa khoshekh li ba-eynaim*" [literally, "It was made dark in my eyes"] instead of "*khashkhu eynay*" [literally, "My eyes darkened"]—from Russian. And we must fight such jargonization and Russification of the Hebrew language, as we must fight Germanization, Anglicization, and Arabization. But not every barbarism is dangerous and deserves to be weeded out. A limited number of barbarisms is natural: no language was ever developed without a conscious or subconscious influence of another language. Sixty years ago, when I wrote "*She'ela bo'eret* [literally, "A Burning Question"] for the first time, I was attacked from all sides: how dare you? A coarse Germanism: *Eine brennende Frage*—and now who does not use this "coarse Germanism" in Hebrew? Furthermore, those who do use the "burning question" no longer sense that this expression was ever felt to be non-Hebrew.

Of course, *Hodot l'*—["due to"] and *Lamrot* ["despite"] are expressions influenced by German *dank* and *trotz*; but if our writers have used such expressions for a hundred years, we have no right to disqualify them today: otherwise we shall have to disqualify dozens of expressions from the *Mishna* that were influenced by the Aramaic language. [. . .] The "pure" German expression *Bekanntschaft machen* is nothing but a translation of the "pure" French expression *faire la connaissance*, which in turn, is a translation of the English expression *make acquaintance*; and who is to decide what is a barbarism and what is not!

It is certainly not my intention to abandon the language of the Bible, the *Mishna*, and the Tibbonites and their special Hebrew expressions. We will always teach our schoolchildren Bible, *Mishna*, and *Midrash*, and our language will always be influenced by the two earliest strata of our language, the Biblical and *Mishnaic*, for when they emerged, the Hebrew language was still spoken among the Jews. And we shall always write poems and religious treatises in a language close to the holy texts and the Talmud—the language of our poetry and the language of our oral teachings. Poetry and religion favor archaisms in all languages; not to mention in the Hebrew language of poetry and religion. But in simple prose, we too must approach the spoken language, as other languages do, even if to a lesser degree. For in other languages, too, there is a difference between the language of the marketplace and the language of literature; but *a difference is not an abyss*. And in our literature today, there is not a difference between those two, but a gaping abyss. This abyss must be bridged by bringing the literary language closer—in prose a great deal and in poetry more and more—to the spoken Hebrew language, which, after all, is the living language only coarsened and distorted by the market-place.

Once, if you wanted to write simple Hebrew for children, you would write in the Biblical language: for the Hebrew language was known even sixty years ago not from speech but from study, and children studied Bible first of all. Now the situation is reversed: if you write for children in the Biblical language, you make it hard for them to understand. Our children in Eretz-Israel speak modern Hebrew from childhood and study the language of the Bible in school, so they don't know it well before the age of thirteen or fourteen. Hence it is a sin that many books intended especially for our children are written basically in the language of the Bible, even if they occasionally use Mishnaic Hebrew: this blended language is dead for them compared with the living language of our time; and when they read a book written in that language—even in the most "grammatical" and "exquisite" language—it is hard for them to understand and, in any case, they don't savor the living language, which is the only language of their lives and spirits. [. . .]

All this must end. Our language must be a real language, not an exhibit of more or less successful imitations of the ancients. We must speak and write as free men in their own language and not as slaves to Isaiah and Rabbi Yehuda ha-Nasi. That certainly does not mean canceling grammar and writing anything a fishwife in the marketplace may say or a casual journalist may write; but we must undo the *superfluous* chains—archaic forms, words, and expressions—that bind the legs of those who speak and write Hebrew; if not—our language will never live a full life! If not—it will never be a unified language but will forever remain "a mixed tongue"—mixed in with Bible, *Mishna*, Tibbonite. And this is not a language, but a linguistic hocus-pocus. [. . .]

Of course, there is a need to compose a special Biblical grammar, a *Mishna* grammar, and even a Tibbonite grammar to recognize the special character of every period of the Hebrew language and to study Bible, *Talmud*, and medieval literature; this is an important issue for academic science, for the scholars of language at the Hebrew University and outside of it. Of course, Ben-Yehuda's dictionary, which includes—or tries to include—all the words of the Hebrew language in all its periods and strata is a great and necessary achievement, and the Academy of the Hebrew Language, which will sooner or later be formed, must expand and perfect it, include in it all the words used in all times in Hebrew literature in the thousands of years of its existence—even the Aramaic, Greek, Latin, and Arabic words and words from other living languages incorporated in Hebrew literature throughout the ages. But for the needs of the living language and the living literature, for the needs of vital usage, we need a short and new grammar[86] and a short and new dictionary that will give us only what is alive and breathing today and what may be the most recent station, for the time being,

---

86. I published a *Short Grammar of Modern Hebrew*, with Mitspe, Tel Aviv, 1935, and it even went into a second edition; but the fanatics of *ancient* Hebrew prevented its acceptance in the schools of Eretz-Israel and overseas, in spite of the fact that it would have eased the study of the difficult Hebrew grammar that has long been obsolete. [Author's footnote]

in the development of modern Hebrew, a station from which our language will move forward unhindered.

I can end my remarks with the same words that closed the introduction to the second part of my book *Creators and Builders*:

We must and want to be the heirs of our forefathers, but not their graves!

(Jerusalem–Talpiot, 8 Sivan, 1929)

Tsvi Shats

1890–1921. Born in Romny, Ukraine. Immigrated to Eretz-Israel in 1911. Served in the Jewish Legion. Was murdered with Brener during an Arab riot in Jaffa.

EXILE OF OUR CLASSICAL POETRY

The only language in which genuine classical poetry is created is the language of the working people. In the early days of humanity, when folk poets like Homer walked around reciting their poetry to the people, their language was the language of the people. There was no difference then between the language of the people and the literary language. But in the course of generations, the language of the people became raw material also in the hands of those whose situation in society had changed and allowed them to live a more intuitive life. As an expression of their life, they created the second language for themselves—the literary language. Thus, a certain distance was created between literature and the people; and the real life of the people, the life of the worker, remained without a poetic or artistic expression. Since then, the misunderstanding that lies like a deep abyss between the class of the working people and the artist began and grew. Thus the seed of jealousy and class hatred, that chronic social illness, was born. A cure for these ills can only come if the working people will also be the creating people.

In our world, ostensibly, we could have avoided that shameful situation. For we are just about to build our own society, to lay its first bricks. And yet, a schism deeper than that of other nations is also emerging among us. The fact is that the language of the people in Eretz-Israel is not our literary language. The pronunciation stressing the ultimate syllable is completely different from that in which our great poets wrote their poetry, where the stress is on the penultimate syllable. To the working people in Eretz-Israel, the entire new generation that is now arising, their poetry is incomprehensible.

As we begin gathering in the exiles of the nation, mending the divisions, destroying all the barriers that have arisen between its various strata and creating a ground of deep, intimate, and purposeful understanding—we must pay special attention to the creation of a single language, and a single pronunciation. So far, proper attention has not been given to that. We must first of all avoid the reality of two languages, a language of the people and a literary language. Let us remember that our people is the People of the Book, and even here in Eretz-Israel, the worker who holds the plow remains a man, with the burning desire to be a man, and his need for spiritual nourishment is no less—and perhaps is even stronger—than the need of some idler lying on a silk sofa and spitting idly at the ceiling. In the new Russia, which is now in Messianic pangs, a new generation of the *intellectual worker* will arise. He is the product of the new education of physical labor for everyone, from childhood on, with no exceptions. A generation of the intellectual worker who will work with his hands and conquer and create with his mind will arise instead of the hostile classes. He will carry within him the candle of the future culture and he will erect it.

That same model of the worker is being created in the pioneer movement in our land too. For the desire for work and the desire for life do not contradict each other in the heart of our youth, and these two desires will finally blaze a trail to a perfect world and will drive out of their way all other desires that lie in wait for him... For he is no longer the same oppressed man, who serves only as material for exploitation, who lets others enjoy poetry and beauty at the expense of his own time which is stolen and his own needs which are stifled.—

There is not yet any poetry that will enfold this intellectual worker who is being absorbed here and there, bursting forth and sprouting in our land, who is the seed of the future nation. His language, which is different in pronunciation from our literary language, is not yet material for poetry. His independent and full life has not yet found any echo, any joyful, comforting expression. At dawn, he will brace himself like a lion, when he comes out to the field—but his poetry will not accompany him! He will come out like this, as overseas. His poetry remained in exile... He will not read the poetry of Bialik, Shneur, Tshernikhov-ski[87]—for he will not understand it . . .—And not because of that schism between his life and exile. Nor because of that vital sorrow—"the sorrow of yesterday." Let us allow that sorrow of yesterday to still shade our faces and evoke sad voices in our hearts.—The main reason why poetry cannot be absorbed among us is its foreign accent. With all its beauty and depth, it will not make our heart beat because it is not molded from the coarse clods of our life or from the harsh or joyous tones of our life, which vibrate on our lips every day... Its value is like that of poetry written in a foreign language... And, with all good will, if we wish to bring it close to our own lives and read in our own language, whose stress is on the ultimate syllable—we will not understand it, not to mention enjoy it. It will be ridiculous and pitiful, like that wonderful Beethoven sonata written by mistake according to garbled notes, like a musical instrument corrupted by a drunkard... It will come out whole from the treasure of the artist's soul and maimed with

87. Major Hebrew poets of the Renaissance Period, beginning at the end of the nineteenth century, and still central to Hebrew poetry in Europe at the time.

defective form, it will assault our ears. For the most exalted idea will not occur unless it assumes its own fitting and unique expression, and if the latter is defective and alien to us, how shall we envision the soul of the creation in its untainted purity as it emerged in the soul of its creator?—No, the worker in Eretz-Israel has no classical poetry that will comfort him and educate him, for the poetry that is available will not lift his hard life from the low level, will not enlighten the weariness of the evenings after work, and, when he rises at dawn, will not sing within him, will not even cheer him. It will not evoke in him the spirit of revolt or the courage to bear his life or the calm of happiness... It will not make our future history...

And the worker is so attentive, so thirsty for that melody! And perhaps it is because of that vague hope that he came to Eretz-Israel... Where is it?

It is not the poverty of our life that is against us! We talk in Eretz-Israel about influencing the Diaspora and about stirrings of creativity within us. But not one original popular poem, not even one melody was created in this center in Eretz-Israel throughout all those years, nor could they have been created! And there is no need for them, there is no need for premature fruit that testifies only to the sickness of the young seedling. Let us exempt Eretz-Israel from the obligation to create, from the obligation to influence, etc., etc. (See Sh. Yavnieli, "Imparting the Language to the People," in the collection Aḥdut Ha-Avoda.)

But this is a profound error, comrade Yavnieli! For poetry never was contemporary or a mirror of its period, as other faithful genres of the culture of their time, like the realistic novel, science, or essays.

Poetry in itself cannot be a loyal contemporary either. *Like prophecy, poetry anticipates and heralds the generation.* It expresses life in potential, reveals what is hidden to the naked eye, the sweet, exuberant, and hidden dream... Poetry is the perfume of the future, the aromatic fragrance of the offering of the yearning soul, and rises to the eternal god; it is a distant echo of those voices which were only destined to be born! The freshest poetry, with slivers of night still in its curls, will shine at the time of the ferment of aspirations and not at the time of their fulfillment in life. In fact, our lives are rich, invisibly influencing, profound tones... For perhaps in no other generation were there so many "artists of the beautiful silence" as in ours. No, it is not the poverty of our lives, not the lack of substance, but the absence of form, of a framework; the absence of a vessel for the essence that is falling into chaos; the absence of an instrument for the player and for the hands stretched out "toward every stirring of beauty and vibration of splendor." Tshernikhovski sensed the hidden tragedy that was created by "the opposition between the melody of speech and the melody of poetry damaging the music and causing Hebrew poetry not to strike roots." But he sensed the other side of the tragedy, which was his—the one who sings; but greater than that is the tragedy of the many whose name will not be famous and whose heads will not be crowned with wreaths in their longing to listen. For, in the beginning was listening, the holy need to receive, and it was this that created the second need: to give. You can wipe out books but you can't hinder the course of life... And life in Eretz-Israel is already fused organically with our accent and we now want to receive what belongs to us.

Until today, we have been forced to read our poetry in a pronunciation that is foreign to our lives. The most marvelous poem will suddenly, on a certain borderline, abandon me—and my life remains unsung—the life is separate from the poetry. How shall we put our lives into poetry? Or how shall we return the exile of our poetry?

The fate of our very revival may depend on this question.

Klatzkin writes about this: "It [the revival] is still playing with the national idea and sporting secretly with the revolution hidden in that idea. But the time has come to take the thought of revival to the ultimate conclusion and to reveal it in all its genuine cruelty."

Indeed, the time has come, and what can be sensed in the dark there in exile—we see clearly here in Eretz-Israel. The great hour is approaching, the hour of encounter of the reviving nation with its great poets, the poets of Exile. Who will give way to whom?

Shneur writes about our literature in Eretz-Israel in [the journal] *Miklat*: "A stream of such barbarism always erupts into the breaches of every language during times of revolution and days of transition to new cultural goals, to national revivals and political expansions, until the Sanhedrin of that language comes, led by great poets, whose artistic sensibility was and always will be the highest and most correct judge in all languages, and sweeps the barbarism out to that chaos of licentiousness and that mass fog whence it came."—Yes, the great poets have the right to enact the laws of language... But not the laws of life, for life paves its own way without asking the poets of the generation or its legislators! And we mustn't look down on the "mass fog."

At this decisive hour, I, one of the people, the ignorant people of the land, dare to turn to them. You must lend an ear to the pulse of our lives.—Here, Bialik demands the "obligation," he bends his head and asks for the iron yoke on his neck. Indeed, the yoke is ready and the obligation is clear. *To immigrate to Eretz-Israel and, out of the clods of her black earth, to mold the truth of real life, the poetry of life!* Some by manual labor and some by intellectual talent, for only the poetry of life is victorious.

Is it not a riddle (shameful at any rate) of our revival that the pillars of our poetry still stand far away, beyond the borders of Eretz-Israel, and have not yet felt their direct obligation and have not immigrated to Eretz-Israel and have not yet absorbed within them the voices of life, and have not yet set up a living god among them and have not yet tuned the strings of their instruments anew?!

How will the encounter be? We shall see; we still want to return our poetry from Exile, for we cannot and do not want to cut all threads that tie us with the Diaspora, for there are also veins of life among them, which draw from blocked ponds in the heart of the people. We will not be deluded in our wish to create "anew," and we will not be in despair in postponing the vision of creation to the distant future. We will call to the great men of the nation: Don't let us start from scratch, build a bridge and come to us and influence our lives with that hidden happiness which throbs in the source of life! Give us, us too, that juice, the ancient vision, and we will fill with it the cup of our fate, we will dress it in the tones of our life, we will serve it with splendor, we will return it from the wanderings of Exile to our hearts!!

Come to us not to "sweep away" but to listen attentively and to create.

"Then a poet will sing a new song"...

The corrupt "Ashkenazi" accent achieved its existence thus far because our language was still only in the book. But other days arrived, the language was absorbed in our heart and found utterance, and the corrupt accent no longer has any place in our daily life and certainly not in the temple of poetry.

Other nations also have various dialects, in various strata of the "simple" people; but not in the language of creation. To create one such language, both popular and literary, we have to bring together all three of our pronunciations, for only then will the national accent be created. It will be strong, lucid, and plastic as the Sephardi, lyric as the Ashkenazi, and manifold in its tones and nuances as the Yemenite. But the body, the base, the river that receives the other streams—will be and must be our Sephardi accent, in which the working and creating generation thinks—for from it will rise the nation.

And when and who will start building this new accent? I still believe that our great poets, after they strike root in Eretz-Israel—for this is their function, their national obligation—will create for us the one national accent, as they created from various languages—the language of the Bible, the Haggadah, and so on—one language understood by everyone.—And let us not postpone this for generations. We live in a period of general melting, the melting of a new world. In the heat of our day, values are created which many generations could not have created in another period.

And meanwhile, the distortions in our language get accepted. A great cultural work is done right in front of our eyes. Enormous sums were donated by the rich of our nation; diligent and talented people are working at full steam. In America they translate Longfellow, Shelley, the classics of world poetry into Hebrew, and a profound grief grips our heart: all that is not for us. Shelley, who is all subtlety and music will be presented to us, speakers of a native language, as a stammerer and a stutterer! The only swallow that has thus far wandered into our street—is Jabotinsky's translation of Edgar Allen Poe's "Raven" [in the Sephardi accent]. But since then, years have gone by and the second swallow has not yet returned. Instead of that, they go on translating diligently the geniuses of poetry into the distorted dialect. And what is the purpose of all this Sisyphean labor? Of all this creativity made from material that will soon be nonexistent? And who is it for? Are the gifted exempt from this concern? Is such toil worthwhile for the doubtful, temporary, and passing majority of speakers of the distorted accent? Where is the good sense of those in Exile and even of the young poets growing here in Eretz-Israel? They didn't learn anything either, nor did they understand anything, they too keep going in the same paved path...

For the emotional recovery of the nation, so that the rent will be united, we need in every aspect the internal fortification—and that is our slogan today: *to concentrate all that is being created in our nation in one language and in one pronunciation.* Therefore, we now need translations of A. Reyzen and Morris Rosenfeld[88] perhaps much more than of Shelley and Longfellow.

And may we wish that Shneur, Tshernikhovski, and Bialik be translated into our pronunciation!...

Our forefathers, just exiled from Eretz-Israel and still feeling its aroma and holiness, were more Jewish. What did they do? They immediately all stood and took advice and hung their violins on the willows there and controlled their souls and put their thumbs in their mouths *and squeezed and chopped them.* That is what was said: How shall we sing, how shall we sing the song of our Lord in an alien land? And yet the generations that came after them did not keep the vows of their fathers; the grief of wandering in foreign lands, memories of the past, and yearnings for the homeland demanded expression but could no longer be played on the strings of the ancient violin which were stretched in their crushed hands, in their chopped fingers. What did they do? They took advice and weakened them and prepared them according to the structure of Exile.

And now we must stretch the harpstrings anew and strengthen them as before. For our hands are strengthened by work, the hands of the worker in Eretz-Israel have gathered force and returned to their firmness.

So much for the obligation and the talented. And who, therefore, will do the work of building?—All of us, the workers who live and speak... But imposing one language and one correct accent demands the radical, concentrated, and immediate work of one higher institution, selected by the Hebrew World Congress that is to convene during our lifetime. This Sanhedrin, which will emerge here in Eretz-Israel, will also have the authority and the means that will make its laws and its instructions mandatory in every school in Exile and in Eretz-Israel. Textbooks, dictionaries, and encyclopedias that will be published by it will teach the nation to speak, and when it speaks—it will also give expression.

(Rafah, September 1919)

---

88. The Yiddish proletarian poets in America.

REFERENCES

The notation [H] indicates a publication in Hebrew; other languages are noted; all unmarked items are in English.

Academy of the Hebrew Language
  1970   [H] *Collection of Documents on the History of the Language Committee and the Academy of Hebrew Language 1890–1990 and on the Revival of Hebrew Speech* (Jerusalem: Academy of the Hebrew Language).
Aḥad Ha-Am
  1950   [H] "Truth from Eretz-Israel," in *Collected Writings*, 2d ed. (Tel Aviv: Dvir; Jerusalem: The Jewish Publishing House), pp. 28–40.
Aliya Shniya
  1947   [H] *Sefer Ha-Aliya Ha-Shniya*, edited by Brakha Khabas, with the participation of Eliezer Shokhat (Tel Aviv: Am Oved).
Alter, Robert
  1975   Ed., *Modern Hebrew Literature* (New York: Behrman House).
  1988   *The Invention of Hebrew Prose: Modern Fiction and the Languages of Realism* (Seattle and London: University of Washington Press).
Amichai, Yehuda
  1987   "My Parents' Migration," in "Five Poems by Yehuda Amichai," translated by Barbara and Benjamin Harshav, *Orim* 3, no. 1:28.
Azaryahu, Yosef
  1954   [H] *Hebrew Education in Eretz-Israel* (Ramat-Gan: Masada).
Bacchi, Roberto
  1956a   "A Statistical Analysis of the Revival of Hebrew in Israel," in *Studies in Economic and Social Sciences* (Jerusalem: Magnes Press).
  1956b   [H] "The Revival of the Hebrew Language as Reflected in Statistics," *Leshonenu* 20:65–82; 21 (1957): 41–68.
Bar-Adon, Aaron
  1975   *The Rise and Decline of a Dialect: A Study in the Revival of Modern Hebrew* (The Hague and Paris: Mouton).
  1977   [H] *Sh. Y. Agnon and the Revival of the Hebrew Language* (Jerusalem: Mosad Bialik).

1988   [H] "The 'Galilee Dialect' and Its Pronunciation: A Chapter in the History of the Revival of Hebrew in Eretz-Israel," *Katedra* 46:115–138.

Ben-Gurion, David

1947   [H] "On the Twenty-Fifth Anniversary," in *Aliya Shniya*, pp. 15–19.

1972   *Letters*, vol. 1 (Tel Aviv: Am Oved).

Ben-Sasson, H. H.

1976   Ed., *A History of the Jewish People* (Cambridge, Mass.: Harvard University Press).

Bentwich, Norman

1912   *Jewish Schools in Palestine* (New York: reprinted from the *Jewish Review* and published by the Foundation of American Zionists).

Ben-Yehuda, Eliezer

1986   [H] *The Dream Come True: Selected Writings on Topics of Language*, edited by Reuven Sivan (Jerusalem: Mosad Bialik).

[Berditshevski] Bin-Gorion, Mikha Yoseph

1987   [H] *Poetry and Language: Selected Essays and Sketches* (Jerusalem: Mosad Bialik).

Bialik, Hayim Nakhman

1990   [H] *Poems: Academic Edition*, edited by Dan Miron, vol. 2 (Tel Aviv: Dvir).

Blanc, Haim

1957   "Hebrew in Israel: Trends and Problems," in Morag 1988, 1:167–155.

Blau, Yehoshua

1983   [H] "Remarks on the Multi-Layered Character of Modern Hebrew," in Morag 1988, 1:214–219.

1984   *The Renaissance of Modern Hebrew and Modern Standard Arabic: Parallels and Differences in the Revival of Two Semitic Languages*, University of California Publications, Near Eastern Studies, vol. 18 (Berkeley, Los Angeles, London: University of California Press).

Braslavski, Moshe

1955   [H] *The Eretz-Israel Labor Movement: History and Sources* (Tel Aviv: Ha-Kibutz Ha-Meuchad).

Brener, Yoseph Chaim

1910   [H] "In Newspapers and Literature: Notes and Remarks," *Ha-Poel Ha-Tsayir*, vol. 4, 24.11.1910, pp. 6–8.

1947   [H] "Rise and Fall," in *Aliya Shniya*, pp. 20–22.

1978a   [H] "From Here and From There," in *Writings*, vol. 2 (Tel Aviv: Ha-Kibutz Ha-Meuchad), pp. 1265–1440.

1978b   [H] "Bereavement and Failure," in *Writings* 2:1443–1688.

Chomsky, William

1986   *Hebrew: The Eternal Language* (Philadelphia: Jewish Publication Society of America).

Cohen, Israel

1918   *The German Attack on the Hebrew Schools in Palestine* (London: Offices of the "Jewish Chronicle" and the "Jewish World").

Deytsh [Deich], Lev

1923   [Russian] *For Half a Century* (Berlin: Grani).

Dubnov, Simon
1958   *Nationalism and History: Essays on Old and New Judaism*, edited and trans-
            lated by K. S. Pinson (Philadelphia: Jewish Publication Society).
Eisenstadt, Shmuel
1967   [H] *Our Living Hebrew Language* (Tel Aviv: Tekuma).
Eliav, Benjamin
1979   [H] Ed., *The Jewish National Home: From the Balfour Declaration to Inde-
            pendence*, rev. ed. (Jerusalem: Keter).
Eliav, Mordekhai
1978   [H] *Eretz-Israel and Its Settlement in the Nineteenth Century: 1777–1917*
            (Jerusalem: Keter).
Engelmann, Bernt
1984   *Germany without Jews*, translated by D. J. Beer (New York: Bantam Books)
            [original: *Deutschland ohne Juden*, Munich: Wilhelm Godmann, 1979].
Even-Zohar, Itamar
1979   "Aspects of the Hebrew-Yiddish Polysystem: A Case of a Multilingual
            Polysystem," in Even-Zohar 1990, pp. 121–130.
1980   "The Emergence of a Native Hebrew Culture in Palestine: 1882–1948,"
            in Even-Zohar 1990, pp. 175–191.
1984   "The Role of Russian and Yiddish in the Making of Modern Hebrew," in
            Even-Zohar 1990, pp. 111–120.
1985   "Gnessin's Dialogue and Its Russian Models," in Even-Zohar 1990, pp.
            131–153.
1990   *Polysystem Studies* (= *Poetics Today* 11, no. 1).
Fellman, Jack
1973   *The Revival of a Classical Tongue: Eliezer Ben Yehuda and the Modern Hebrew
            Language* (The Hague: Mouton).
1976   [H] "Eliezer Ben-Yehuda and the Revival of the Hebrew Language" [with
            discussions by Reuven Sivan, Uzi Ornan, Chaim Rabin], *Katedra* 2 (Nov.
            1976): 83–107.
Frankel, Jonathan
1981   *Prophecy and Politics: Socialism, Nationalism and the Russian Jews,
            1862–1917* (Cambridge: Cambridge University Press).
Gay, Peter
1988   *Freud: A Life for Our Time* (New York and London: W. W. Norton).
Glinert, Lewis H.
1988   "Did Pre-Revival Hebrew Literature Have Its Own *Langue*? Quotation and
            Improvization in Mendele Mokher Sefarim," *Bulletin of the School of Orien-
            tal and African Studies*, University of London, vol. 51, part 3: 413–427.
Greenzweig, Michael
1985   [H] "The Status of Hebrew in the Second Aliya," in Naor 1985, pp.
            198–212.
Grossmann, Stefan
1930   *Ich war begeistert: Eine Lebensgeschichte*, edited by Helmut Kreuzer, Reihe
            Q: Quellentexte zur Literatur- und Kulturgeschichte, vol. 7 (Berlin:
            Scriptor Verlag).

Haramati, Shlomo
1978   [H] *Three Who Preceded Ben-Yehuda* (Jerusalem: Yad Yitshak Ben-Tsvi).
1979   [H] *The Beginnings of Hebrew Education in Eretz-Israel and Its Contribution to the Revival of the Language* (Jerusalem: Reuven Mas).

Harshav, Benjamin
1982   "An Outline of Integrational Semantics: An Understander's Theory of Meaning in Context," *Poetics Today* 3, no. 4:59–88.
1984   "Fictionality and Fields of Reference: Remarks on a Theoretical Framework," *Poetics Today* 5, no. 2:227–251.
1986   *American Yiddish Poetry: A Bilingual Anthology* [with Barbara Harshav] (Berkeley, Los Angeles, London: University of California Press).
1988   [H] "The Revival of Eretz-Israel and the Modern Jewish Revolution," in *Perspectives on Culture and Society in Israel*, edited by Nurith Gertz (Tel Aviv: Open University), pp. 7–31.
1990a   *The Meaning of Yiddish* (Berkeley, Los Angeles, Oxford: University of California Press).
1990b   [H] "Essay on the Revival of the Hebrew Language," *Alpayim* 2:9–54.

Hertzberg, Arthur
1973   *The Zionist Idea: A Historical Analysis and Reader* (New York: Atheneum).

Horowitz, Dan, and Moshe Lissak
1990   [H] *Trouble in Utopia: The Overburdened Polity of Israel* (Tel Aviv: Am Oved).

Howe, Irving
1976   *World of Our Fathers* (New York and London: Harcourt Brace Jovanovich).

Jabotinsky, Ze'ev [Zhabotinski, Vladimir]
1914   [H] "The Language of Education," *Ha-Shiloah*, pp. 405–411, 501–511.
1930   [H] *Hebrew Pronunciation* (Tel Aviv: HaSefer).

Karmi, Shlomo
1986   [H] *First Furrows in Hebrew Education: The Assembly of Hebrew Teachers in Eretz-Israel and Its Place in the History of Education: 1892* (Jerusalem: Reuven Mas).

Katznelson, Berl
1912   [H] "From Inside," in *Writings*, vol. 1 (Tel Aviv: Labor Party of Eretz-Israel, n.d.), pp. 11–19.
1919a   [H] "Proposal for Unity," in *Writings* 1:129–132.
1919b   [H] "Statement of the *Kuntres* (On the Question of Languages)," in *Writings* 1:148–150.
1947a   [H] "The Miracle of the Second Aliya," in *Aliya Shniya*, pp. 11–14.
1947b   [H] "My Road to Eretz-Israel," in *Aliya Shniya*, pp. 67–85.
1990   [H] *The Second Aliya: Lectures for the 'Socialist Youth' (1928)*, new and annotated ed. edited by Anita Shapiro and Naomi Abir (Tel Aviv: Am Oved).

Katznelson, Rachel [Shazar]
1946   [H] "Language Insomnia," in *Essays and Sketches* (Tel Aviv: Am Oved), pp. 9–22.

Klauzner, Yosef [Klausner, Joseph]
1956   [H] "Ancient Hebrew and Modern Hebrew," in *Modern Hebrew and Its Problems* (Tel Aviv: Masada), pp. 36–56.

Klein, Dennis B.
1981   *Jewish Origins of the Psychoanalytic Movement* (Chicago: University of Chicago Press).

Kloyzner, Israel [Klausner]
1978a   [H] "The Pioneers of Hebrew Speech in Eretz-Israel," in *On the Roads to Zion: Chapters in the History of Zionism and the Revival of the Hebrew Language* (Jerusalem: Reuven Mas), pp. 371–384.
1978b   [H] "The Pioneers of Hebrew Speech in the Diaspora," in *On the Roads to Zion*, pp. 384–410.

Laqueur, Walter, and Barry Rubin
1984   Eds., *The Israel-Arab Reader*, 4th rev. and updated ed. (New York: Penguin).

Lessing, Theodor
1984   *Der Jüdische Selbsthass* (Munich: Matthes & Seitz).

Lexicon
1981   [Yiddish] *Biographical Dictionary of Modern Yiddish Literature*, vol. 8 (New York: Congress for Jewish Culture).

Malamud, Bernard
1989   *The People and Uncollected Stories*, edited and introduced by Robert Giroux (New York: Farrar, Straus, Giroux).

Mandel, George
1981   "*Sheelah Nikhbbadah* and the Revival of Hebrew," in Morag 1988, 1:32–46.

Mendele Mocher Seforim
1968   *The Travels and Adventures of Benjamin the Third*, translated from the Yiddish by Moshe Spiegel (New York: Schocken Books).

Mendes-Flohr, Paul R., and Yehuda Reinharz
1980   Eds., *The Jew in the Modern World: A Documentary History* (New York and Oxford: Oxford University Press).

Morag, Shelomo
1988   [H] Ed., *Studies on Contemporary Hebrew: A Selection of Readings*, 2 vols. (Jerusalem: Academon Press).

Nahir, Moshe
1977   Review of Jack Fellman, *The Revival of a Classical Tongue*, in *Language Problems and Language Planning*, vol. 2 (= *La Monda Longvo-Problemo*, vol. 8), pp. 177–181.
1987   "L'aménagement de l'hébreu moderne," in *Politique et aménagement linguistiques*, edited by Jacques Maurais (Quebec: Conseil de la langue française), pp. 259–316.
1988   "Language Planning and Language Aquisition: The 'Great Leap' in the Hebrew Revival," in *International Handbook of Bilingualism and Bilingual Education*, edited by Christina Bratt Paulston (New York: Greenwood Press), pp. 275–295.

Naor, Mordekhay
    1985   [H] Ed., *The Second Aliya, 1903–1914: Sources, Summaries, Selected Problems and Auxiliary Material* (Jerusalem: Yad Yitzhak Ben-Tsvi).

Ornan, Uzi
    1976   [H] "Hebrew as the Creator of a National Society," *Katedra* 2 (Nov. 1976): 98–101.
    1986   "Hebrew in Palestine before and after 1882," in Morag 1988, 1:76–47.

Pollak, Michael
    1984   *Vienne 1900: Une identité blessée* (Paris: Gallimard/Julliard).

Rabin, Chaim
    1988a   [H] "What was the Revival of the Language?" in Morag 1988, 1:16–31.
    1988b   "Language Revival and Language Death," in Morag 1988, 1:114–103.

Roth, Cecile
    1953   "Was Hebrew Ever a Dead Language?" in *Personalities and Events in Jewish History* (Philadelphia), pp. 136–142.

St.-John, Robert
    1952   *Tongue of the Prophets: The Life Story of Eliezer Ben Yehuda* (New York: Doubleday).

Shapiro, Yosef
    1967   [H] *Ha-Poel Ha-Tsayir: Idea and Praxis* (Tel Aviv: Ayanot).

Shats, Tsvi
    1919   [H] "The Exile of Our Classical Poetry," in *Ohel*, edited by M. Kushnir (1921); also in Tsvi Shats, *At the Border of Silence: Writings* (Tarbut ve-Khinukh).

Shkhori, Ilan
    1990   [H] *A Dream That Became a City* (Tel Aviv: Avivim).

Sholem, Gershom
    1982   [H] *From Berlin to Jerusalem: Memories of My Youth* (Tel Aviv: Am Oved).

Sholom Aleichem
    1956   "The Town of the Little People," translated by Julius and Francis Butwin, in *Selected Stories of Sholom Aleichem*, edited by Alfred Kazin (New York: Random House).

Shulman, Kalman
    1911   [H] *The Mysteries of Paris*, translation of Eugène Sue's *Les mystères de Paris* (Vilna: The Widow and Brothers Rom).

Sivan, Reuven
    1986   [H] "Eliezer Ben-Yehuda and His Linguistic Achievement," in Ben-Yehuda 1986, pp. 7–33.

Slutski, Yehuda
    1961   "Criticus," *He-Avar* 8:43–59.

Szmeruk Ch.
    1961   "The Jewish Community and Jewish Agricultural Settlement in Soviet Byelorussia," Ph.D. dissertation, Hebrew University, Jerusalem.

Steel, Ronald
    1980   *Walter Lippmann and the American Century* (Boston: Little, Brown).

Tabenkin, Yitshak
  1947   [H] "The Roots," in *Aliya Shniya*, pp. 23–30.
Toury, Gideon
  1990   "The Hebraization of Surnames as a Motive in Hebrew Literature," in *Actes du XVIe Congrès international des sciences onomastiques* (Quebec: Les Presses de l'Université Laval), pp. 545–554.
Tsemakh [Zemach], Shlomo
  1965   [H] *The First Year* (Tel Aviv: Am Oved).
Tuwim, Julian
  1984   *My, Żydzi Polscy... We, Polish Jews*, edited by Ch. Shmeruk (Jerusalem: Magnes Press).
Usishkin, M.
  1928   [H] "The War for the Language," in *Gdudenu: On the Third Anniversary of the Brigade of the Defenders of the Language in Jerusalem* (Jerusalem: Brigade of the Defenders of the Language in Eretz-Israel, Jerusalem Branch).
Weinreich, Uriel
  1958   [H] "The Hebrew-Yiddish Style of Scribes," *Leshonenu* 22:55–66.
  1965   [H] *Ashekenazi Hebrew and the Hebrew in Yiddish: Their Geographical Aspect* [reprint from *Leshonenu*] (Jerusalem).
Yehoash [Solomon Bloomgarden]
  1917   [Yiddish] *From New York to Rehovot and Back*, 2 vols. (New York: Hebrew Publishing Company).
  1923   *The Feast of the Messenger* [English translation of above] (Philadelphia: Connat Press).
Yerushalmi, Yosef Hayim
  1989   *Zakhor: Jewish History and Jewish Memory* (New York: Schocken Books).
Zuckerman, Yitzhak
  1993   *A Surplus of Memory: Recollections of a Leader of the Warsaw Ghetto Uprising*, translated and edited by Barbara Harshav (Berkeley, Los Angeles, Oxford: University of California Press).

INDEX

CONTRAVERSIONS

JEWS AND OTHER DIFFERENCES